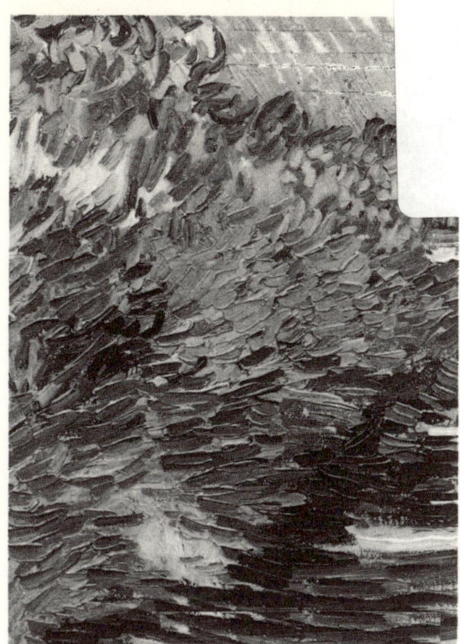

landscape painting in oils

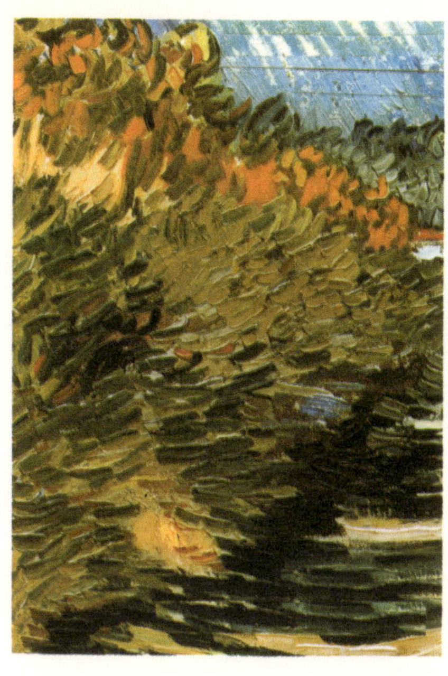

landscape painting in oils

–how to set about it.

by

J. M. Parramón

From the series: "Improve your painting and drawing"

FOUNTAIN PRESS, ARGUS BOOKS LTD., WATFORD, ENGLAND

FOUNTAIN PRESS
ARGUS BOOKS LIMITED,
14 ST. JAMES ROAD,
WATFORD
HERTFORDSHIRE
ENGLAND

First Edition in English 1980
Original Title in Spanish
«El paisaje al óleo»

ISBN: 0-85242-707-7

Printed in Spain by Printer, industria gráfica sa
Provenza, 388 Barcelona-25
Depósito Legal B. 33238-1979
Número de Registro Editorial 785

Index

1

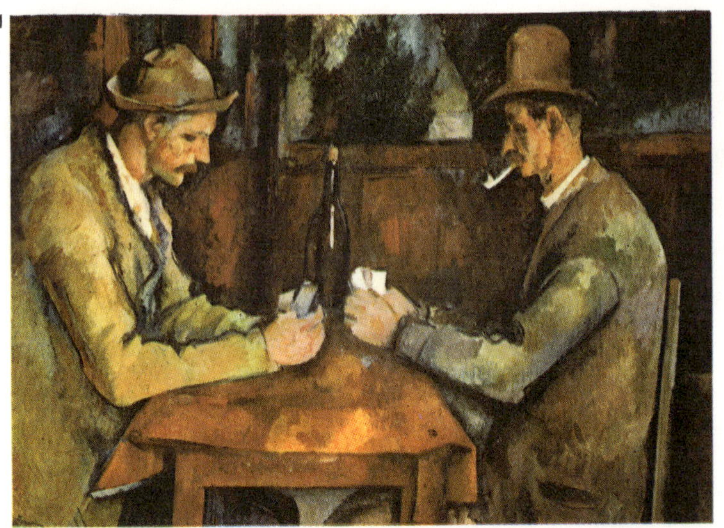

2

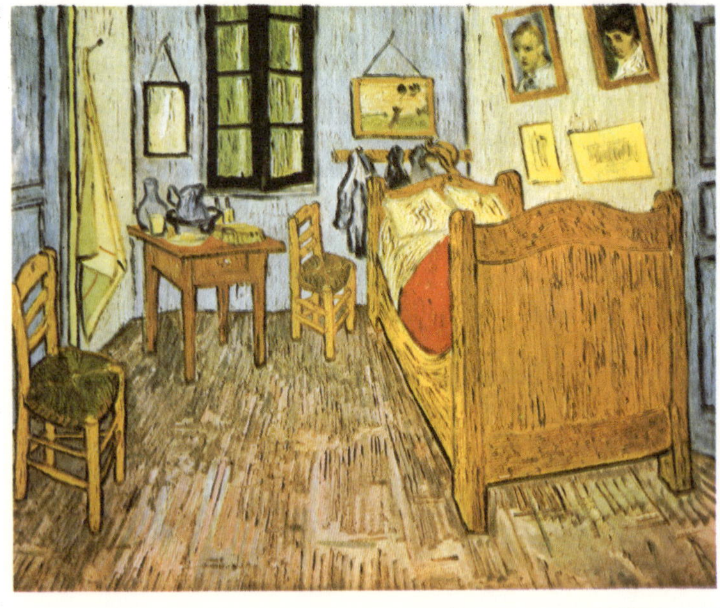

Figs. 1 and 2. The Impressionists rebelled against the traditional "set themes". They painted what they *saw* - perhaps in their mind's eye: everyday scenes such as Cézanne's *The card-players*, above, and Van Gogh's *Vincent's room at Arles*, both in the Louvre.

Introduction

My aim in this book is to teach you how to paint landscapes in oils. One immediately thinks of the landscapes which hang in most art galleries, and one is tempted to conclude that the majority of landscape painters paint like the Impressionists. So we might think we need to know just how the Impressionists painted landscapes. And then we ask ourselves the usual question: should we, in the 1970s, follow the style of, say 1870, and try to paint as Monet, Pissarro, Renoir, Berthe Morisot, Cézanne, Gauguin and Van Gogh did a century ago?

We know that the work of an artist is always the reflection of the age in which he lives. The Impressionists held the first exhibitions of their paintings in 1874. It was the age of the Industrial Revolution, of scientific and mechanical inventions, of the rise of large-scale capitalism, of the beginnings of trade unionism — an age of changes taking place with unprecedented speed, of innovations and new attitudes in every sphere of life. As a reflection of this new society, the "progressive" artist of those days painted dynamic, fleeting, momentary impressions; he rejected the "grand theme", and academic conventions governing composition; he rebelled against the classicists, caught light and freedom and put it on canvas. He painted the underprivileged. His palette carried a range of unusual, bright colours; he used new techniques based on the theories of Chevreul and he chose topical subjects as opposed to the traditional set themes, as can be seen in the two illustrations opposite: Cézanne's *The card players* and Van Gogh's *Vincent's room at Arles.*

Our society and our age, however, are different: we live in a world of computers, television, multinational corporations, the UN, the USA, Nato and OECD, artificial satellites, neo-capitalism and socialism, the consumer society, pollution, high-speed travel, alienation and rebellion... An age of experimentation and of searching, which is also reflected in the art of today by formulae and styles that are new and ephemeral, and are born to die in the space of a few years.

But the methods employed by the Impressionists are still used by the majority of professional artists, sometimes using identical means, sometimes with slight variations, either because they can find no other way to interpret landscape in painting or because this style is, after all, accepted and enjoyed by most people.

These assumptions give rise to a series of questions. Firstly, is landscape still a suitable subject for this day and age? Secondly, what can we art teachers say and teach about this subject today? Finally, must we take as our starting-point the methods used by the Impressionists in order to teach landscape painting today?

I must say again that I have given much thought to the contradiction implied in teaching an amateur painter today on the basis — which seems necessary — of using formulae and techniques which belong to a bygone age. I have reached the following conclusion:

Impressionism is a classic style, well deserving of imitation, and especially appropriate to landscape painting. Of this there is no doubt. It is the inevitable starting point for the purpose of teaching landscape painting, because, among other reasons, it has been the cradle of all the trends, styles and "isms" of our century, from *fauvisme*, initiated by Gauguin and Van Gogh, to *hyper-realism*, the fashion of the present day. It is the way, and the best way, to learn to paint landscapes as they are painted today — and this, incidentally, confirms the contemporary relevance of landscape painting — by such famous artists as Palencia, Ortega Muñoz, Buffet and others. So the lessons taught in this book will be based on the methods of composition and painting used by Monet, Pissarro, Sisley, Cézanne and Van Gogh. But I will try to ensure that these lessons are up to date by adding information regarding techniques, formulae and experiences that have successively achieved prominence since those artists first went out into the open air with their easels.

If, in principle, the reader succeeds in imitating Monet, Pissarro, Sisley and the others, then we can both express our satisfaction. If the reader then carries on and persists in painting landscapes, I would go so far as to promise that his style may develop until it reaches... But that will be his problem. Mine has been solved by providing this brief introduction.

J. M. Parramon

3

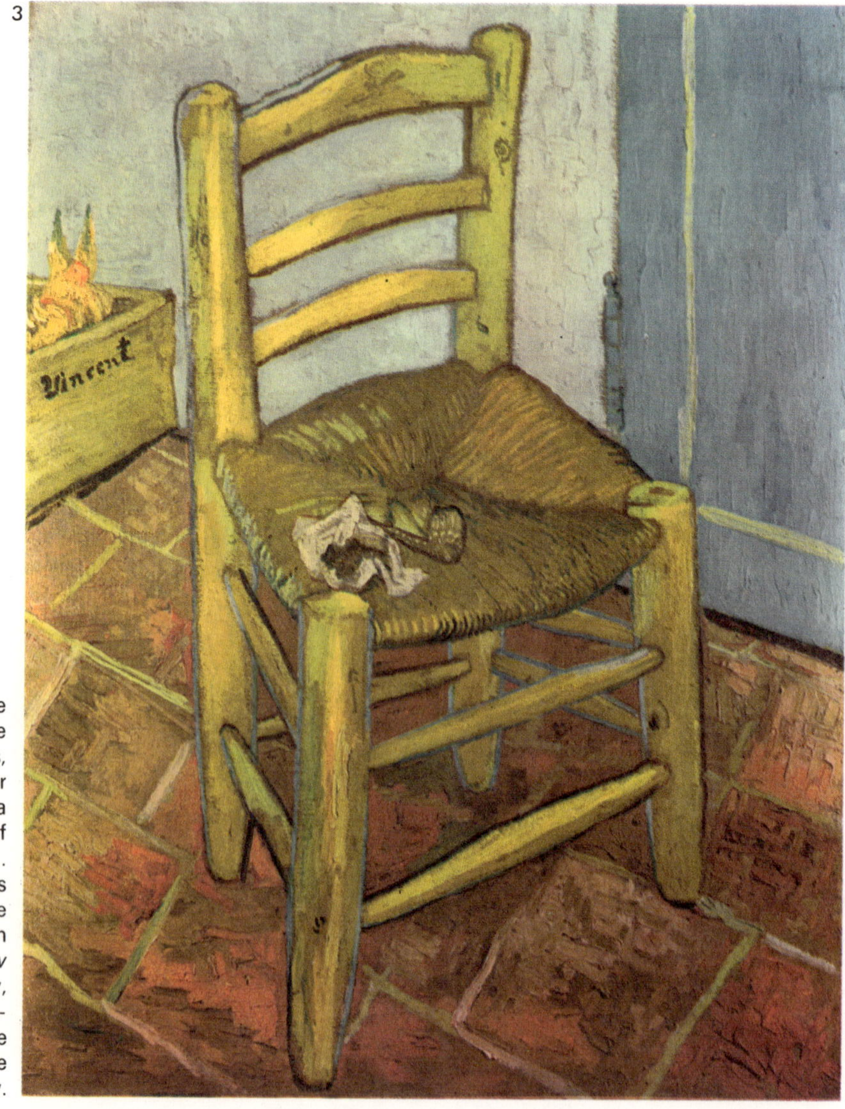

Figs. 3 and 4. To the Impressionists, the choice of subject was, apparently, of little or no importance; just a chair, or a corner of the painter's garden... As an example of this approach, see these two examples from Van Gogh: *The yellow chair* (Tate Gallery, London) and a pen-and-ink sketch of the garden of the Hospice de Saint-Rémy.

Choosing the subject

I am a great admirer of Van Gogh. I am deeply moved by his painting, his life and his madness. In my opinion he is the greatest landscape painter of all time. I believe that the story of his life provides a masterly lesson, even when he had lost his reason, a year before he committed suicide; and yet he discovered colour and light, he continued to develop. And he produced the best pictures he had ever painted in his life.

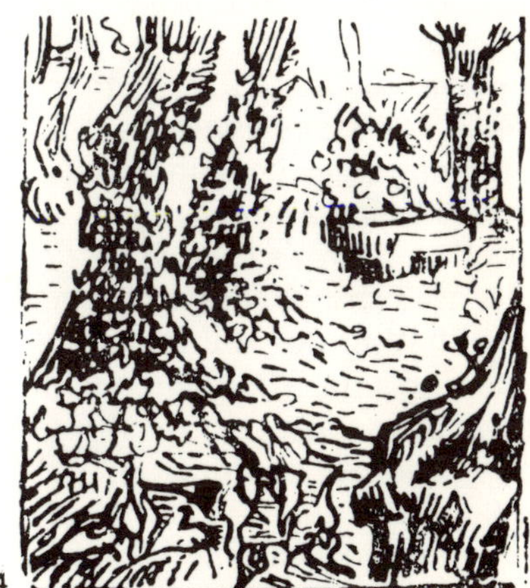

4

"I think I did the right thing when I came here," Van Gogh wrote to his brother Théo from the hospice of Saint-Rémy. "The change of atmosphere has done me good and, little by little, I can come to think of madness as I would of any other illness.

"Since I have been here, the abandoned garden, with its tall pine-trees and high, untended grass mingled with weeds, has provided me with material enough for work. When I send you another four canvasses on which I am still working, you will see that, if one bears in mind that I spend most of my life in the garden, this is not as gloomy as it may seem."

An abandoned garden, resembling some place in the middle of a forest, provided an appropriate subject for Van Gogh to paint several pictures. "I have not yet been outside," he wrote to his brother, "but through the window of my room, which has iron bars, I can see a wheat-field in an enclosure..." It would, however, be a mistake to think that these subjects were just a result of his imprisonment in Saint-Rémy. Not a bit of it. A year earlier, when he was living in Arles, he painted a picture of his room, of a chair and even of an ordinary pair of shoes... Van Gogh, in common with all the Impressionists, was a fervent admirer of his predecessor, Eugène Delacroix. The latter had written:

"The subject is you, yourself, your impressions, your emotions towards nature. You must look inside yourself and not around you."

One of the great innovations of the Impressionists was, in fact, their rejection of the idea of the "academic" subject, the studiously prepared picture, the composition of which was carefully thought out, sometimes down to the most trivial detail. For centuries, landscapes had been painted in the studio, from memory or on the basis of preliminary sketches. As late as the 17th century, Poussin and Claude Lorraine, in the neo-classical period, composed their landscapes with an obvious element of fantasy, idealizing the subject in a way that had no connection with reality (Fig. 5). In contrast to this traditional formula, the Impressionists painted on their canvasses, to use their own terminology, *motifs* rather than subjects: that is to say, topics that were living, spontaneous, ingenuous and natural, without any previous preparation. They painted them just as they were in real life.

There is an obvious lesson to be drawn from these preliminary observations: to find a subject or motif suitable for landscape painting presents no difficulty at all — they are to be found everywhere: in the very street where you live, in or around any village or town, in any garden, field or hillside, on the beach, or in a fishing or industrial port.

"Themes, motifs?" Renoir used to say (he was noted for his crude language), "I can do all right with any old pair of buttocks."

However, even though Renoir, Van Gogh and the other Impressionists emphatically expressed their indifference as to subjects for painting, and even though they painted motifs as trivial — at least they appeared so then — as a gang of workmen repairing a street (Manet's *The stone-pavers of the rue Berne*) or a crowd of people and horse-drawn carriages crossing a city square, viewed from a balcony (Pissarro's *Place du Théâtre Français*), or the interior of a cafe with a billiard-table in the middle (Van Gogh's *Café at night - interior*)... even though they painted these and other pictures for which the models were apparently already there, and all they had to do was to set up their easels and start work, it is also true that before this they had perceived the motif for a picture and had considered that the shape and colour of the motif were agreeable: that is to say, they had analysed the composition, in terms of shape and colour, and had imagined how to interpret it. In fact, they had chosen the subject... and cared little about its content, whether it was a handful of radishes or a bunch of roses.

In their case, as in yours, this selection of the subject depends on three factors:

Factors which determine the choice of subject:

1. Knowing how to see
2. Knowing how to compose
3. Knowing how to interpret

The order in which these factors have been placed is arbitrary, because these three ideas or operations are simultaneous: when the artist is considering a motif to paint, he is also judging the best framework, the best lighting, the best viewpoint and the structure in terms of shape and colour. As he analyses the composition he simultaneously imagines what he can delete, what he can emphasize, the dominant colours in which he can paint, and the contrasts which he can accentuate. He is "looking inside himself". He is engaged in the process of interpretation.

5

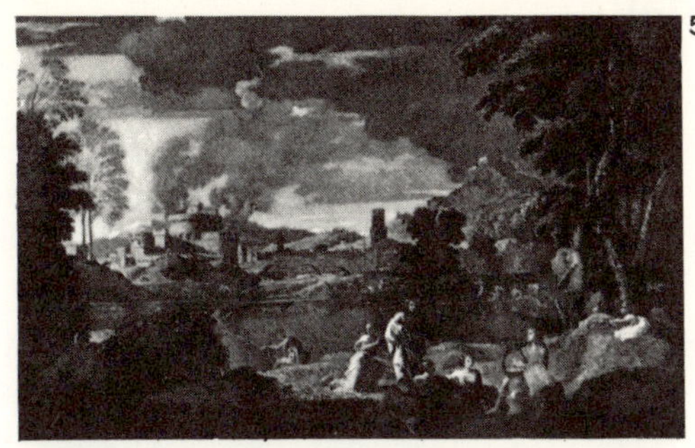

6

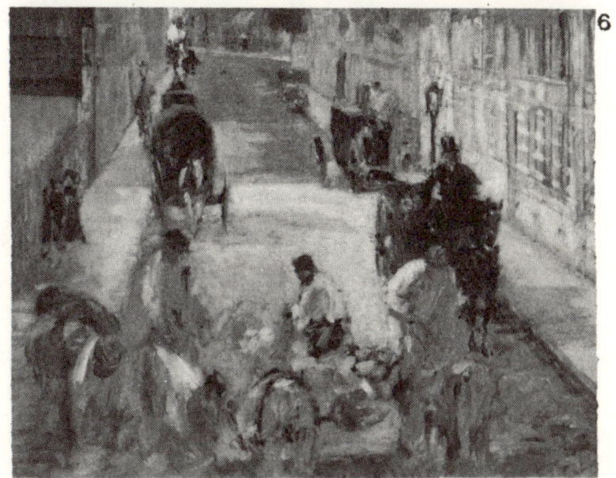

7

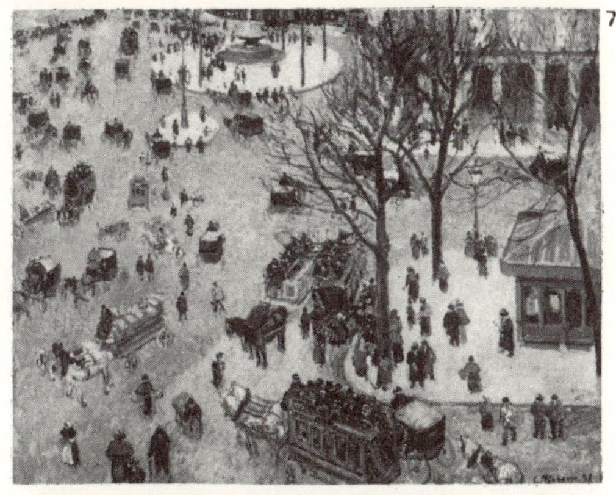

8

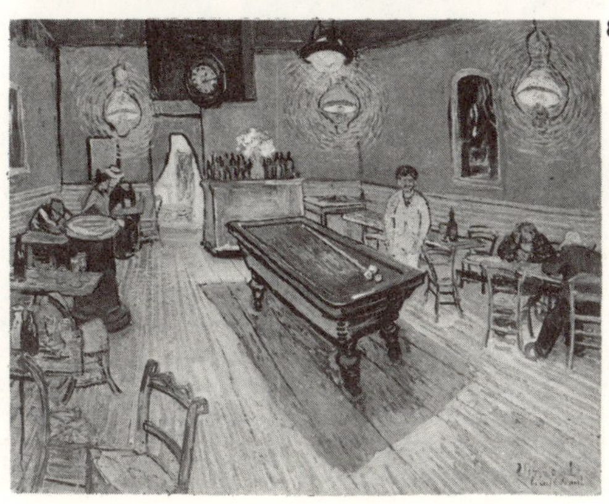

Fig. 5 (top). This landscape by Claude Lorraine, a 17th-century French painter, is based on a preconsidered composition. Even the smallest details are studied and the picture includes classical figures, monuments and buildings. Figs 6, 7 and 8 show how the Impressionists rejected these academic formulae, set up their easels in the street and painted everyday scenes as apparently trivial as Monet's *The stone-pavers of the rue Berne* (Lord Butler's Collection); Pissarro's *Place du Théâtre Français* (Museum of Art, Los Angeles); or Van Gogh's *Café at night, interior* (S. Clark Collection, Yale University).

Subjects for landscape painting most often used by the Impressionists

If one takes a good look at the great number of Impressionist landscapes, it is clear that these artists had a marked preference for certain themes and motifs which frequently recur in their works. To attempt to classify these motifs we can take certain headings as follows:

Landscapes with rivers, lakes or ponds, which generally include the painting of shapes reflected in the water. This is, perhaps, the motif most often painted by all the Impressionists, without exception. They probably regarded this motif as an opportunity to depict impressions, movement and reflected colours (Figs. 10 and 13).

Scenes of roads or tracks leading to towns and villages. These, too, were the subject of many paintings, especially by Pissarro, Sisley and Monet (Figs. 9 and 14).

Snow-covered landscapes. The Impressionists showed a marked preference for such scenes; they no doubt regarded them as the most forceful expression of the theme of light, and also as a confirmation of the latest theories about colour (the blue colour of shadow, for example). (See Figs. 9 and 15).

Landscapes with orchards, with flowers, grass, small trees and houses. This theme was a reflection of the idea of an "unimportant motif", unpretentious and not based on any composition studied beforehand (Fig. 12).

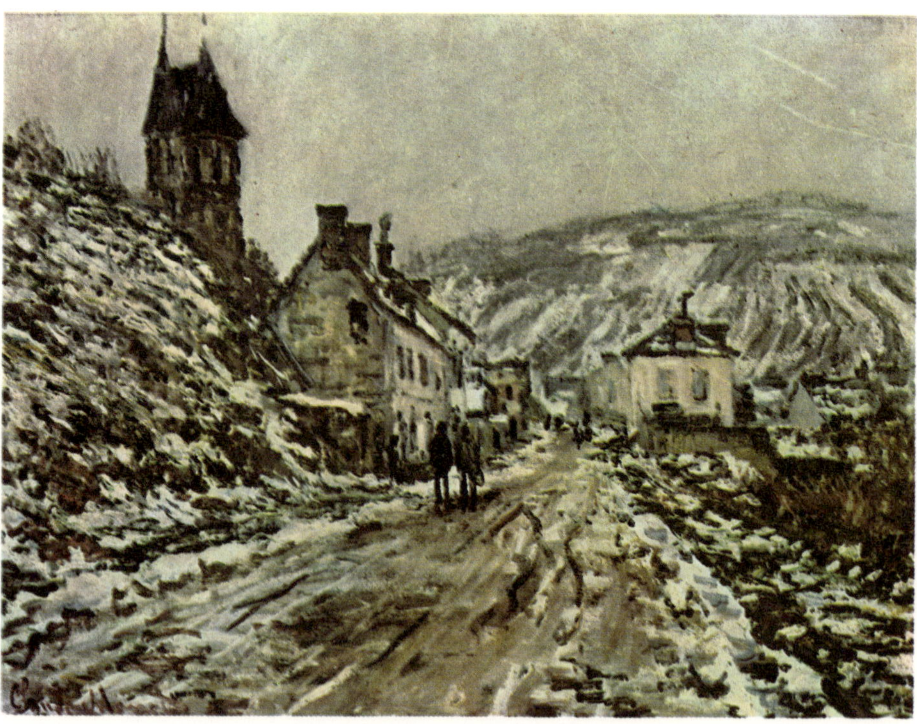

Fig. 9. Monet. *The road in the village* (Museum of Art, Gothenburg).

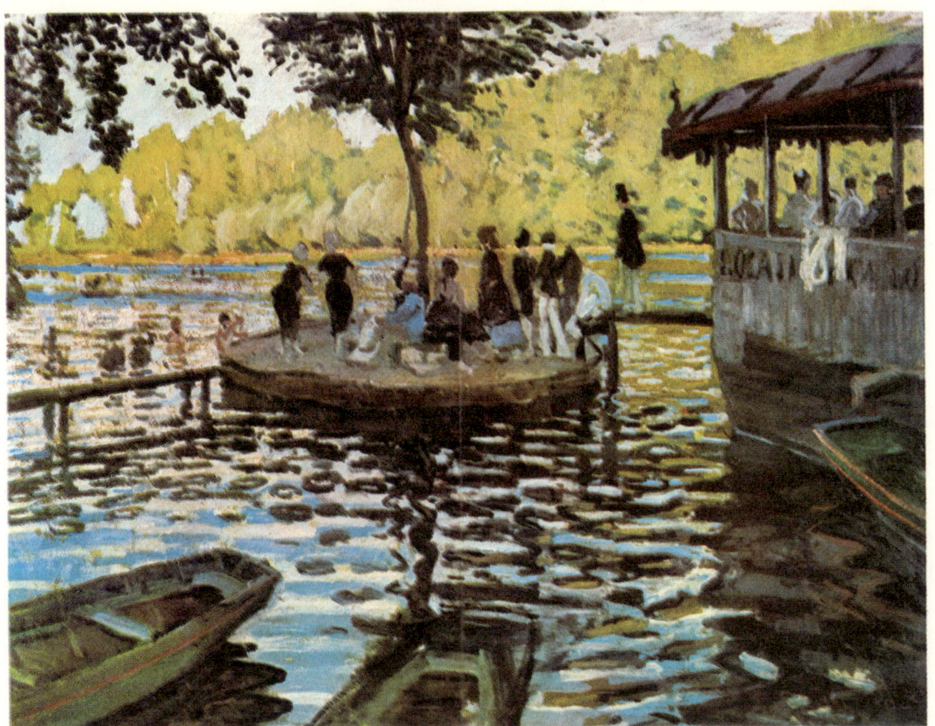

Fig. 10. Monet. *The bathing-place* (Metropolitan Museum of Art, New York).

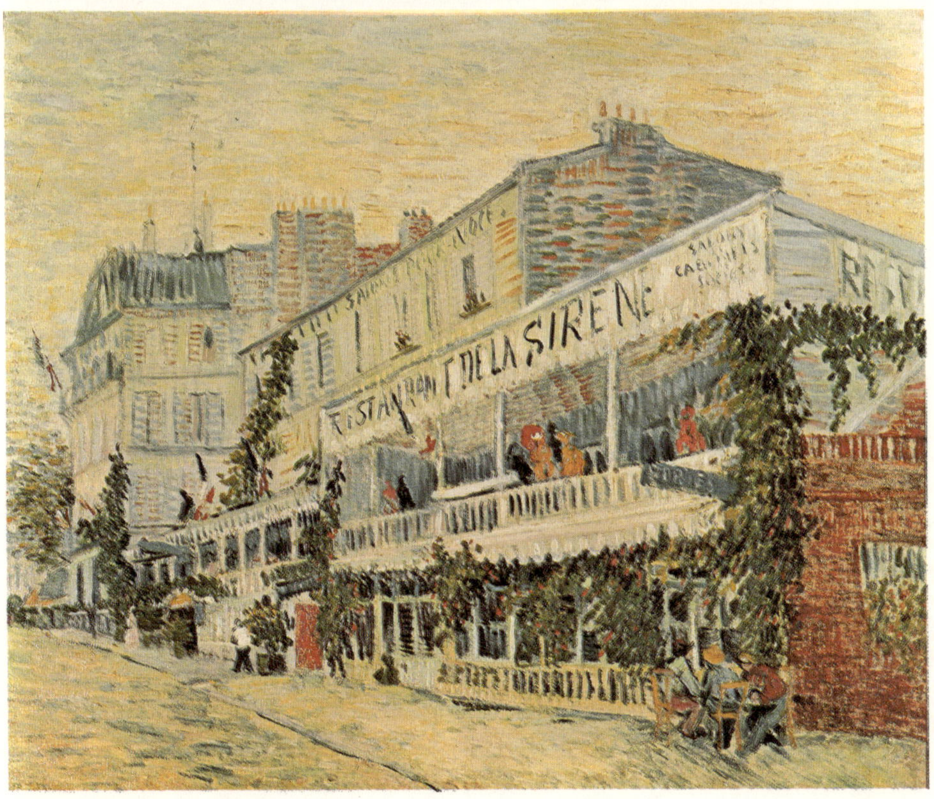

Fig. 11. Van Gogh. *The Restaurant de la Sirène* (Louvre, Paris).

Fig. 12. Pissarro. *Orchard with fruit-trees in blossom, in spring, Pontoise* (Louvre, Paris).
Fig. 13. Monet. *The bridge at Argenteuil* (Louvre, Paris).
Fig. 14. Sisley, *A street in Marley* (Metropolitan Museum of Art, New York).

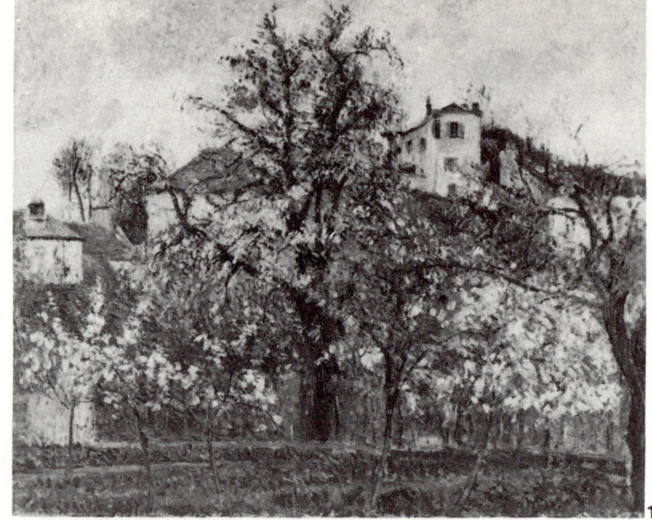
12

Urban landscapes. The streets, squares and boulevards of Paris, complete with pedestrians and vehicles — the depiction of the city as a reflection of the age; this was a real innovation on the part of the Impressionists, and they all painted such scenes (Figs. 11 and 17).

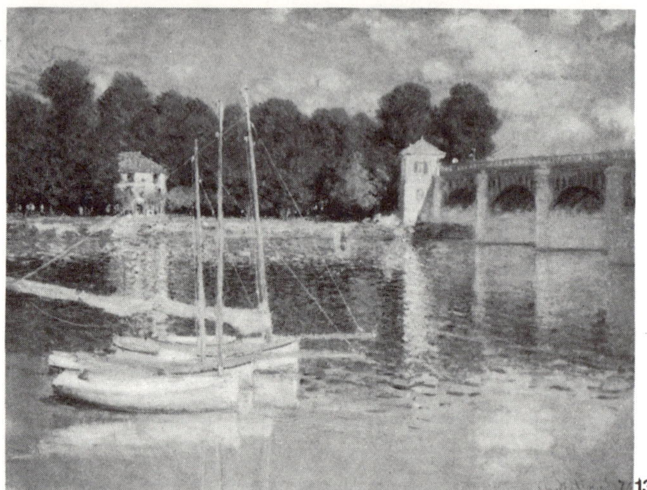
13

Rural landscapes "à plein air", with mountains and vegetation, and sometimes with views of the sea. In these paintings there are almost always some houses and small villages. There are also landscapes consisting entirely of natural scenery, especially woodland. Cézanne was especially fond of such subjects (Fig. 16).

Van Gogh, too, was exceptional in his choice of subjects and he displayed very marked personal preferences. Like his contemporaries, he painted water and reflections, but he never painted a snow scene. In the heart of the countryside he would paint lone cypresses. He painted the sea, the countryside and the city at night, and always tried to express himself in striking, harsh colours.

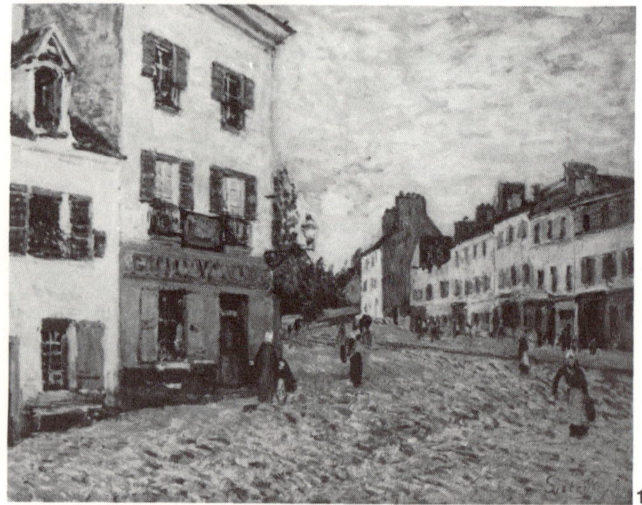
14

Fig. 15. Gauguin. *Breton village in the snow* (Louvre, Paris).
Fig. 16. Cézanne. *Wood with windmill* (Philadelphia).
Fig. 17. Marquet. *Bridge over the Seine* (Louvre, Paris).

15 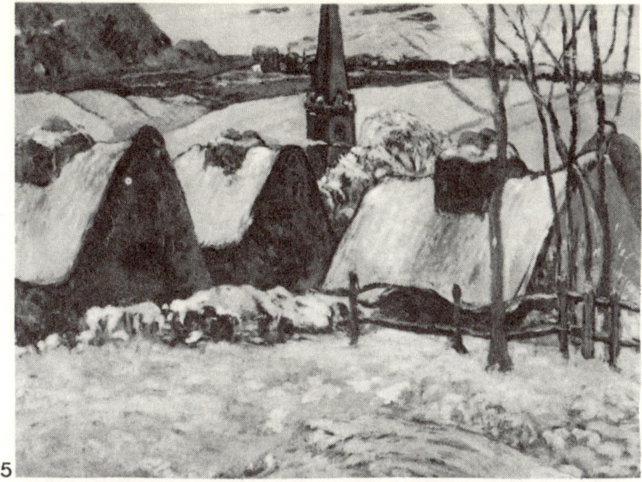

16 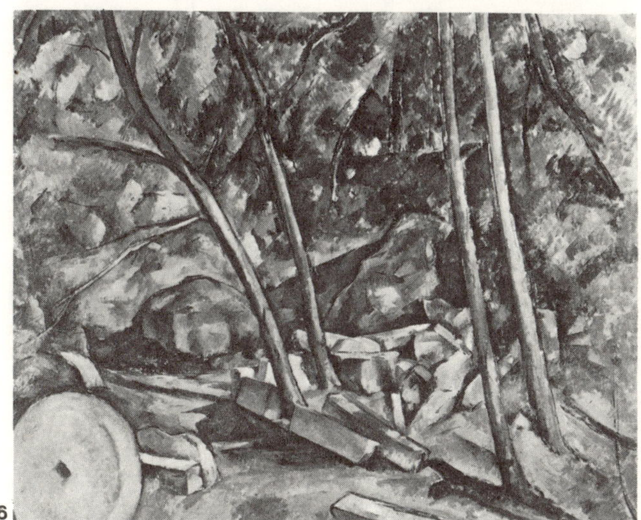

17 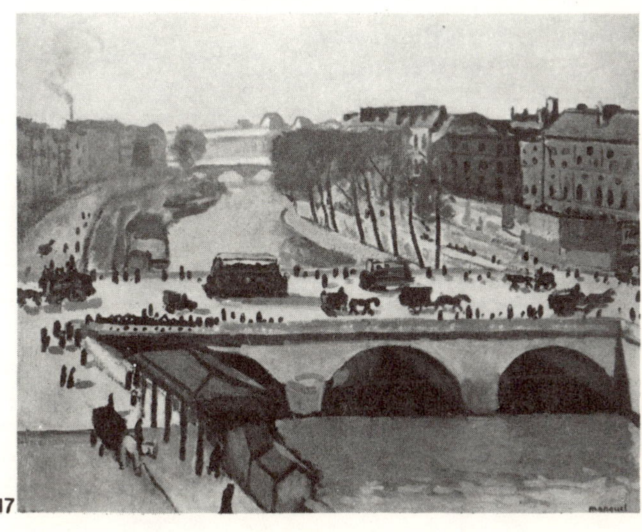

Lastly, if we attempted to classify the subjects most often painted by our own contemporaries, they seem to fall into three major categories:

Landscapes with mountains or rocks, in open country or including houses, small villages, etc.

Urban landscapes - paintings of villages and towns and, especially, city streets and squares, including everyday reflections of society. Markets, suburbs, old quarters and slums are included as are scenes featuring industries and railways, etc.

Seascapes, featuring the sea and rocks or mountains, beaches, ships, and fishing and industrial ports.

Composition in landscape painting

There have been many attempts, with varying degrees of success, to define the art of composition. The famous French painter Matisse used to say, "Composition is the art of disposing, in a decorative manner, the various elements available to the artist for the expression of his emotions". Montesquieu, the French philosopher and writer, said "The things which we see in succession must have variety, and those which we see at one time must have symmetry". The most perfect definition, however, was formulated centuries ago by the ancient Greek philosopher Plato, who expressed the task of the artist in a few words. Plato stated quite simply:

Composition consists of finding and depicting diversity within unity

There must be variety as regards to shape, colour, the position and stituation of the elements included in the picture — a diversity which makes an impact on the spectator and arouses his interest, encouraging him to see and then giving him the pleasure of looking and contemplating. But the artist must not achieve this variety at the expense of disturbing and distracting the interest first aroused in the spectator. In other words, this diversity must be organized within a framework of order and unity. It may be said that these two ideas are complementary, so that one must combine the two factors together, in this way achieving:[1]

Unity within diversity
diversity within unity

We shall illustrate this and study the essential factors underlying this important principle:

Factors which determine unity within diversity

1. The organization of shapes and space

Imagine that you are looking at a landscape. You are in open country, you can see a bell-tower, a church surrounded by a few houses, all situated

1. As regards composition, see *How to compose a picture* in this series.

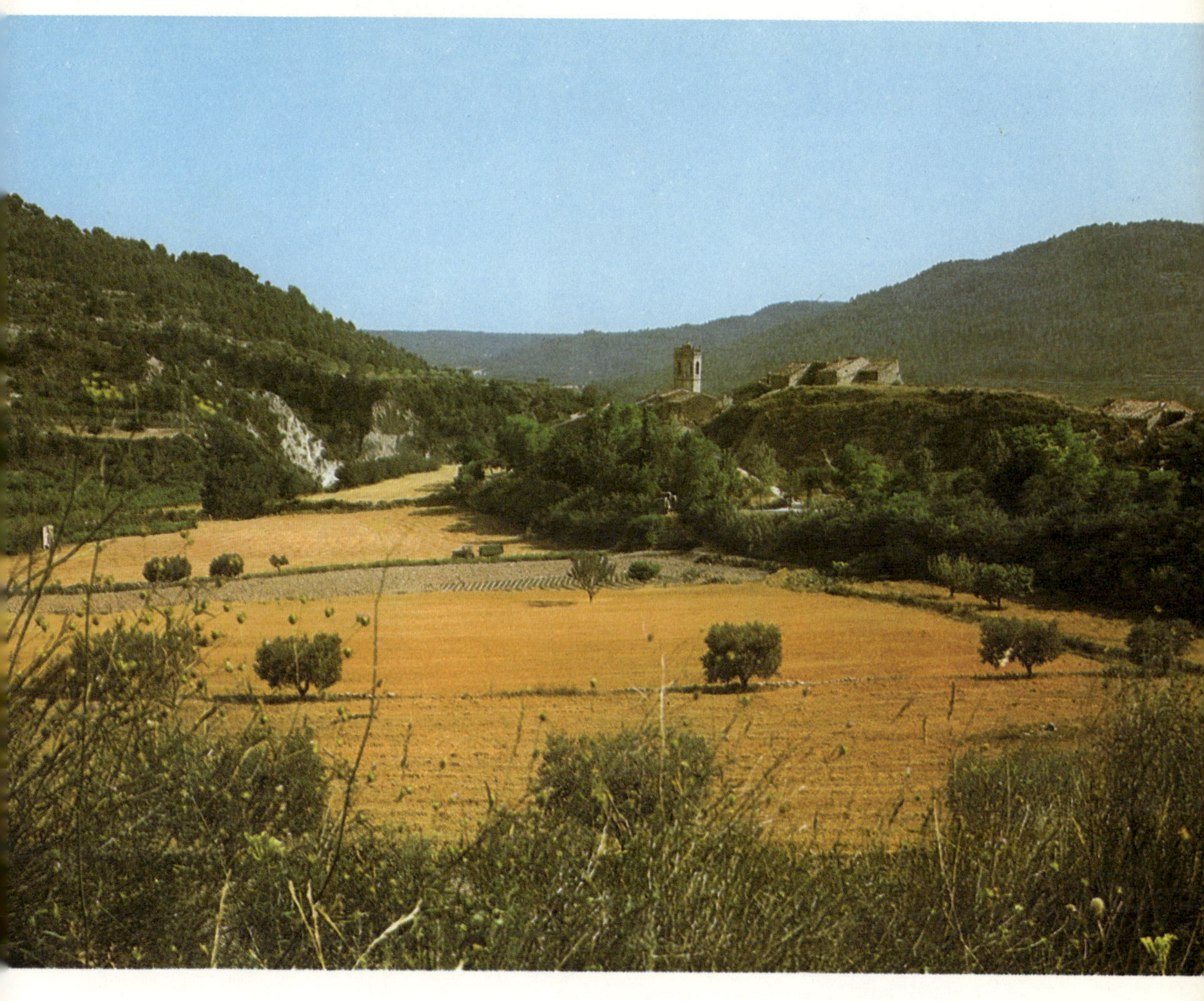

on a small hill, and in the background, the deep blue of a range of mountains. At the foot of the hill, stretching from behind it, as though it were the delta of a river, you can see a yellow patch of flat ground formed by several fields of wheat stubble. On the left, bordering this golden flat surface, is a hill with stones, bare earth and vegetation, while in the foreground are stalks and branches of grasses and shrubs (Fig. 18).

If you were to paint this broad panorama, the result would most probably be a picture with too much diversity; which would distract the attention of the viewer. He would look at the church tower and the houses — which are the principal motif of the picture — but he would also look at the stalks of grass in the foreground, the house on the right of the picture, and the hill stretching out to the left. To create unity, it is vital to come closer to the principal motif. This, however, is the first problem that we encounter in the process of discovering unity within diversity... How is one to organize these elements? How can one arrange these shapes within the space or surface of the canvas? Or, to put it another way, by giving specific examples:

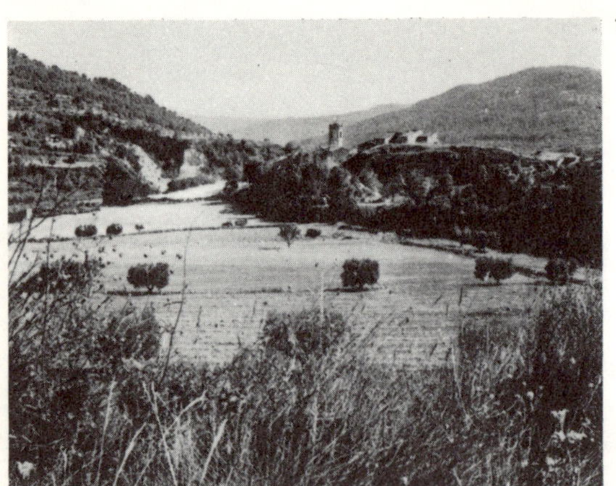

19

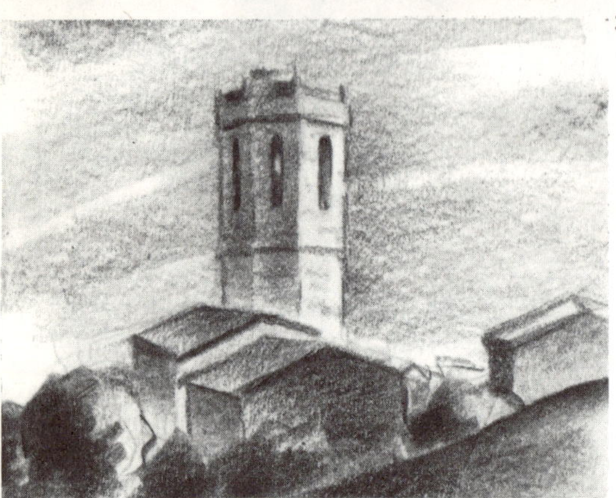

20

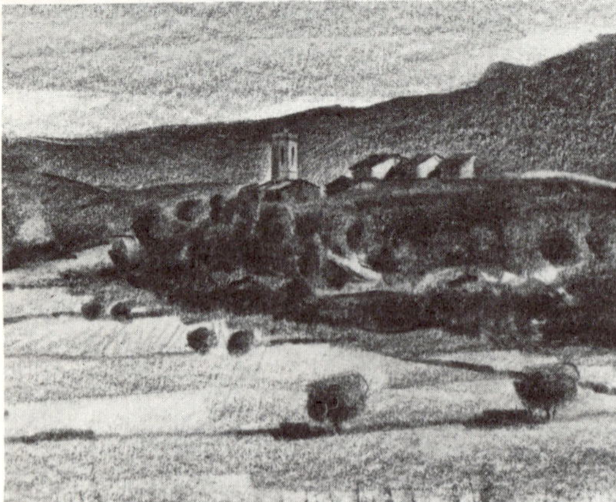

21

Fig. 19. If this is the landscape you have decided to paint (see previous page)...

Fig. 20. Which part of it is best to tackle? Just the church and a couple of houses, perhaps, as if you had a camera with a telephoto lens?

Fig. 21. Or include the wheat stubble in the foreground, more houses and the hills behind?

I think we all agree that the approach shown in Fig. 20 is pretty dull. There is not much here of any interest: the colours are monotonous and the shapes uninspired, with few contrasts.

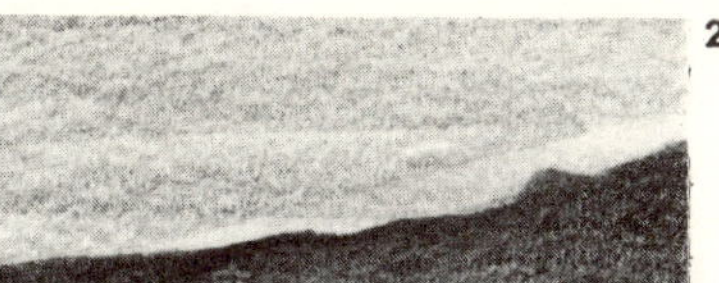
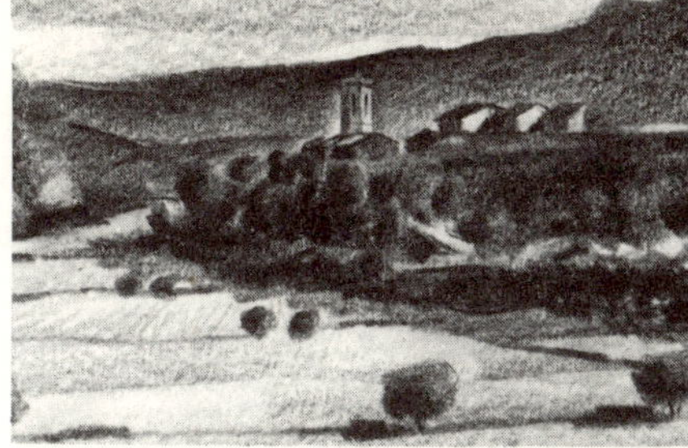

22

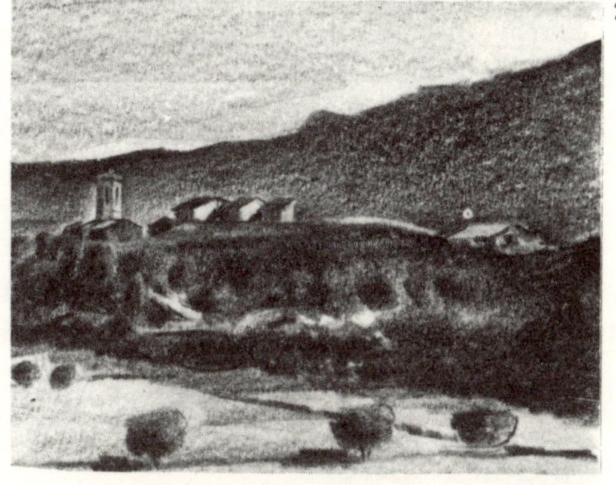

23

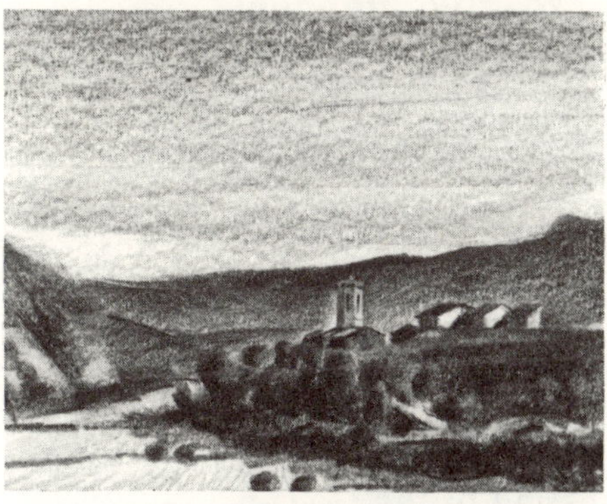

24

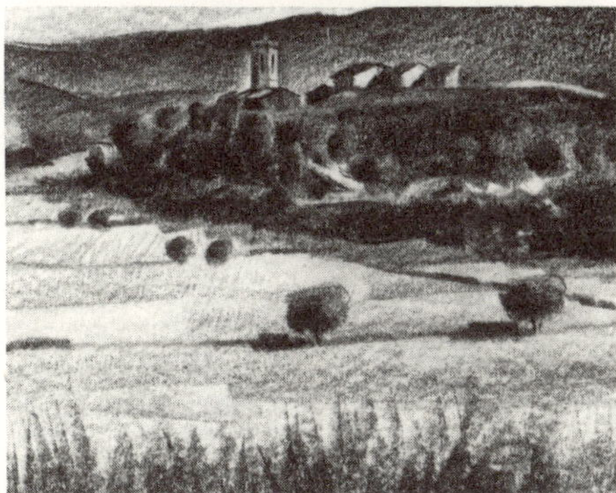

25

Fig. 22. Ask yourself whether centring the church tower gives the best result.

Fig. 23. Or moving it to the left?

Fig. 24. Or putting the horizon and the church tower in the lower half of the picture, leaving a large space for the open sky?

Fig. 25. Or going to the other extreme, painting the church and the houses in the upper part of the picture, and giving more prominence to the field of golden wheat stubble?

• There is no rigid principle here. But when considering the two problems of proportion and that of deciding on the framework, there are two rules or principles which may be expressed as follows:

1. Create a centre of attention in our composition and use it to emphasize the wholeness of the picture.

In our case we have already noted a church, some houses, a blue background of mountains and some fields of wheat, so try to choose a framework which will include these features and exclude the rest, eliminating the stalks of grass in the foreground, reducing the sky area, including the wheatfields, and leaving out features on the right and left of the picture — see Fig. 21. One must get close enough to the subject to be able to emphasize the church tower as the centre of attention. One of the mistakes most commonly made by the inexperienced artist is to paint great empty spaces, minimizing the features which are really the essential motif of the picture.

The second principle, which is related to the location of various shapes within the picture (as depicted in Figs. 22-25), is based on a well-known law of aesthetics discovered by Vitrubius, a Roman architect who lived during the reign of Augustus:

2. The law of the Golden Section: "If a space divided into two unequal parts is to look good and be aesthetically pleasing, there must be between the smallest and the largest part the same proportion as that between the largest part and the whole."

The numerical factor in this division, "in medium and extreme ratio" (to use mathematical terms) can be established as follows:

The arithmetical expression of the Golden Section is equivalent to 0.618.

In order to achieve this ideal division, which is perfect from the aesthetic point of view (and which, as we shall see, provides the basis for the correct ordering of the various elements in the picture), we need only apply the following formula in this and all other cases:

Multiply the width of the canvas by 0.618, and the Golden Section is automatically obtained.

If this operation is repeated with the height of the canvas, a point considered to be ideal for the location of the principal feature, or focus of interest, of the picture will be obtained. This can be demonstrated by means of a few examples:

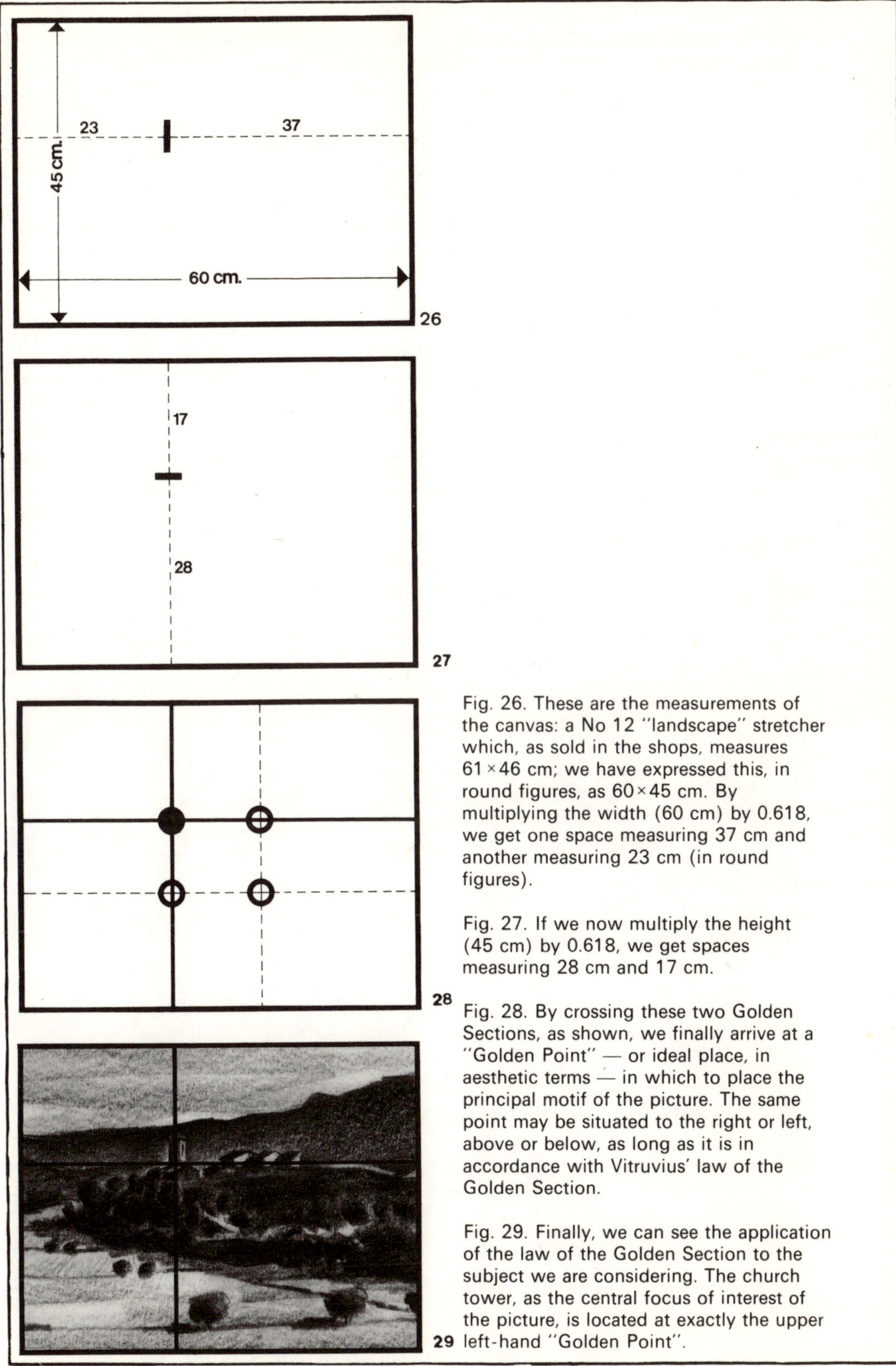

Fig. 26. These are the measurements of the canvas: a No 12 "landscape" stretcher which, as sold in the shops, measures 61 × 46 cm; we have expressed this, in round figures, as 60 × 45 cm. By multiplying the width (60 cm) by 0.618, we get one space measuring 37 cm and another measuring 23 cm (in round figures).

Fig. 27. If we now multiply the height (45 cm) by 0.618, we get spaces measuring 28 cm and 17 cm.

Fig. 28. By crossing these two Golden Sections, as shown, we finally arrive at a "Golden Point" — or ideal place, in aesthetic terms — in which to place the principal motif of the picture. The same point may be situated to the right or left, above or below, as long as it is in accordance with Vitruvius' law of the Golden Section.

Fig. 29. Finally, we can see the application of the law of the Golden Section to the subject we are considering. The church tower, as the central focus of interest of the picture, is located at exactly the upper left-hand "Golden Point".

It is worth repeating that, as regards these and all other rules of artistic composition, there are no hard and fast principles. The church tower might be situated further to the right, and painted from apparently further away or closer, and the resulting composition might be equally sound. Nevertheless, apart from the fact that a knowledge of these principles may help to resolve problems involved in deciding the framework and situating the principal features, it is an undoubted fact that, either consciously or unconsciously, following his usual habits with regard to display, organization of detail and basic framework, the professional artist actually puts these principles into practice.

2. Symmetry and asymmetry

Symmetry is synonymous with unity: in itself, it expresses order, formality and authority; asymmetry is synonymous with diversity: it expresses movement, contrast and originality (Figs. 30, 31). In the composition of still-life paintings, figure painting and portraits, it is possible for the artist to keep control of these factors — symmetry and asymmetry — by simply placing and moving the model as he wishes. In landscape painting the model cannot move, but the artist can. The painter can place himself further to the right or the left of the model until he finds the most satisfactory viewpoint. Symmetrical composition is not, generally speaking, suitable for landscape painting — the expert at composition in this sphere always tries to

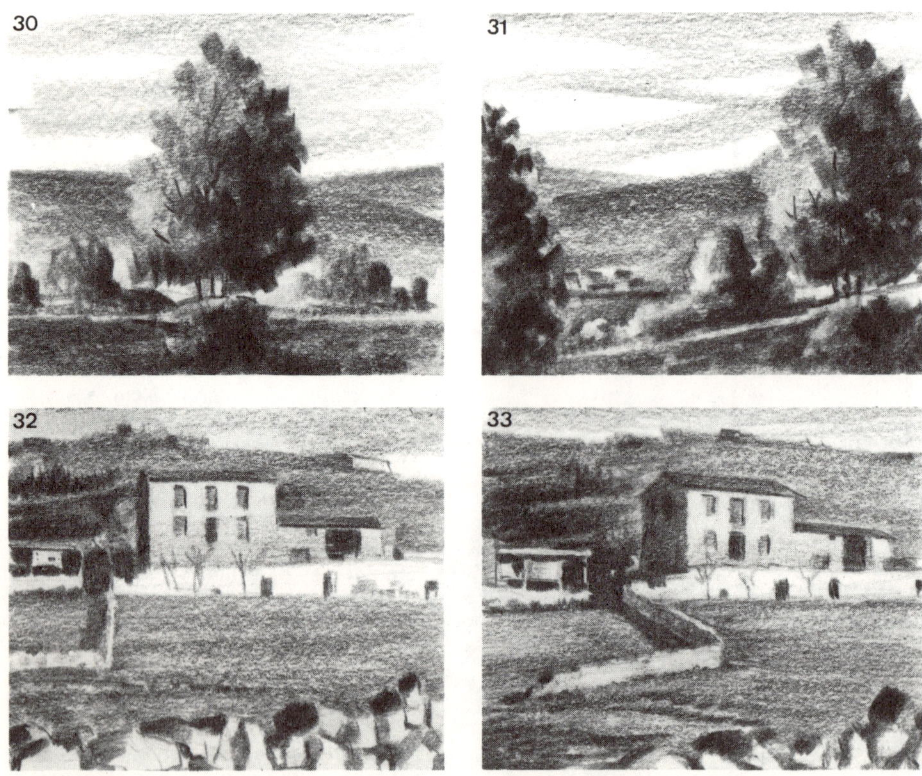

Figs. 30, 31, 32 and 33. Symmetry, and also the direct frontal view of bodies, are not the most appropriate methods to employ when selecting a viewpoint for a landscape. In fact, asymmetrical composition and an oblique viewpoint achieve a greater degree of diversity, which favours the achieving of diversity within unity.

find an asymmetrical arrangement of bodies and of the picture as a whole. This serves to remind us of the need to depict shapes from an oblique viewpoint rather than providing a direct frontal view (Figs. 32 and 33) and to try to find the most effective visual angle which most accurately reflects the principle of unity within diversity.

3. Balance and compensation of masses

In order to understand what is meant by the balance and composition of masses as part of the process of asymmetrical composition in landscape painting, think of a set of old-fashioned scales: these have two weights, at differing distances from the fulcrum, which are kept in equilibrium because one is bigger, and so is heavier than the other. In the process of asymmetrical composition in landscape painting, the fulcrum corresponds to the ideal axis of the picture — which can be deduced from the law of the Golden Section — whereas the role of the weights is played by the patches or volumes — referred to as masses — which constitute important parts or elements of the picture (Figs. 34, 35 and 36). To achieve perfect balance in the picture, which is the same as achieving perfect unity, it is necessary for some masses to be compensated by others. This depends on the size, distance and tonal value of some masses as compared with others.

34

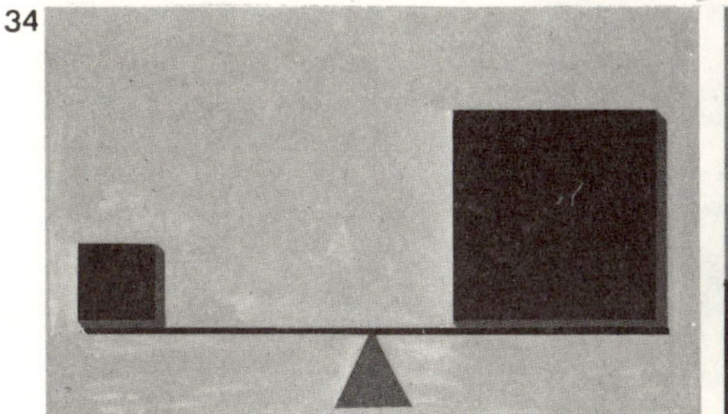

35

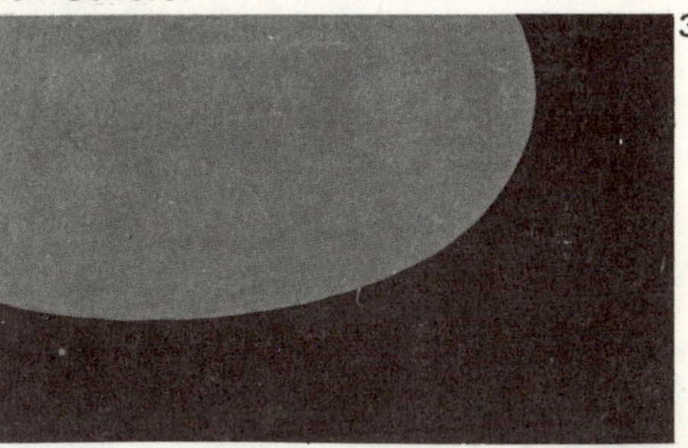

36

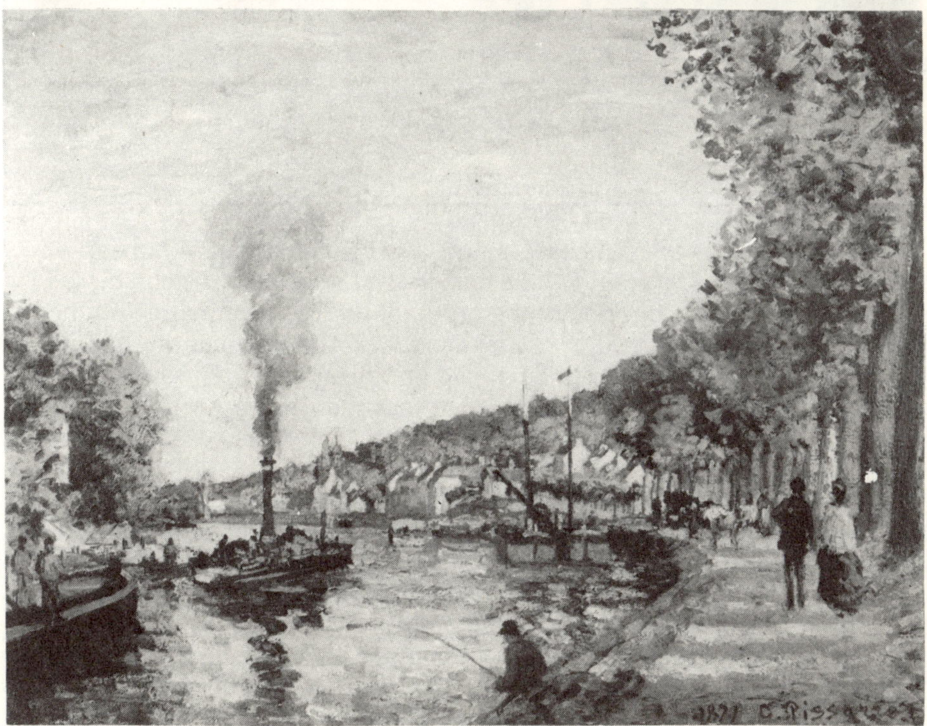

Figs. 34, 35 and 36. In this picture, Pissarro's *The Seine at Marly*, the artist has chosen a viewpoint which enables him to balance the "weights" and "masses" which make up the work. (Private collection).

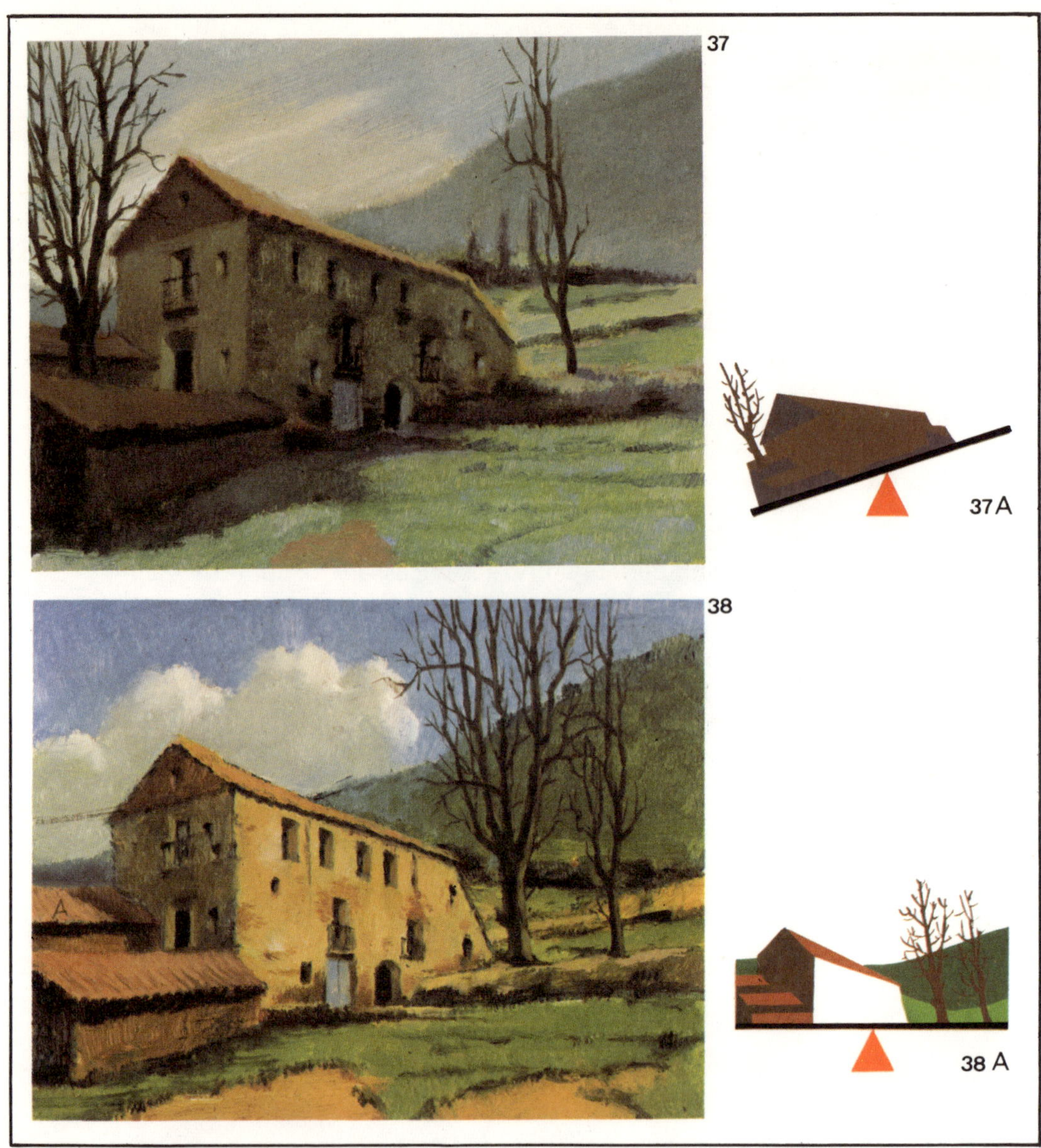

In Fig. 37 above we see a landscape with a small group of houses, a few trees, a hill in the background and a field in the foreground. As can be seen in sketch 37A, the mass or body of the group of houses and the tree on the left constitute a greater weight in comparison with the features on the right of the picture. The result is an unbalanced composition. In Figs. 38 and 38A, however, the features on the left weigh less than those on the right, with one group compensating the other. In this way, equilibrium is re-established.

One might well object: "True. But the model is no longer quite the same". This is a valid objection, up to a point. The fundamental difference is that in Fig. 37 the light comes from behind, leaving the group of houses in shadow, whereas in Fig. 38 the light comes from the right. As regards to the trees, it is true that they are situated differently: in Fig. 38 both are placed on the right of the picture. However, changes such as this are perfectly legitimate and they should be made if they result in the improvement of the

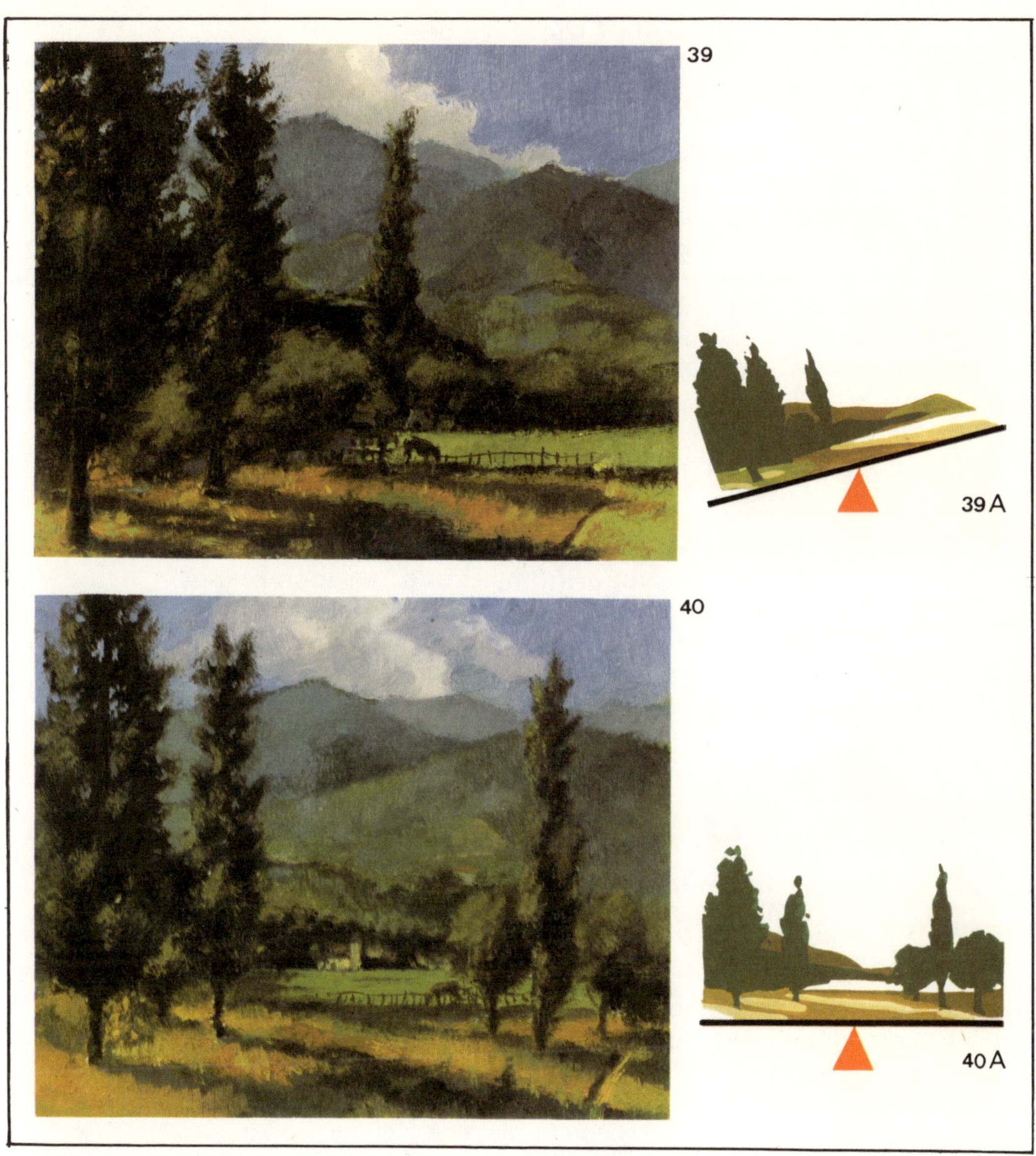

picture. They all form part of the process of interpretation, about which more will be said later.

As another example of this, in Fig. 39, the mass of the trees on the left of the picture is not sufficiently compensated on the right. Slight changes in the location of certain features (Figs. 40 and 40A) achieve a better composition.

It must be emphasized that this is not a decisive factor in composition; but it is worthwhile bearing in mind when deciding on the framework, the viewpoint and the method of lighting.

Sometimes a mere change of position or a different form of illumination, can achieve a marked improvement in the final picture.

4. Graphic portrayal of the third dimension

We will now move on to a different topic.

The study of this factor in composition will need a somewhat more detailed description, since the success of the picture depends on it to a very great extent. The problem consists of overcoming the limitations of a flat picture or surface, which has only two dimensions — width and height — and of reproducing on it a subject which has three dimensions — width, height and depth. Up to this point, all this may seem perfectly obvious. The fact is, however, that in landscape painting depth is an essential factor. One must make it possible for the spectator to "enter the picture" and walk along the paths, the fields and the streets. And this is by no means a statement of the obvious.

In order to achieve the impression of depth, the artist can make use of the following five factors:

a. The inclusion of a foreground;
b. The superimposition of various planes;
c. The effects achieved by perspective;
d. Emphasizing contrast and atmosphere;
e. The use of "close" and "far-away" colours.

We shall have a look at each of these factors and see how the Impressionists made use of them in their paintings.

a. Emphasis on depth by the inclusion of a foreground

If a prominent foreground is included in the composition of a landscape painting, this automatically provides an illusion of depth, because the spectator instinctively compares the size or dimensions of this foreground with the size of features located further away. Let us suppose, for example, that one has chosen as the subject a village in the mountains, as in the photograph in Fig. 41. Theoretically, this scene has a foreground consisting of the houses of the village and a background consisting of the snow-covered mountain in the distance. But this does not sufficiently emphasize the sense of depth. Let us now imagine that, by slightly changing the viewpoint, we manage to include, in the immediate foreground, a tree like that which appears in Fig. 42. Doesn't this make all the difference? The sensation of depth is splendidly emphasized: anyone who looks at the picture will instinctively make a comparison between sizes and a calculation of distances, which will create the illusion that he can walk from the tree to the houses in the village.

This appears perfectly simple, and in fact it is. Moreover, a foreground such as this is a classic method of organizing the composition of a landscape. The Impressionists often employed this technique. Figs. 43 and 44 show two typical examples of the inclusion of foreground features to emphasize the sensation of depth.

41

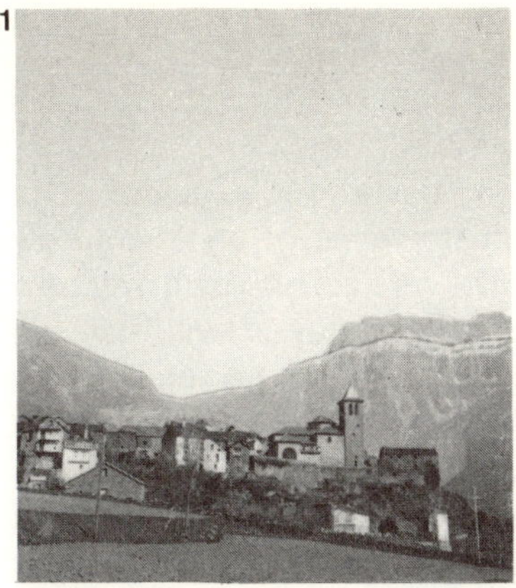

42

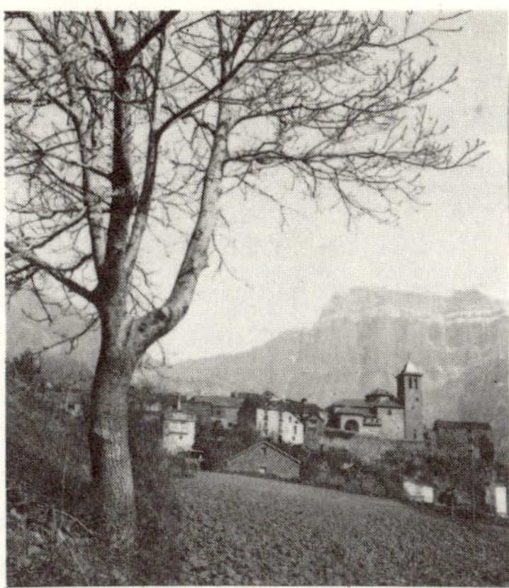

Figs. 41 and 42. The inclusion of a foreground feature (in this case, a tree) is one of the classic methods of emphasizing the sensation of depth. In order to find this foreground, it is usually necessary only to change the viewpoint, by standing a little further back. Or a little more towards the right or left.

43

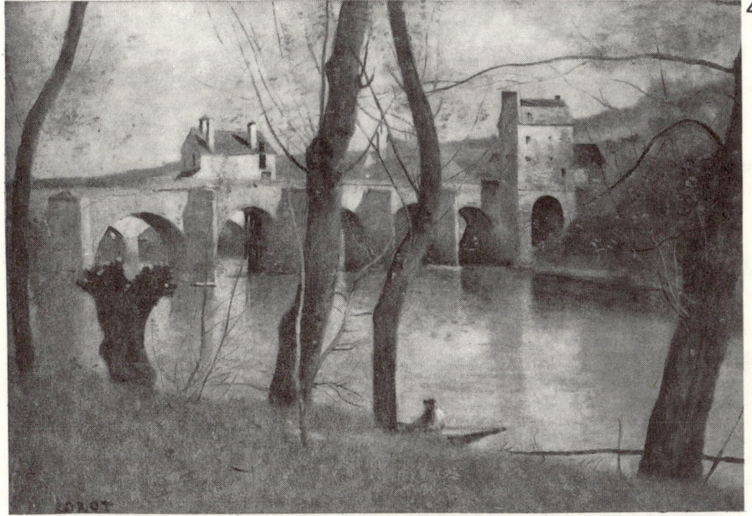

44

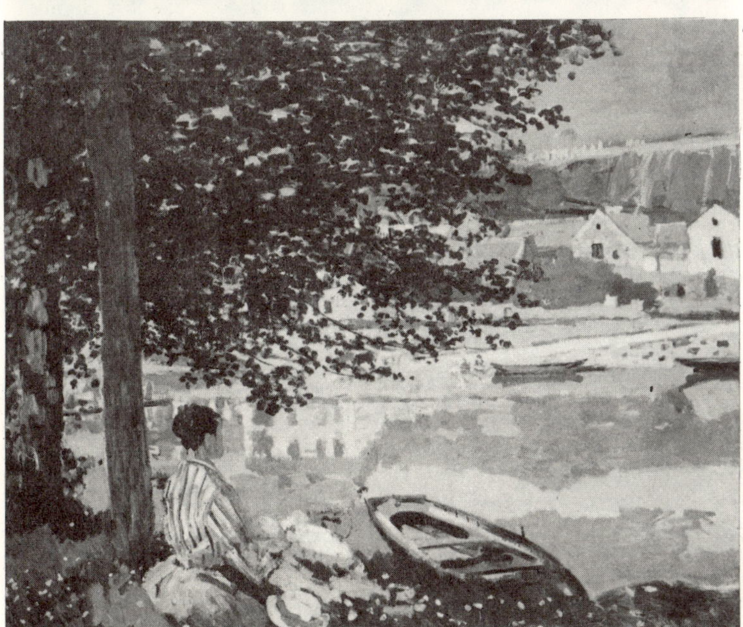

Figs. 43 and 44. Look closely at these two pictures, in which the sensation of depth is emphasized by the inclusion of a striking foreground: the tree-trunks and the edge of the river, in Corot's painting *The bridge at Nantes* (Louvre, Paris), and a tree, a human figure and a boat, in Monet's *The river* (Art Institute, Chicago).

b. Achieving the sensation of depth through the superimposition of various planes

We must now analyse this second factor. Firstly by explaining its underlying theory. Let us suppose that the artist places in an absolutely horizontal plane a series of features, one beside the other. The result will be a picture virtually lacking any third dimension: that is to say, it will have no depth (Fig. 45). If he inclines the plane and places some features closer, and others further away, he will achieve a certain sensation of depth owing to the effects of perspective (Fig. 46). If, however, he places some features behind others, superimposing them in a series of successive and vertical planes, he will increase this sensation of depth by emphasizing the concepts of foreground, middle, distance, background, etc. (Fig. 47).

This is the classic formula. The Impressionists employed it frequently, as can be seen in the two pictures opposite (Figs. 48 and 49). Bearing this formula in mind also means that one has found an effective method of achieving unity within diversity.

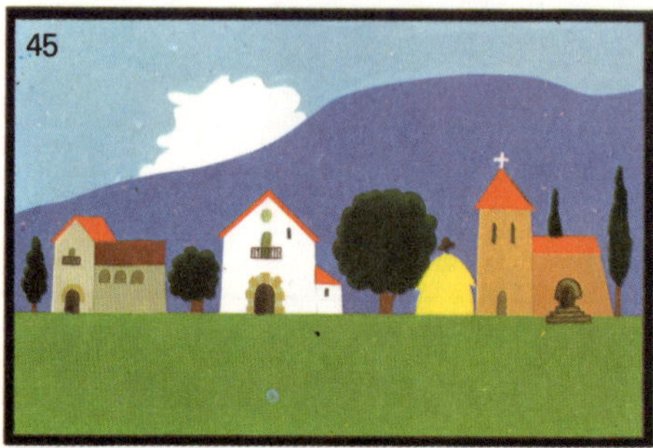

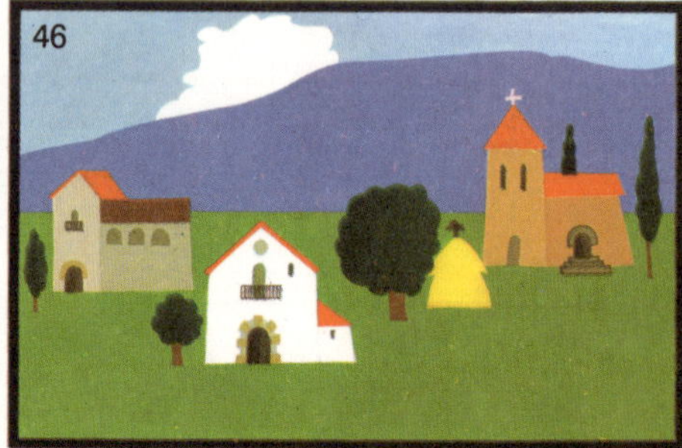

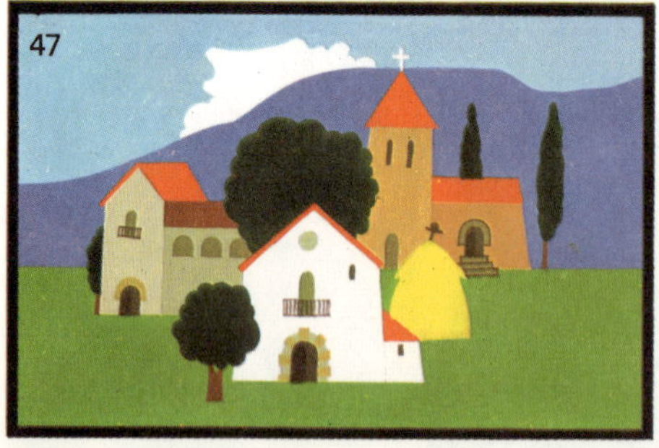

Figs. 45, 46 and 47. This is a graphic representation of the sensation of depth achieved through the superimposition of successive planes. Below, in the sketches for Figs. 48 and 49, the application of this formula in two famous pictures — Monet's *Snow effect at Bétheuil* (Louvre, Paris) and Pissarro's *The red roofs* (Louvre, Paris) — can be seen.

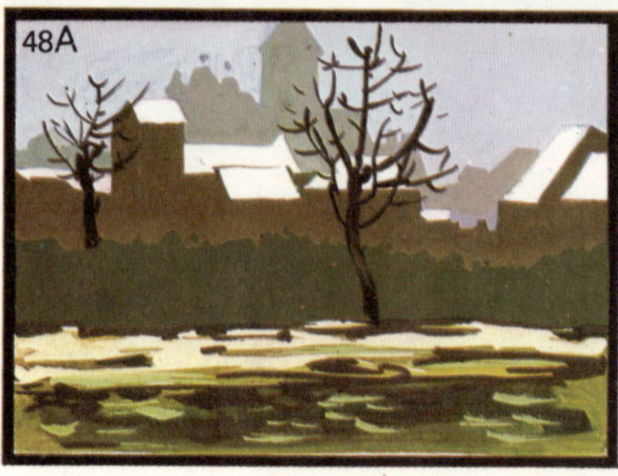

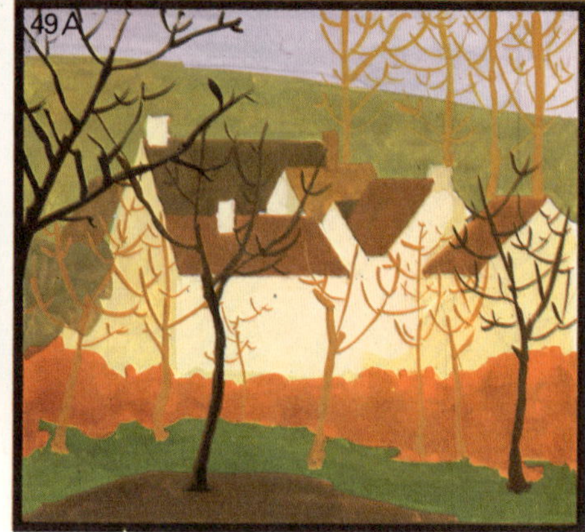

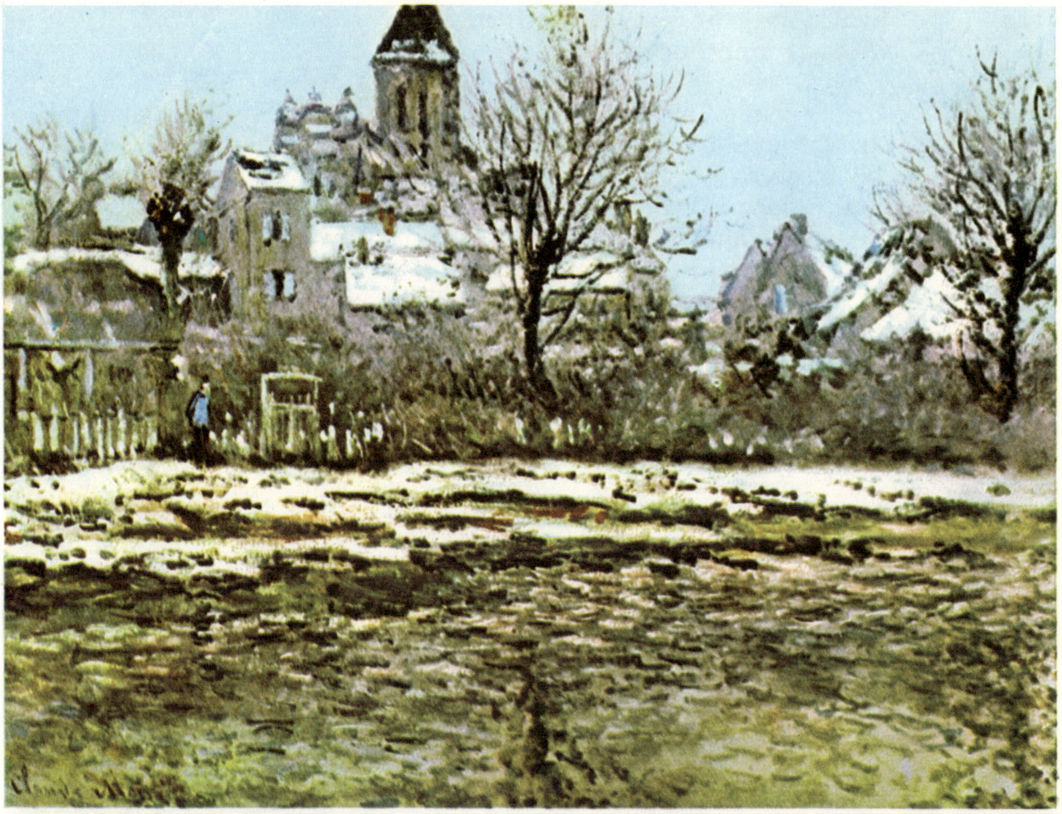

48

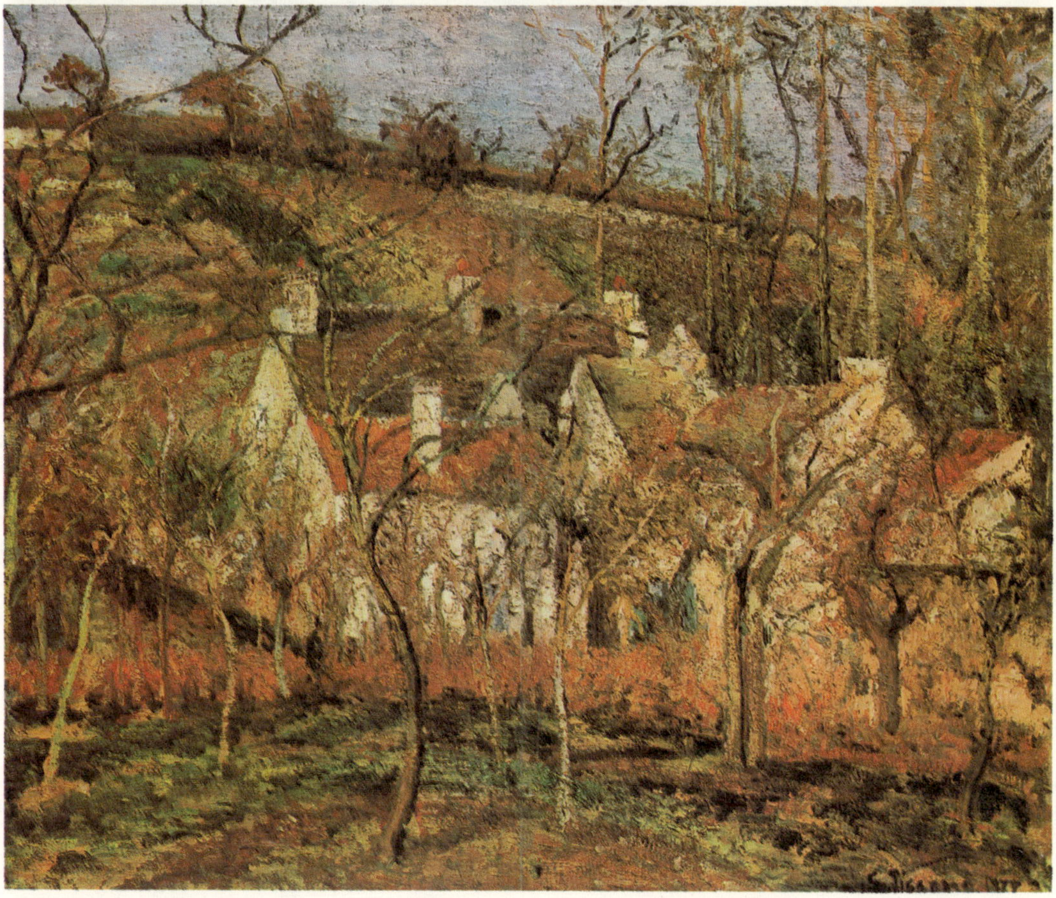

49

c. Increasing the sensation of depth through perspective

Corot, Pissarro, Sisley and Van Gogh himself frequently made use of perspective in order to increase the sensation of depth in their pictures. We do not need to go into any detailed reasoning to understand this. It is enough to look at a few paintings by these famous artists and notice that Corot and Pissarro preferred scenes in which there was a road or highway which, beginning in the foreground, ran towards a group of houses or a small village (Figs. 50 and 51). Sisley often painted houses and streets, rivers with houses on their banks, and even scenes of flooded villages, in all of which perspective was an essential factor in creating the illusion of a third dimension (Fig. 52). In fact, perspective played a vital role in a great many of Van Gogh's and Monet's paintings (see Figs. 53 and 54).

Later in this book we will give a brief description of perspective as it affects landscape painting, since in many cases it is essential for the construction and composition of the picture.

50

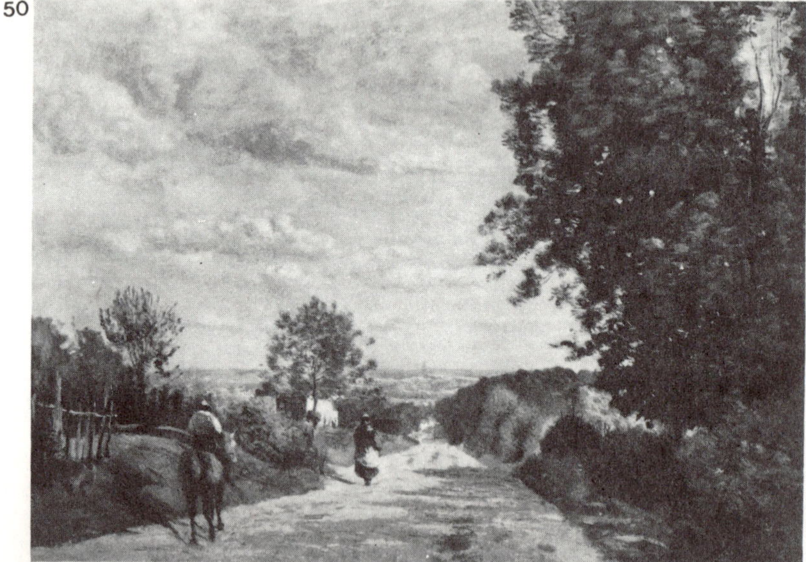

51

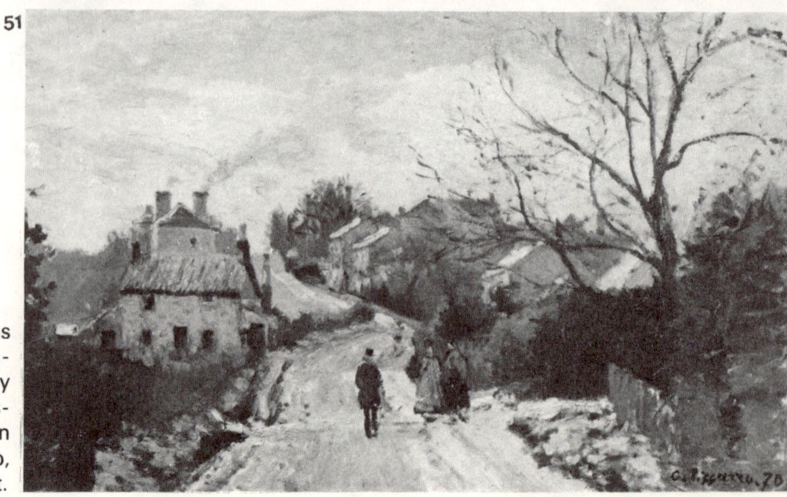

Figs. 50 to 54. Perspective, as means of increasing the sensation of depth, was used by all the artists of the Impressionist period, as can be seen in these paintings by Pissarro, Sisley, Van Gogh and Monet.

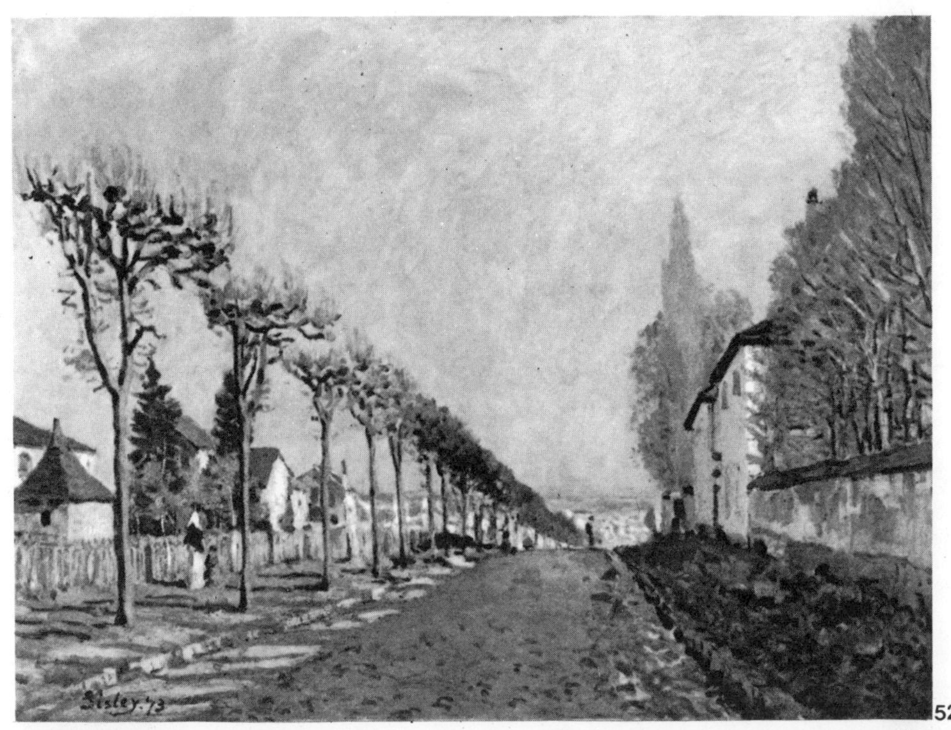

52

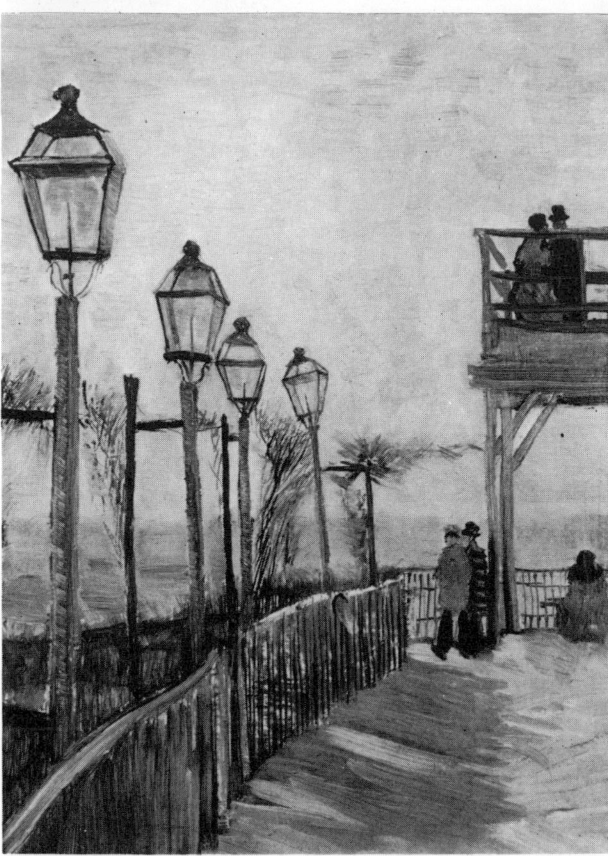

53

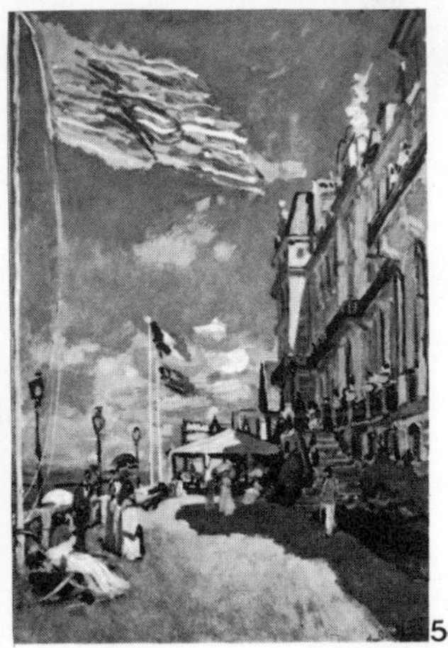

54

Fig. 50. *The road to Sèvres* by Corot (Louvre, Paris).
Fig. 51. *Lower Norwood* by Pissarro (National Gallery, Paris).
Fig. 52. *The road to Sèvres* by Sisley (Louvre, Paris).
Fig. 53. *Montmartre* by Van Gogh (Institute of Art, Chicago).
Fig. 54. *Roches Noires Hotel* by Monet (Laroche Collection, Paris).

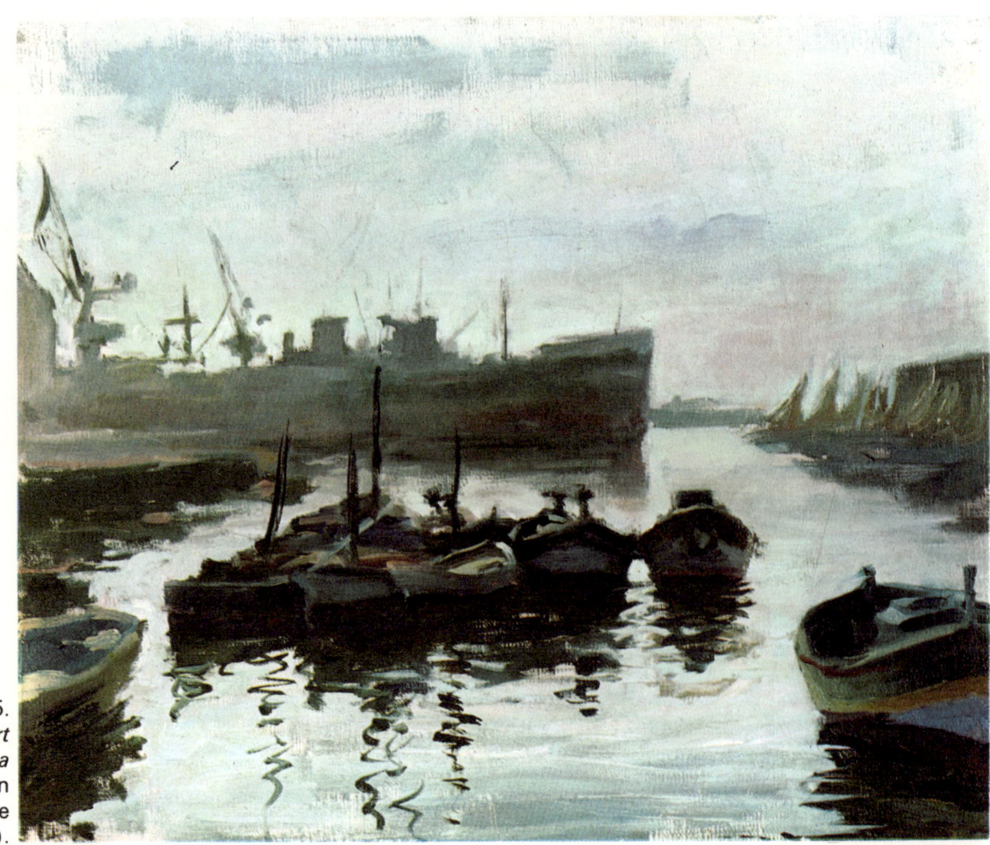

Fig. 55. *The port of Barcelona* by Parramon (private collection).

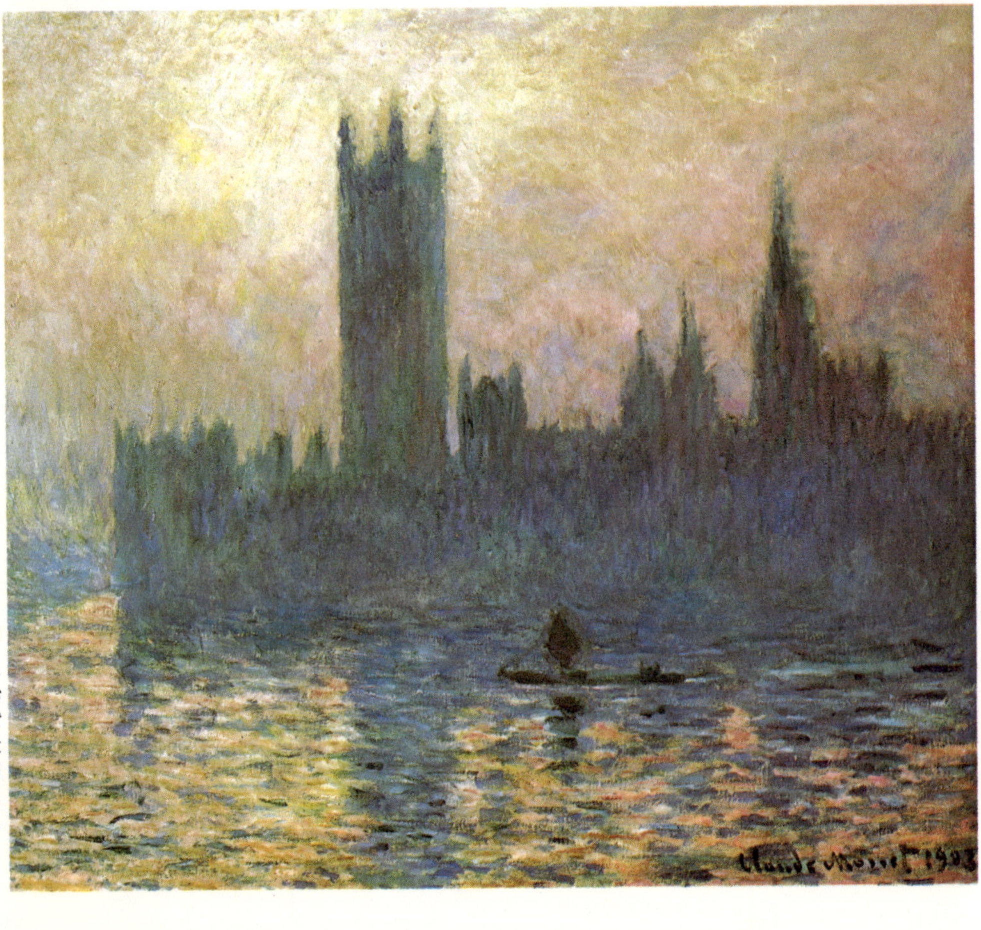

Fig. 56. *The Houses of Parliament* by Monet (National Gallery, London).

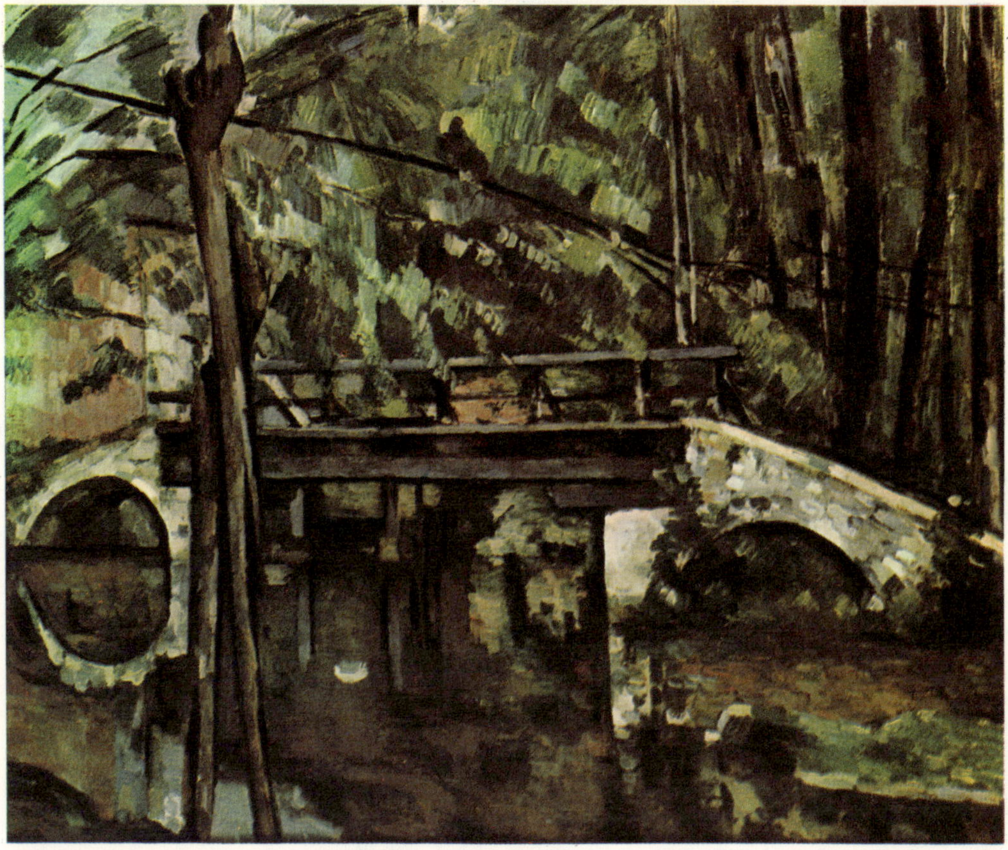

57

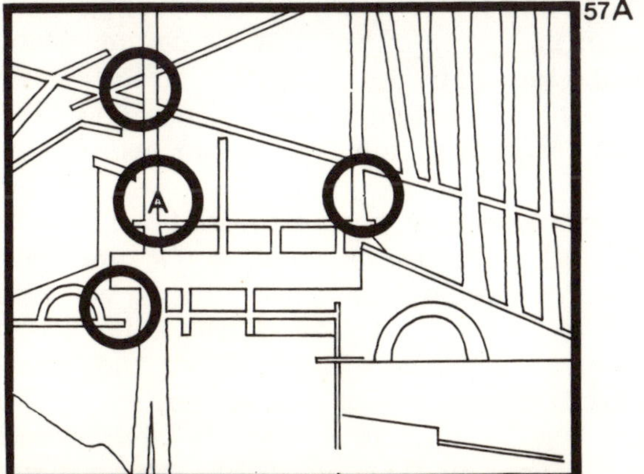

57A

Figs. 57 and 57A. The sensation of depth enhanced by "contrived contrasts" (for a fuller description, see p. 37). Look closely at this picture, Cézanne's *The bridge at Maincy* (Louvre, Paris). Here you can see a series of false contrasts, contrived by the artist, in order to emphasize the outline of some objects in comparison with others and, at the same time, creating an enhanced sensation of depth. As an example of this, note the small area marked A in the sketch of the picture: you can see how this tree-trunk, on its shady side, stands out clearly because of a kind of clarity or aureola, whereas on its sunlit side it is emphasized by the intensely dark colour of the leaves in the background. Similar effects may be seen in the other areas demarcated by small circles, and one realizes that these emphases are not really part of the subject as such: they have been thought out by the artist — in the form of "contrived contrasts" which emphasize certain shapes and distinguish them from others.

d. Enhancing the sensation of depth by use of contrast and atmosphere

The German philosopher Hegel, in his book *The System of Art* has provided us with a magnificent introduction to this new method of enhancing the sensation of depth. He said: "In the real world all objects undergo a variation in colour on account of the atmosphere which surrounds them". And he added:

"The further away objects are, the more they lose the intensity of their colours, and the more indeterminate do their shapes become, because the contrasts between light and shade become increasingly blurred...

"It is usually believed that the foreground is the lightest and the objects furthest away the darkest, although this is not the case. The foreground is the darkest and at the same time the lightest: that is to say, the contrast of light and shade has its most intense effect when closest to us, and so makes shapes more sharply defined."

This guiding principle is so important and so comprehensive, that it is worth attempting to summarize it in the form of two general rules:

The further away from us objects are, the more they lose their intensity of colour, and blue, violet and grey colours tend to predominate.

The foreground is always more clearly defined and offers sharper contrasts than distant objects.

In Fig. 55 you can see an example of these principles. You have the foreground, formed by the parts of two boats on either side, and also by their reflections in the water, which can be seen as clearly defined shapes. In the middle distance — in the case of the group of boats in the centre — and, more especially, in the background formed by the steamship and the mass of sails and the building on the right, the colour is less intense and tends towards grey and blue shades. Moreover, the shapes are less sharply defined.

The concept of blurred outlines had already been expressed by Leonardo da Vinci, in Renaissance times, in his *Treatise on painting:* "If one draws distant objects too distinctly and in too great detail", he wrote, "it will seem as if they are close instead of far away. Try to imitate the subject with discernment, taking into account the distance of each object and, where they are confused and with blurred outlines, depict them as they are and not in excessive detail". Velázquez, himself, in order to achieve his "abbreviated" manner (to use Palomino's term), used to eliminate details, blur outlines, enveloping shapes in air, as can be seen in his splendid painting *Las Meninas* (The maids of honour). The Impressionists, especially Manet and Monet, who are known to have visited the Prado to study Velázquez's style, were past masters at conveying the idea of atmosphere by means of the blurred outline of shapes. In Monet's paintings there is even, at times, an exaggerated concept of the sensation of atmosphere (see Fig. 56). But it must be emphasized that this method of painting is better and more appropriate to the present day than that of the earlier painters who depicted the outlines of shapes as sharply as if they had cut them out with a knife.

Translator's note: is this meant to be Hegel's *Philosophy of Fine Art?*

Mention must also be made, in connection with the enhancement of the sensation of depth by means of contrast and atmosphere, of the experiments of Corot, which were later put into practice by some Impressionists. One of the revolutionary principles underlying painting in France in the 19th century stated that the sensation of depth would be achieved by the neutralization of the foreground. In 1830, Théodore Rousseau wrote that "a spectator looking at a landscape does not see what is lying at his feet". As early as that date it was thought that a landscape without an "accentuated" foreground was a landscape without balance (that is to say, badly composed) and without space (or depth). Corot, repeating experiments carried out by some English painters, reached the conclusion that without the typical foreground formed by figures and tall trees, one could achieve, by just painting a few shrubs, and some blurred stones and edges, the sensation of a foreground closer to the spectator, as compared with the middle distance, with its more sharply defined shapes, and the somewhat more blurred background.

Contrived contrasts

The illusion that one object is in front of another, with air or atmosphere between the two, can be increased by contriving contrasts, even though the latter are not present in the subject. This is something which all professional artists know and put into practice. Leonardo da Vinci expressed it by means of the following formula:

> The background of a particular body should be dark on the sunlit side and bright on the shady side.[1]

In this case, Leonardo was referring to the placing of the model in such a way that the light falling on it, in relation to its background, should display these characteristics (see Fig. 58). However, the experienced artist also applies this technique by superimposing one shape upon another, by painting a bright outline on a dark body or area, etc., in such a way that both bodies and areas "stand out" and are distinguished from one another, so creating the illusion of air and space between them. In Figs. 57 and 57A one can see an example of this technique applied in practice by Cézanne.

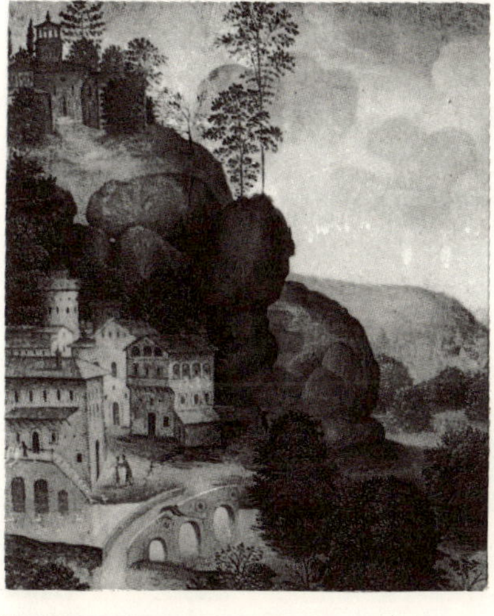

Fig. 58. Here is a detail of Leonardo da Vinci's famous painting *Leda*, where the landscape provides the background for the central figure. Here the great Renaissance artist has put into practice his principle of painting dark tones on the side exposed to light, and bright tones on the shady side. This effect is especially notable in the hills and the flat surfaces of the houses, where there come into play a series of contrasts which have been imagined and accentuated in order to distinguish and emphasize the shape and depth of some bodies as compared with others. There is also a succession of closer planes placed in relation to objects further away.

1. See *Light and Shade for the Artist* in this series, where the problem of light and contrast is dealt with in detail.

e. Enhancing the sensation of depth by the use of "close" and "distant" colours

If the artist paints a patch of mid-blue or bright blue adjoining a patch of yellow, he will notice that yellow is a colour which "comes closer" and places itself in the foreground, whereas the blue "moves away" and appears more distant. In this connection, it is a well-known fact that:

"Warm" colours "bring bodies closer".
"Cold" colours "move bodies further away".

Furthermore, an order of relative "proximity" has been established as follows:

Warm colours in order of "proximity":	Cold colours in order of "distance":
Yellow	Green
Orange	Blue
Red	Bright violet
Carmine	Bright blue-grey

If you find a landscape in which the foreground is yellow or yellowish, and the background is bluish, paint it just as it is: this is a good subject, in terms both of colour and conveying the sensation of depth.

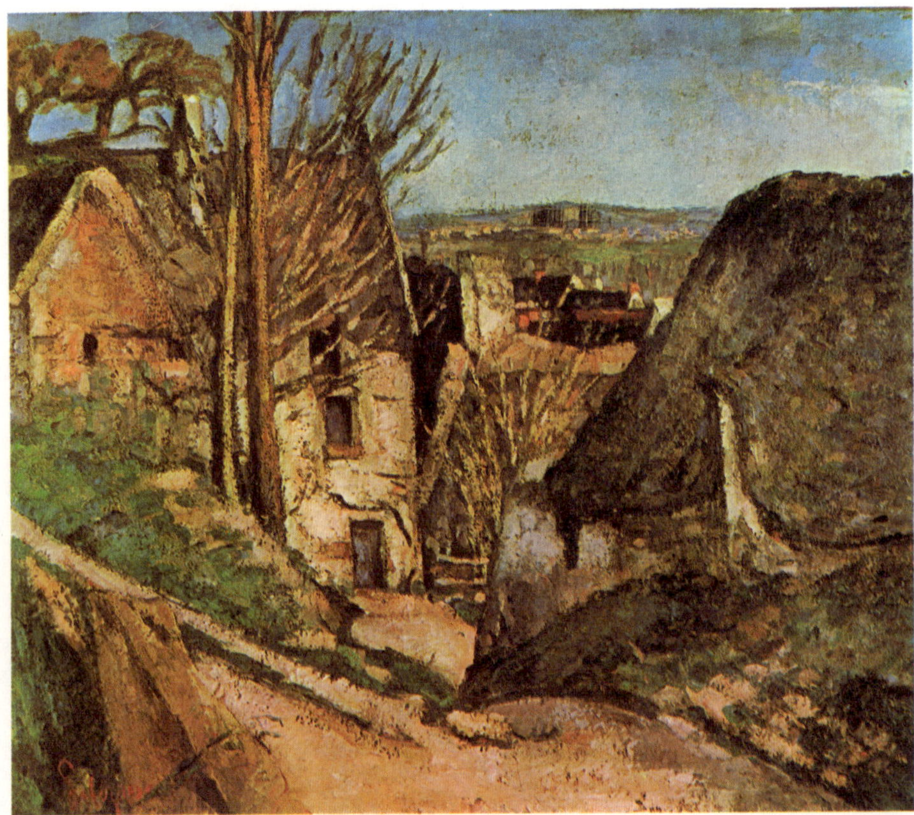

Fig. 59. In this picture by Cézanne, *The house of the hanged man* (Louvre, Paris), one can observe how the sensation of depth is enhanced by the yellowish tone of the foreground, which contrasts with the bluish tone of the background.

Interpretation

Interpretation involves change. In the sphere of music, it is considered that a good "interpreter", in addition to stamping the interpretation of the work concerned with his own style, is capable of improvising variations on the original theme, transforming the work into a new piece. This is the case, for example, with Beethoven's famous "Diabelli Variations", which consisted of 33 variations on an original waltz.

In the field of painting, interpretation conflicts even more sharply with the exact copy of the original model. This is because one takes for granted that a real artist, faced with a model or a natural landscape, feels the excitement of seeing it in his own way — Courbet, for instance, used to say, "I always paint in a state of excitement". The artist looks inside himself and paints "his" landscape, often going as far as to modify reality.

Is it right to change the shapes and colours of the subject in this way, and try to interpret the subject in one's own way? It most certainly is. The idea of painting the picture in the way in which one sees it "inside oneself" has been advocated by many artists, from the earliest to the most modern, from Titian to Picasso, and including Delacroix. "The early artists did not copy Nature exactly: Titian, Rubens and even the classicist Raphael interpreted far more than they copied" (Bousset). "Painters who simply copy their subject will never give the spectator a living sensation of Nature" (Delacroix). "We look on Nature as something routine in character. The artist must see it and paint it as something fantastic and fabulous" (Chagall). "The painter must mould in the picture his own internal impressions and visions" (Picasso).

> "My great desire is to learn how to make such inaccuracies, such anomalies, such modifications, such changes in reality, that... Of course, paint lies if you like, but let them be more true than the literal truth."
>
> Van Gogh

To interpret, to modify, to change... That is what constitutes real art. That is the true basis of inspiration.

Have you, yourself, never felt the emotion of seeing a landscape, imagining it already painted, seeing its shapes, colours and contrasts in "your" way, interpreting it in "your" way?

The difficult art of interpretation

This process is difficult because interpretation is closely connected with the artist's imagination. What is involved is teaching someone how to imagine.

But I must give you some rather abstract ideas about this processs of imagination and the fantasy of the artist, and also emphasize certain definite principles governing artistic interpretation.

Fantasy and artistic imagination are subject to these three factors:

The ability to represent.
The ability to combine features.
And, as a result of these,
The ability to create.

The ability to represent. When the artist stands in front of the subject and sees it for the first time, even before setting up his easel, he spends a long time observing and studying the artistic potential of the subject. He analyses the general formal framework, the peculiar shapes of each feature, the predominant colour of the foreground as compared with those of the middle distance and the background, the contrast of tones and colours... In the course of this analysis, there springs to the mind of the artist, perhaps instinctively, representations of other images seen and remembered for their impact, their beauty or personal style. He may well recall colours used by Van Gogh, shapes used by Cézanne, the chromatic harmonies of a film, the effects of atmosphere observed at another time and in another place, the contrasts of a photograph in black and white, and so on. The ability to recall these images visually, while he is looking at the subject, prompts him to dream, to modify reality and to effect changes.

The ability to combine what is now seen with what remains to be seen. The ability to see other colours and other shapes, to achieve an overall visual image of some idea differing from the actual reality, makes the latter (the landscape before him) give place to the landscape which the artist "sees" within himself. On the basis of this, the artist combines what he is seeing with what remains to be seen: he "works" his landscape, discovers combinations between reality and his memories, studies fresh approaches, emphasizes, accentuates, reduces and eliminates... Then he easily attains the stage of creativity.

The ability to create. On the basis of the processes described above, creativity now begins to play its part. It is, essentially, the result of a fresh attitude towards something that we wish to change. The significance of the word "attitude" is of decisive importance in this context: it represents the sum total of all our knowledge, thoughts and reactions, reflected as the conscious desire to find a new approach, to paint a future picture, which will be different from present reality and from the representation of the past, and which can therefore take the form of something that has never been seen or thought of.

Three technical secrets of the art of interpretation

These are easy to remember. It is, perhaps, unnecessary to explain them; it is sufficient to assert that they are:

1. Amplification

2. Reduction

3. Elimination

To *amplify*, emphasize, exaggerate or intensify a particular colour. The yellow of that pile of straw, the dark green behind it... And so one increases the contrast: that house in the middle distance which looks somewhat small... that tree... that cloud...

To *reduce*, tone down, soften, diminish the size of the thickets in the background, the width of the road, the bright colour of the roof, the edges of the background...

To *eliminate*, suppress, paint over, get rid of those rocks on the left, the telegraph-pole in the middle, the modern house in the background, the grass in the foreground...

"It is the first impression that counts" or the major problem of interpretation

What happens is that the artist is going along with his easel and his paintbox on his back (or in the family car) when suddenly, as he rounds a corner or after he goes up or down a hill, he sees a likely subject. He stops, looks, then looks again from a little further away, or a little closer, and then... "Splendid", he thinks. "That background predominantly blue, this almost black foreground cut out like a silhouette, the houses in the background standing out in sharp contrast and surrounded by a patch of yellow so bright that it might almost have come straight out of the tube... What a picture! It reminds me of those fields in Provence painted by Van Gogh... I'll paint that hill with four broad strokes of the brush, and those thickets with black and green streaks. I will paint a picture almost without shadows. In full colour!"

What happens is that he sees the picture within himself: he sees it with real excitement. He becomes enthusiastic when he thinks what it will be like... He sets up his easel, places the canvas in position, takes up his brushes and palette knife... He is in a hurry: he sees the picture as something extraordinary. He begins to paint.

And, of course, half-an-hour after rushing into it like this, the painting no longer looks like anything that he had imagined: it is just one more picture, correct enough in the usual style and with the usual "perfection".

What has happened?

Let us take note of the explanation offered by the French post-Impressionist painter, Pierre Bonnard, a real authority on modern painting as regards the failure of an interpretation which promised to be extraordinarily good:

"The basis of a picture is, in principle, an idea. This idea determines the selection of the subject and the picture itself; by means of it, the picture can become transformed into a work of art. However, this initial idea tends to fade away and give place to the visual image of the actual subject which, unfortunately, invades and dominates the painter's consciousness. When this happens, the artist is no longer painting 'his' picture."

Claude Monet was terrified of the possibility of the subject's gaining control over him: he knew that he would be lost if he spent more than a quarter of an hour being guided by what he saw in the subject. Bonnard himself admitted: "I have tried to paint directly from the subject, exercising scrupulous care and, unintentionally, I have allowed myself to become absorbed by what lay in front of me. I have ceased to be myself. I need, therefore, a very personal system of defence. I paint only in my studio. I do everything in my studio."

How, then, can one resist this temptation, this seductive appeal offered by the subject?

In this connection, Cézanne said:

"I have, in relation to the subject, a firmly established idea of what I want to do, and I accept from Nature only what is compatible with my ideas, and the shapes and colours of the landscape as they are according to my initial conception."

One can imagine Cézanne looking at his landscape for a long time, until he succeeded in formulating that firmly established idea which was to guide him during his painting of the picture. One can imagine him later, while he was painting, continually repeating to himself "as I see it", "as I see it", never allowing himself to be seduced by the siren-song of the subject. This is not easy, of course, but it is the only way.

A final and decisive factor in the composition and interpretation of the subject

All the advice and instructions given in these pages about the art of composition and interpretation of a landscape are completely futile unless the painter has a broadly based artistic culture. In this context, culture must be understood to mean not only the knowledge of history, names, dates, epochs and styles but, especially, the knowledge and remembering of pictures, paintings in museums, exhibitions, good books and reproductions, etc.

The serious painter or student should devote a few hours every week to visiting museums and art galleries. He should acquire encyclopaedias and books on art containing good and plentiful reproductions of pictures. (There are, for example, many good books on Impressionism.)

The camera is an extremely useful instrument for learning to select subjects and finding the best viewpoint, the best framework for the picture, and the best system of illumination. One must consider the idea. — I would almost say the need — of taking a photograph of the subject which has been painted, not only to have a real souvenir of the place where one has been but also to be able to compare at home, later on, the results of "one's own" pictures as compared with the actual subject. This will, moreover, give the opportunity of rectifying, repainting or finishing the picture.

It is also worth considering the possibility of keeping a file, for later study, of cuttings from newspapers and magazines with good colour reproductions of landscape paintings.

Lastly, follow the advice given by Picasso to Geneviève Laporte when she asked him what she should do to learn how to paint. "You want to be an artist? Then observe. Observe what is going on around you." What about the cinema, for instance? What wonderful landscapes in colour can be seen there! Take in the effects of light and shade, the patches and contrasts of colour. These are all potential pictures, which you can remember when you come to paint a landscape.

Technical aspects of landscape painting in oils

I have taught painting to hundreds of amateurs and one of the most absurd notions that I encountered was that drawing was a prosaic activity, of little value, whereas painting was something sublime and poetic. So as soon as they could, they gave up drawing... and they proved complete failures when they tried to paint. Van Gogh once said to his brother Théo:

"There are laws governing proportion, light and shade, and perspective, and they are vital to any painter: if one does not possess this knowledge, one is involved perpetually in a fruitless struggle and will never succeed in giving birth to a work of art."

Hence, we will give some account of this prosaic activity and the incubation period. We will remind the reader of certain principles of the art of drawing, so that we can then give birth to splendid pictures.

The principles of boxing up and their application to landscape painting[1]

"Every body can be reduced to the shape of a cube, a cylinder and a sphere", Cézanne used to say to his friends. With this observation, Cézanne was laying the foundations for the Cubist style, but at the same time he was expressing a general law governing the art of drawing.

A house does, in fact, have essentially the shape of a cube (or of a parallelepiped, which for this purpose amounts to much the same thing). The trunk and the boughs of a tree can be reduced basically to a series of cylinders. And the top of a tree, a thicket or a heap of straw are all basically in the form of a sphere (see Fig. 60).

Of course, when the artist is an expert draughtsman, he does not draw cubes or cylinders or spheres, although these shapes are certainly present in his mind and he takes them as a basis for constructing and painting the various features of the picture.

Similarly, the proportion of certain features as compared with others can certainly be determined more easily if one begins by drawing simply "boxes" or cubes to represent the various shapes (Fig. 61) and "within" these, once the proportions have been correctly calculated, the actual shapes can be drawn.

---

1. The reader is advised to consult the first book in the present series entitled *Drawing*, where the problems involved in good draughtsmanship are studied in greater detail.

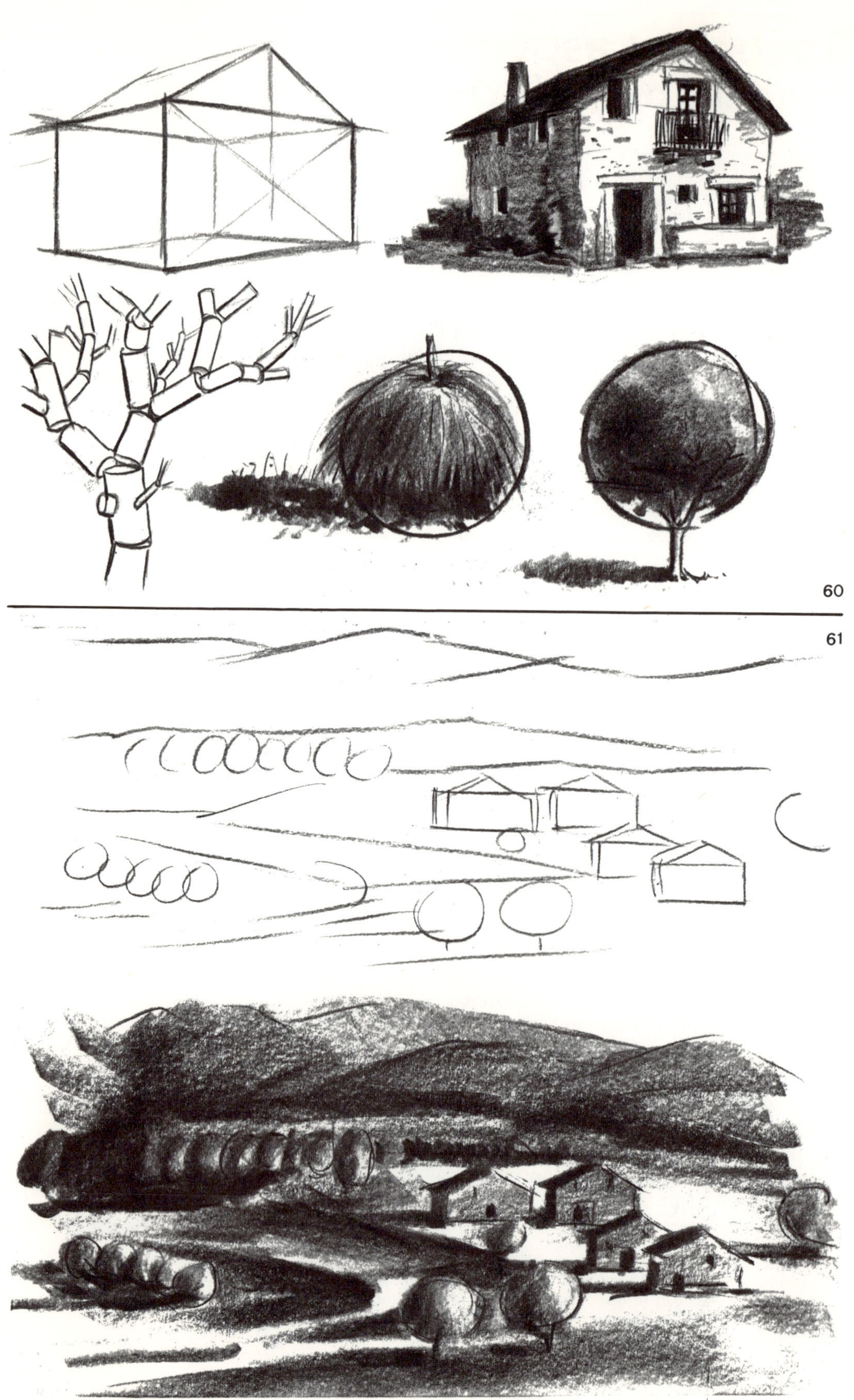
60
61

The laws of perspective and their application to landscape painting

A knowledge of the laws of perspective — a practical knowledge which enables one to trace, draw and paint with confidence — is absolutely essential for good landscape painting.

Firstly, it is important to recognize that there are three types or forms of perspective:

1. **Parallel perspective, or perspective from one vanishing point.**
2. **Oblique perspective, or perspective from two vanishing points.**
3. **Aerial perspective, or perspective from three vanishing points.**

The third type is not, in practice, used in landscape painting and will therefore not be dealt with in this book.[2]

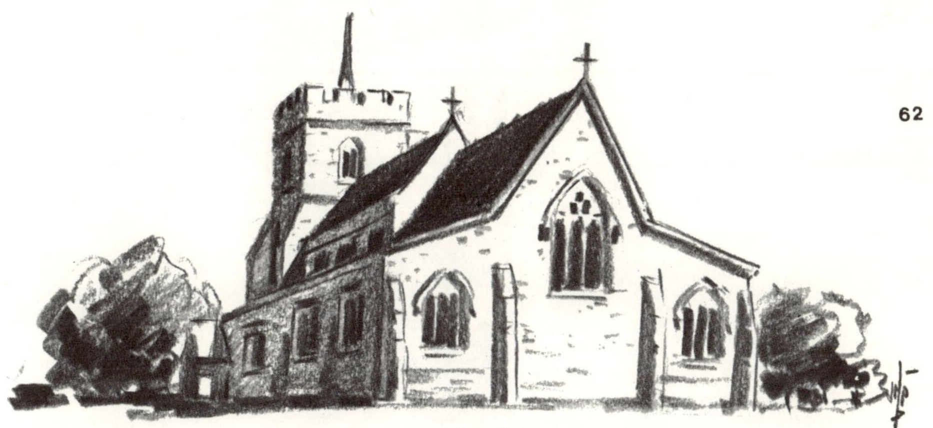

62

Parallel perspective

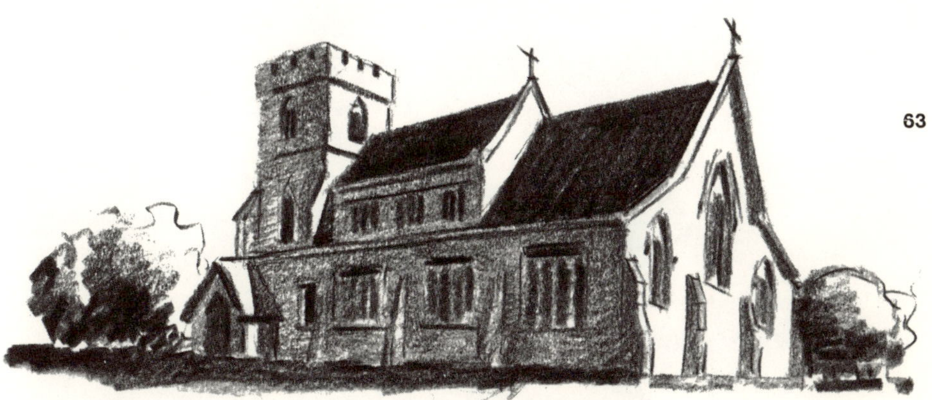

63

Oblique perspective

2. The reader is advised to consult *Drawing in Perspective* in this series, which contains a full study of perspective as it applies to drawing and painting.

As the reader should know, the vanishing point or points are the place where the perpendicular lines and edges of the model meet. It will also be remembered that the vanishing points are always to be found on the so-called "horizon line". The latter, in turn, is situated exactly level with the viewpoint of the spectator, when he is looking forwards — i.e., that of the artist, when he is painting — whether he be standing, sitting or crouching. Lastly, there is the important consideration that, in the case of parallel perspective, the vanishing point (there is only one) and the viewpoint meet at the same place on the horizon. This does not happen in the case of oblique or aerial perspective where the vanishing point and the viewpoint are independent of one another (even though they both meet on the horizon).

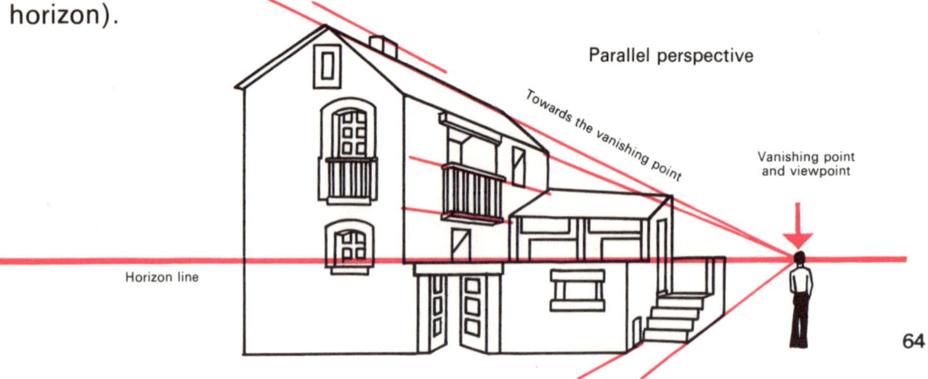

64

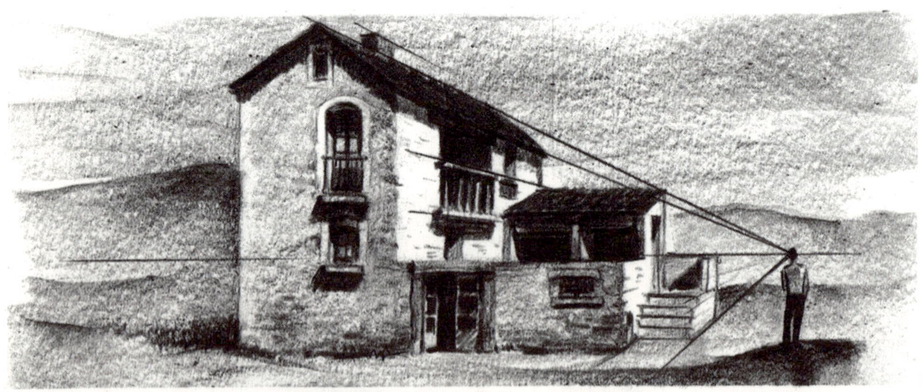

65

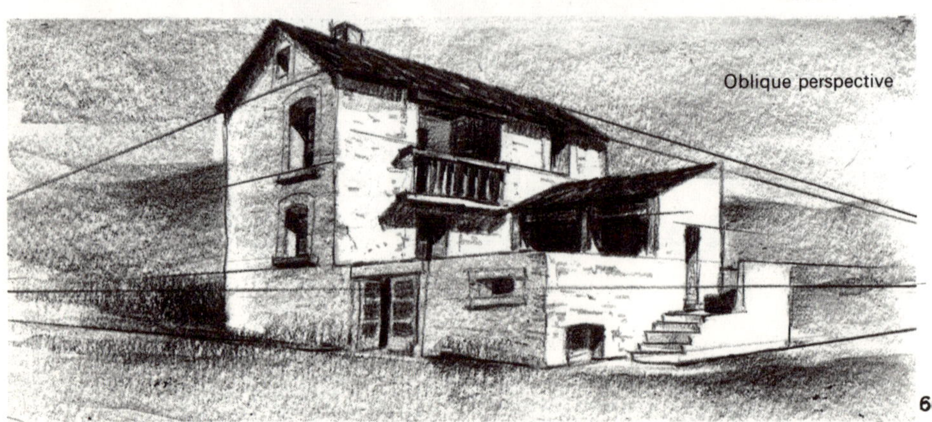

66

One problem often encountered in connection with perspective as applied to landscape painting, especially the painting of urban scenes, is that of dividing the spaces according to their degree of depth (Fig. 68). In such cases, the following formulae are to be applied:

Drawing the centre of a square or rectangle in parallel perspective

To find the centre of a given square or rectangle, and also its division for perspective purposes, based on the centre, it is enough to draw diagonal lines across it (Figs. 67-70).

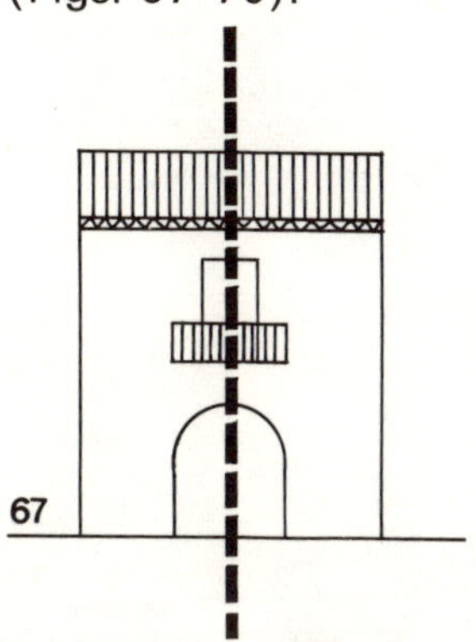

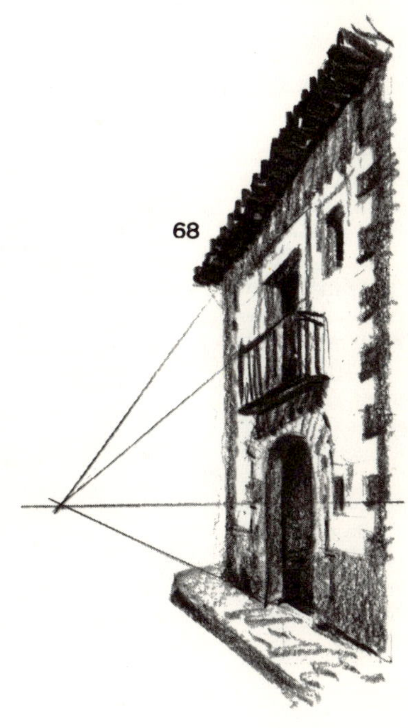

Figs. 67-70. In order to find the centre of the rectangle for the purposes of perspective in the case of this house-front, and to situate the balcony and the doorway correctly (Figs. 67 and 68), one has only to draw a cross which will give one the perspective centre required (Figs. 69 and 70).

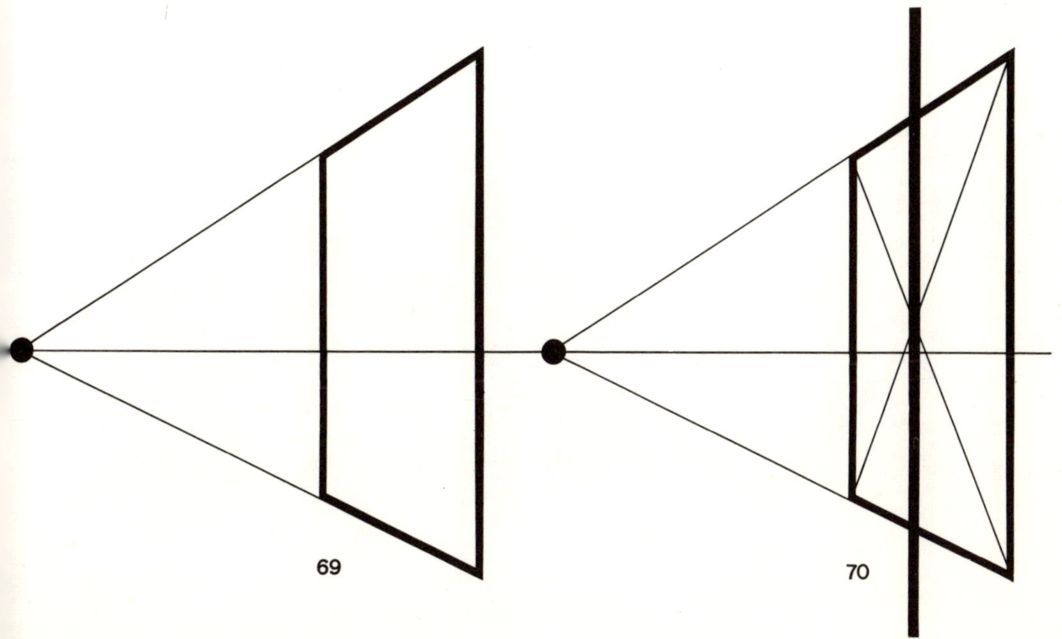

Drawing the division into equal parts of a space, in terms of parallel perspective

The simplest formula consists of dividing into two parts the nearest horizontal or vertical line, then drawing from Point A a perpendicular line towards the vanishing point (Figs. 72 and 73), calculating by eye the first division, which is the nearest, B (Fig. 74). Then draw the diagonal line C (Fig. 75) and repeat this operation as often as necesssary, so obtaining lines D, E, F, etc. (Figs. 76 and 77).

This is quite enough (once it has been learnt by heart) for solving problems of this kind.

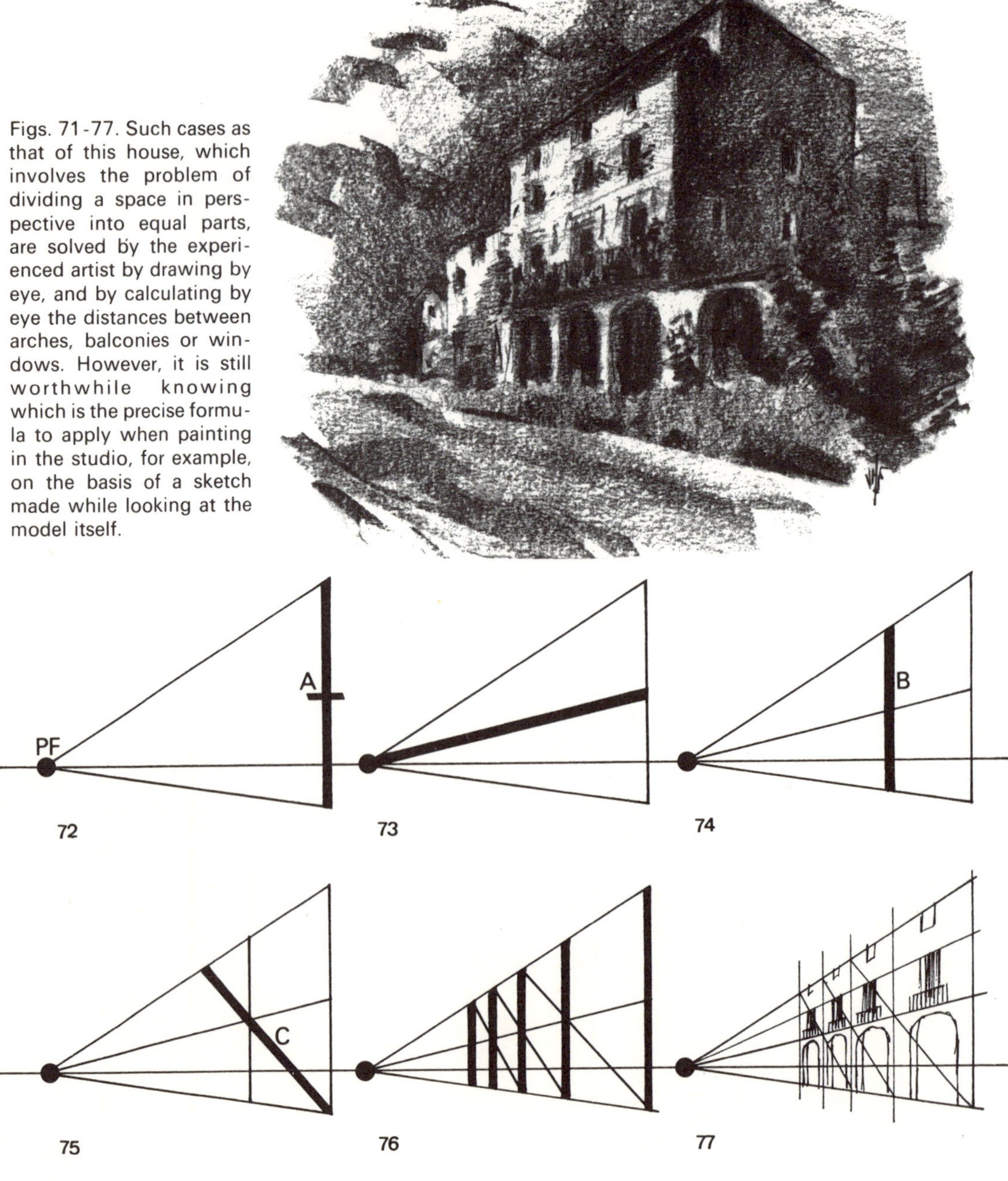

Figs. 71-77. Such cases as that of this house, which involves the problem of dividing a space in perspective into equal parts, are solved by the experienced artist by drawing by eye, and by calculating by eye the distances between arches, balconies or windows. However, it is still worthwhile knowing which is the precise formula to apply when painting in the studio, for example, on the basis of a sketch made while looking at the model itself.

Evaluation of tones and problems of light and shade

Ever since the Impressionists made their impact on the art of painting with their pictures filled with light and colour, landscape painters — and, indeed, painters of all other subjects — can be divided into two major categories:

1. Those who, when painting, prefer to express the volume of bodies by means of colour, making only a limited use of the effects of light and shade.
2. Those who paint in colour but tend to express the volume of bodies through the effect of light and shade.

The first group might be termed "chromatists", and the second "intensificationists" (because they make use of local colours and shades to determine the proportions of bodies). The first group gives priority to colour rather than draughtsmanship, whereas the second group is content to draw the bodies of the subject just as they are. It all depends on the temperament of the artist, which is undoubtedly reflected in his style: for example, Van Gogh was definitely a "chromatist" whereas Dalí is a brilliantly skilful "intensificationist". There is no question, at this stage, of analysing which procedure or which artist is the better of the two. In the words of the present-day painter Lhote: "There are no good or bad methods, but simply good or bad ways of applying them". There is, however, no doubt that each style is determined to a great extent by the method of illumination, and it seems that one can also assert — especially as regard to landscape painting — that the "chromatist" style is more closely related to the techniques of modern painting that the "intensificationist" style.

The "intensificationist" style

It must be borne in mind that to "intensify" a picture means presenting the different tones of the subject with an intensity differing in each case. In painting, this intensification is provided by the local colour, or colour in the true sense of the term, of the subject concerned (the red of a poppy, the green of a field, the yellow of a heap of straw, and so on) and "tonal" or darker colour is the result of the subject's being in shadow. Lastly, with regard to shadow, one must distinguish between real shadow and projected shadow (Fig. 78).

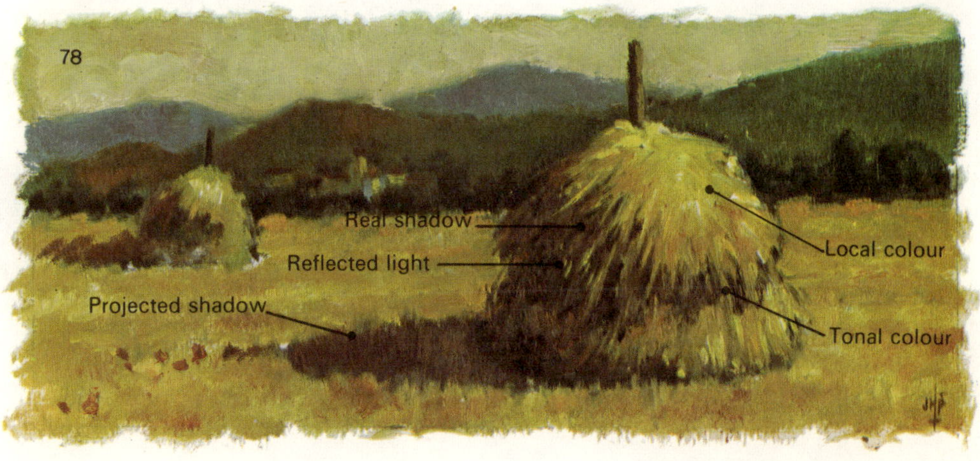

Of course, in order that a subject show the effects of light and shade, the lighting must be partly frontal and partly lateral, with the subject seen partly or wholly against the light.

There are two further factors connected with lighting which affect the "intensificationist" style, namely quantity and quality. The quantity is influenced by the time of day, and depends on whether it is noon (with considerable light) or dawn or dusk (when there is less light). The quality, on the other hand, is determined by the sun itself and depends on whether it is a clear day or whether the sky is partly or completely clouded over. Both quantity and quality have a marked effect on the contrast of tones and values, to such an extent — this must be emphasized — that on a very cloudy day bodies throw practically no shadow at all. This brings us to the question of the "chromatist" style.

The "chromatist" style

Is it possible to paint a landscape without shadows? Can the volume of bodies be represented without the help of the effects of light and shade?

The answer is definitely "Yes", for the simple reason that:

Colour — in itself — diversifies, separates and brings out the shapes of the bodies.

If we were to paint a subject without shadow, simply in black and white (and varying shades of grey), we should find it difficult to bring out the shape of a house coloured red, a tree coloured green, and a field of natural earthen colour: these three colours, represented as grey, would be almost identical (Figs. 79). Our only hope would be to wait for the sun to come out, in order to bring out and correctly depict the shape, location and volume of each feature (Fig. 80). In colour, however, it is a different matter — the three colours are so different. Each colour brings out positions and builds up, on its own, the shapes of the subject (Fig. 81).

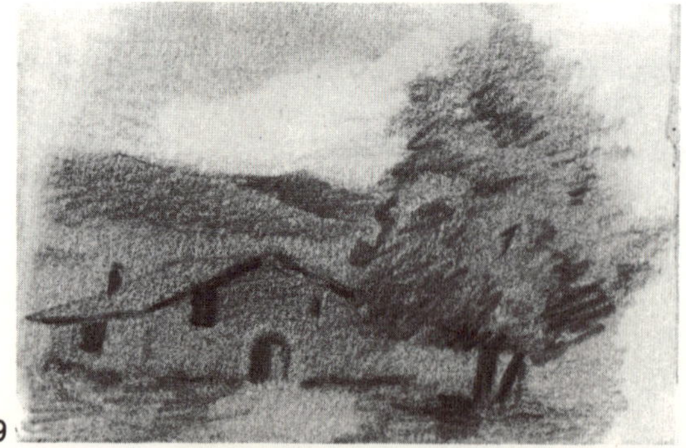

79

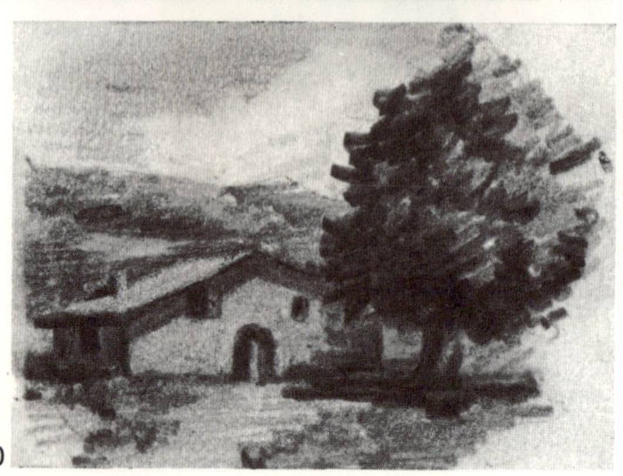

80

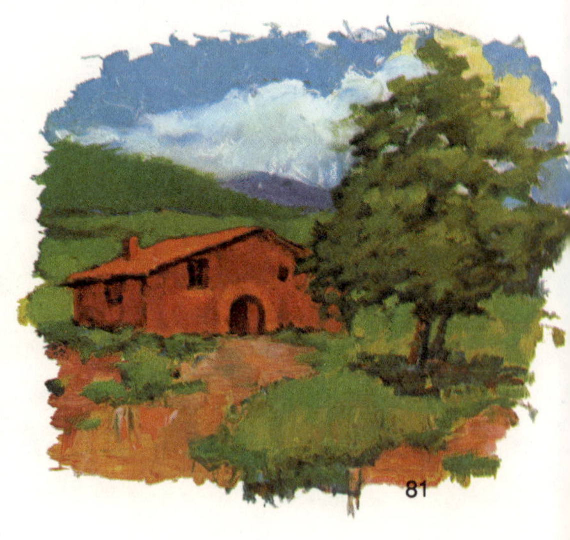

81

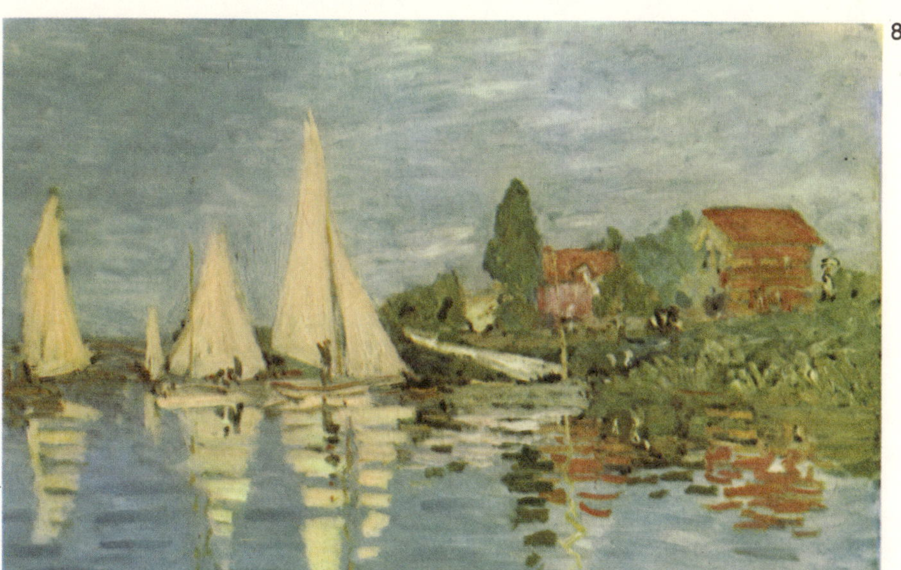

82

82. Monet's *Regatta at Argenteuil* (Louvre, Paris).

83. Van Gogh's *The Crau plain* (or *Market gardens*) (private collection, Laren).

83

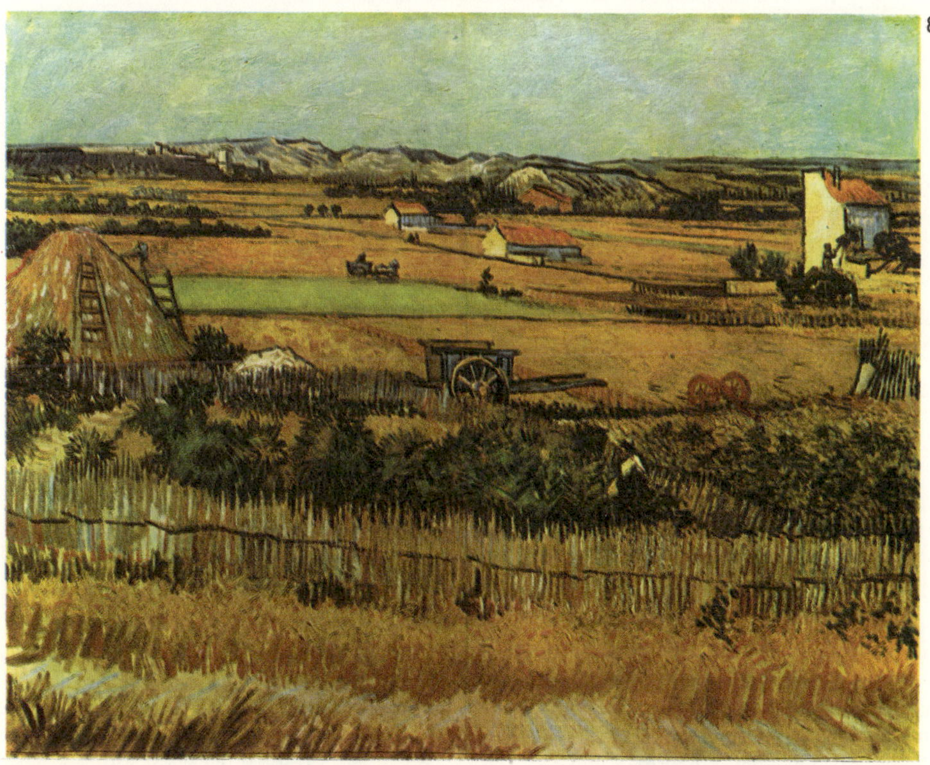

Two spendid examples of the theory underlying the "chromatist" style can be seen in these pictures by Monet and Van Gogh (Figs. 82 and 83). Note that lighting is frontal, so that there are practically no shadows. Nevertheless, the shapes of the bodies stand out perfectly.

The reader must now take note of the following point, in connection with the "chromatist" style and the method of lighting of the subject:

> **In order to achieve the most satisfactory results when using the "chromatist" style, it is advisable to paint with frontal-cum-lateral or completely frontal lighting when the sun is shining, or with diffused light and when there is no sun and the sky appears cloudy.**

It must also be noted that, in these circumstances, the quantity and quality of light are of only relative importance.

One must not exaggerate, however. It should be remembered that even the artists most attached to the "chromatist" style did not impose on themselves, as an obligation, the elimination of shade. Van Gogh painted very little shade, but he accentuated outlines and shapes with the peculiar style of his which involved drawing objects with broad strokes of colour, while Monet did not hesitate to emphasize particular points with dark colours in order to assert more categorically his depiction of certain shapes (see again Figs 82 and 83).

My advice to the reader is that he should try to paint in the "chromatist" style, because, as I have said before, this is the style that corresponds most closely to that of present-day painting.

THEORY OF COLOUR

Some time ago, I came across a delightful passage written by Van Gogh regarding the theory of colour. Which, if one modernizes and explains certain concepts more fully, can serve as a perfect summary for use by the artist of today:[1]

"It is one of the great truths in which Delacroix placed his faith: the ancients admitted only three primary colours, and the modern painters do not admit any others."

Van Gogh said:

Primary colours:

Purple (violet-pink)
Yellow
Blue

---

1. Vincent Van Gogh, *Letters to Théo*: Referring to the spectrum of light, and quoting Newton, Van Gogh distinguishes seven colours: violet, indigo, blue, green, yellow, orange and red. He makes it clear that there are only three primary colours and three secondary ones, and goes on to explain: "With regard to indigo, it cannot be included among the primary colours, since it is merely a variant of the colour blue". Here, Van Gogh was already adumbrating the present-day theory that the spectrum of light consists of only six colours. On the other hand, Van Gogh, in accordance with the theory current in his time, classifies red as a primary and violet as a secondary colour whereas, according to present-day theory, red is considered to be a secondary colour and purple (a sort of violet-pink, referred to in artistic terminology as "magenta") is regarded as a primary colour. These theories are explained and expressed in contemporary terminology in the course of this book.

"These three colours are the only ones that cannot be broken down and reduced any further. It must, therefore, be recognized that in Nature there are only three really basic colours". (See Fig. 84.)

In fact, as Van Gogh asserts, all the colours in Nature can be obtained by means of mixtures of the three primary colours alone. For the purposes of oil-painting, these three colours are:

Yellow .... Medium cadmium yellow
Purple .... Madder red
Blue .... Prussian blue

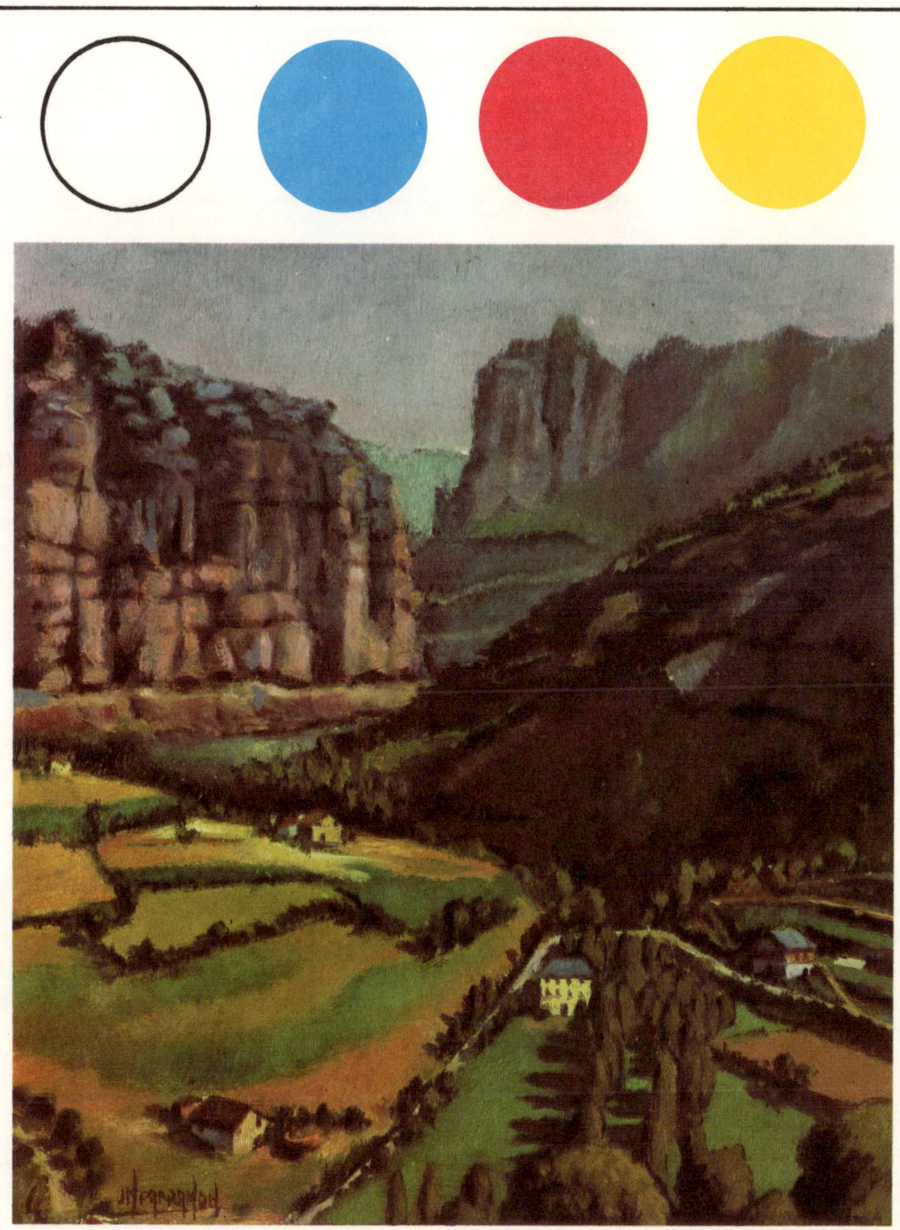

84

Fig. 84. This is a landscape which I painted myself, using only the three primary colours Prussian blue, madder red and medium cadmium yellow, in addition to white: this shows how all the colours in Nature, even black, can be obtained by mixing these three primary colours.

The remaining colours generally used by the professional artist amount to ten or twelve, and a list of these will be given below. These colours, whether applied directly or mixed with the primary colours, make it possible to obtain various shades or tones. However, if the artist's palette lacks even one of the three primary colours mentioned above, it is practically impossible to paint the colours found in Nature.

To quote Van Gogh again:

"These three basic colours, when mixed with their equivalents, produce a further three compound colours, called secondary colours."

Secondary colours:

Red . . . . (mixture of purple and yellow)
Green . . . . (mixture of blue and yellow)
Deep blue . . . . (mixture of blue and purple

At this point, we can broaden Van Gogh's indications by adding to these compound colours the so-called tertiary colours, which are produced by mixing a primary colour with a secondary one:

Tertiary colours:

Bright green . . . . (mixture of yellow and green)
Emerald green . . . . (mixture of green and blue)
Ultramarine . . . . (mixture of blue and deep blue)
Violet . . . . (mixture of deep blue and purple)
Carmine . . . . (mixture or purple and red)
Orange . . . . (mixture of red and yellow)

It would, of course, be possible to compile further series of colours. By mixing secondary and tertiary colours, we could increase the range by a further twelve colours, and so on, until we obtained a theoretically infinite number of shades and colours.

The reader can see, in Fig. 85, the chromatic circle, as it is called, in which the primary colours appear in the apices of an equilateral triangle (A, B, C), the secondary colours (resulting from a mixture of the primary colours) in the apices of a second triangle (D, E, F), while the tertiary colours (a mixture of two secondary colours) each appear between the apices of these two triangles.

To continue with an account of Van Gogh's views on this subject...

"If two primary colours are mixed, in order to make a secondary colour, this will achieve the greatest brilliancy if it is put beside the third primary colour not used in this mixture." (Fig. 86.)

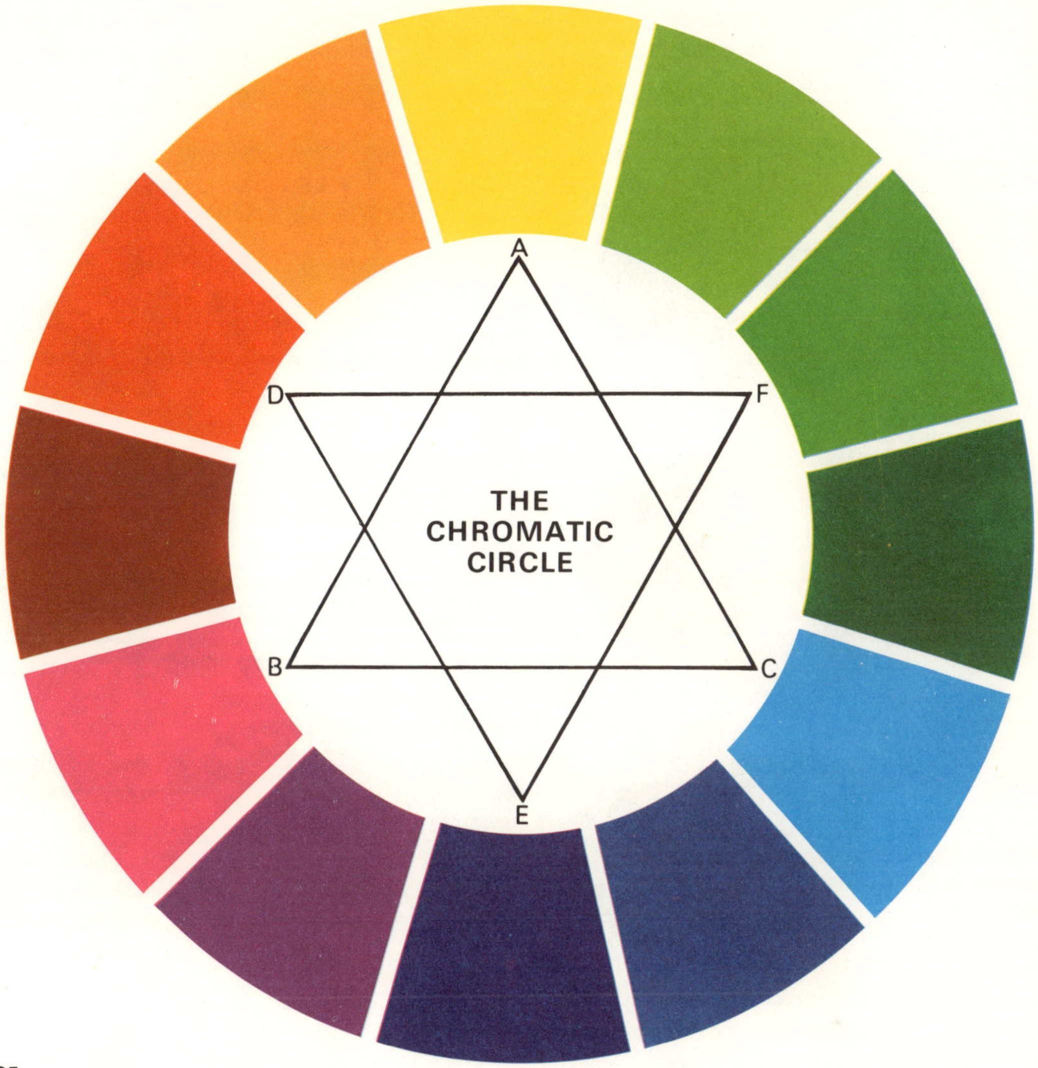

A

D F

THE CHROMATIC CIRCLE

B C

E

85

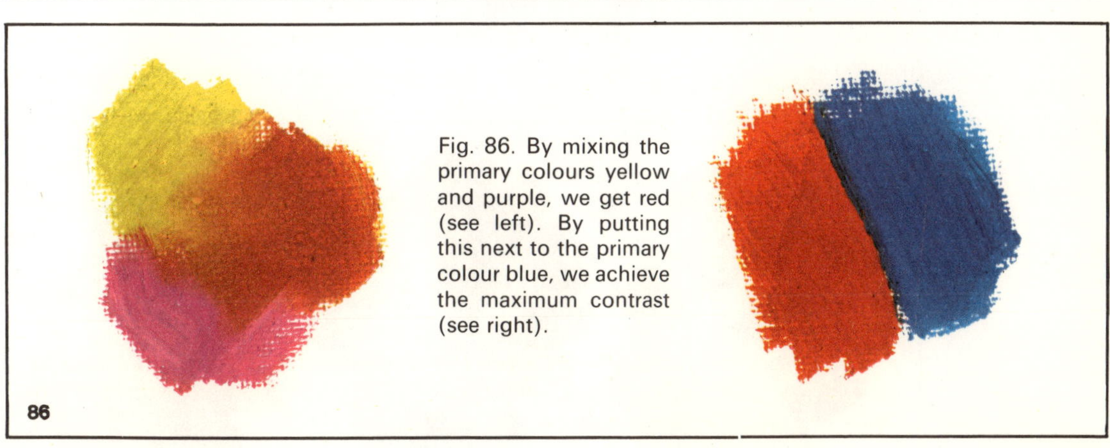

86

Fig. 86. By mixing the primary colours yellow and purple, we get red (see left). By putting this next to the primary colour blue, we achieve the maximum contrast (see right).

Complementary colours

"It is correct to use the term 'complementary' for the three primary colours, because this expresses their relationship with the corresponding secondary colours". (Fig. 87.)

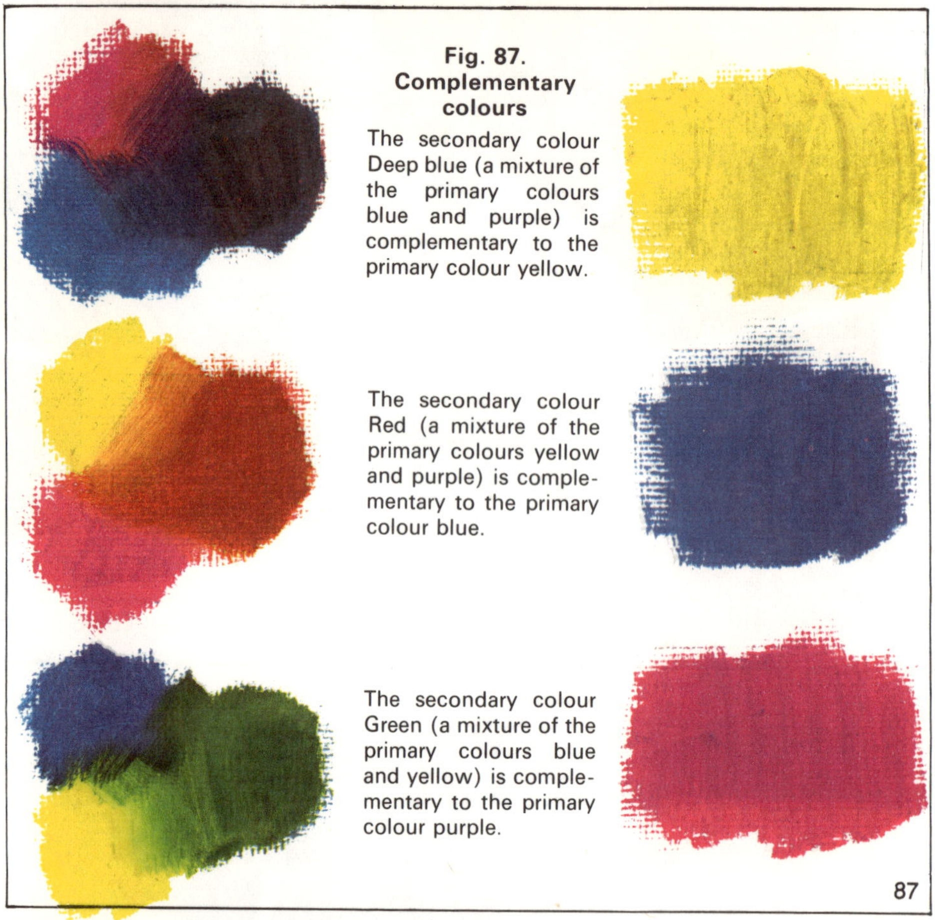

Fig. 87. Complementary colours

The secondary colour Deep blue (a mixture of the primary colours blue and purple) is complementary to the primary colour yellow.

The secondary colour Red (a mixture of the primary colours yellow and purple) is complementary to the primary colour blue.

The secondary colour Green (a mixture of the primary colours blue and yellow) is complementary to the primary colour purple.

87

Maximum contrasts of colour

"If the complementary colours are placed beside each other, with an equal degree of intensity", Van Gogh went on to say, "each one induces in the other an intensity so harsh that the human eye can hardly stand it. This process of reciprocal intensification is what we call the law of simultaneous contrasts". (Fig. 88.)

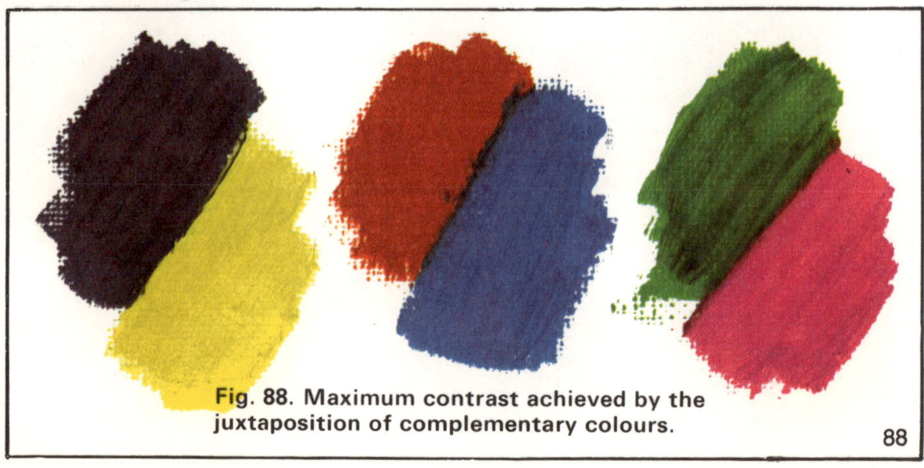

Fig. 88. Maximum contrast achieved by the juxtaposition of complementary colours.

88

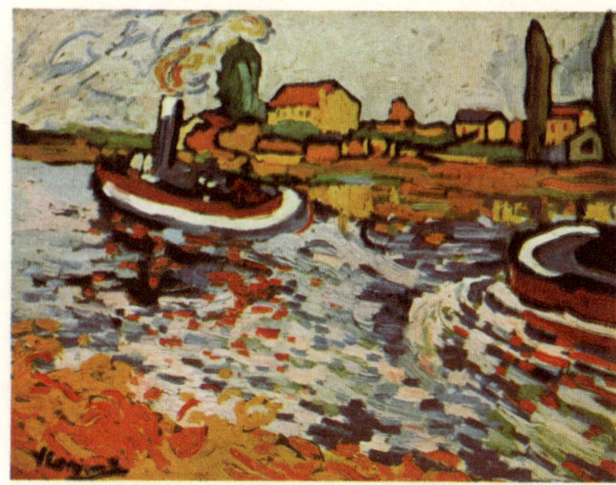

89

Fig. 89. After the Impressionists, the next vogue was that of the "Fauvists", so-called on account of the savage *(fauve)* stridency of their colours, based on the technique of painting in even, harsh colours, establishing strong contrasts, which were often based on the juxtaposition of complementary colours (Vlaminck's *Tug at Chatou*, Whitney Collection, New York).

The following point must be emphasized: the achieving of contrast between two complementary colours through their juxtaposition is extremely dangerous, because it creates clashes between colours (colours that do not harmonize, that simply do not go together). At the same time, however, precisely because of this clash and stridency of colours, it is possible to achieve very striking tonal effects. The juxtaposition of complementary colours was used unhesitatingly by the artists of the Fauvist style who followed the Impressionists (Fig. 89).

"For some curious reason", Van Gogh explained, "when complementary colours are mixed together, the resulting mixture is grey, almost black, absolutely colourless."

We would go on to say that, when one adds white to such mixtures, the colours tend to become greyish (Fig. 90).

The "trap of the greys"

This is an important warning. In this passage, Van Gogh is advising us of the danger of falling into what I call "the trap of the greys": a trap which is especially hazardous for the beginner who, through inexperience, makes excessive use of white, incorporating white into all his mixtures of paints, making it the principal element in all bright colours and shades... and then he "paints", even without realizing it, in dirty grey colours and shades, as a result of badly made mixtures which include colours which are complementary to one another.

Fig. 90. The mixing of two complementary colours results in a greyish-black which, when mixed with white, gives a series of grey and dirty tones.

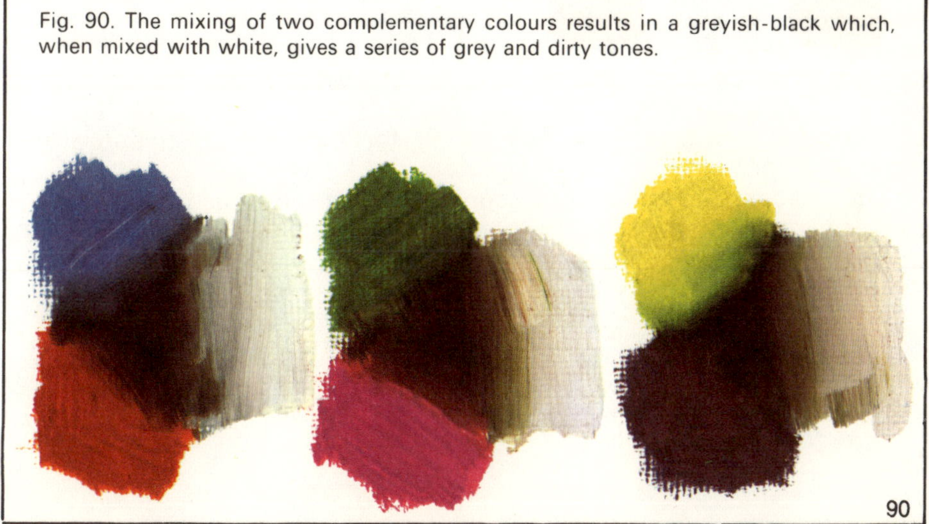

90

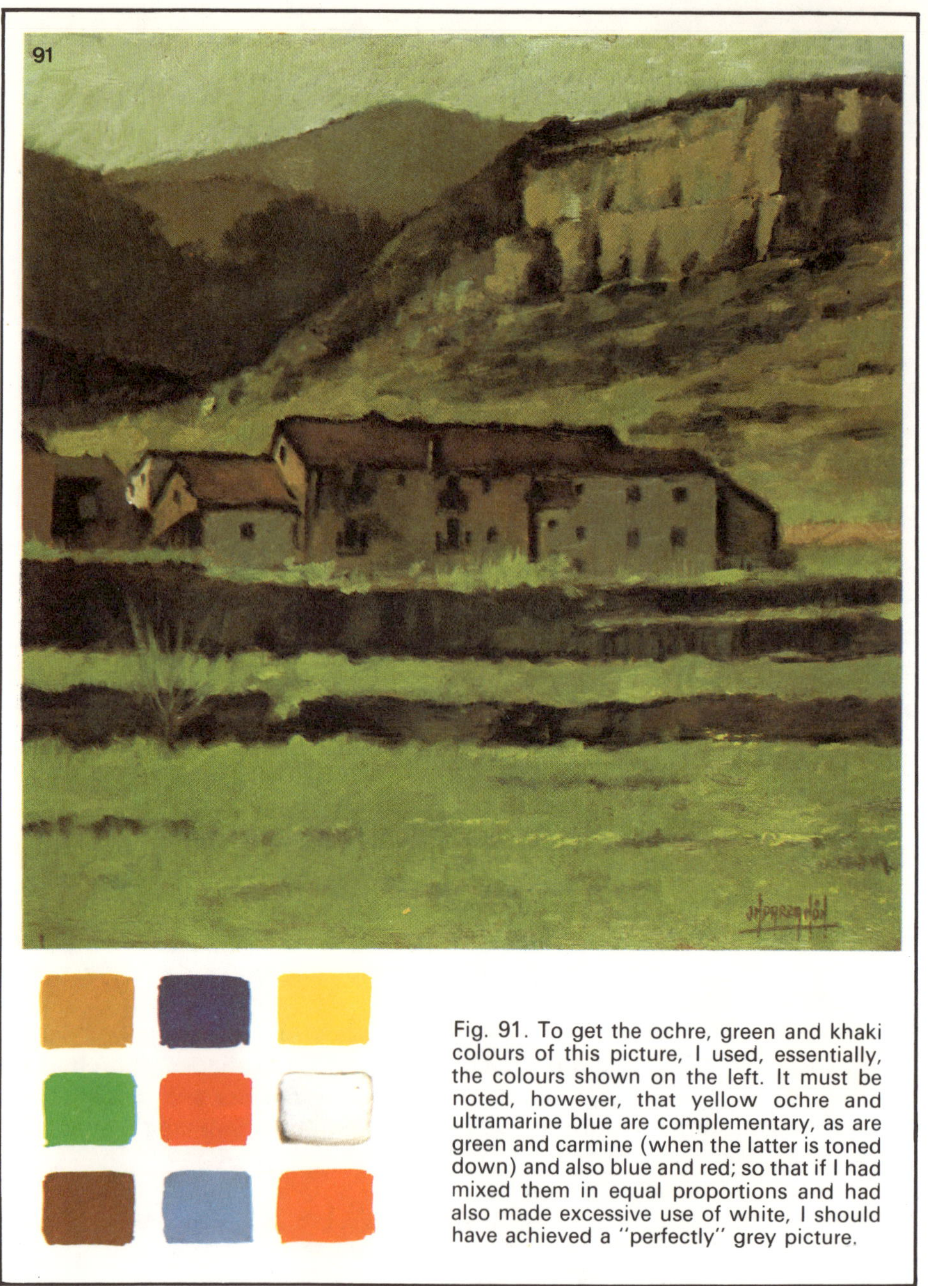

Fig. 91. To get the ochre, green and khaki colours of this picture, I used, essentially, the colours shown on the left. It must be noted, however, that yellow ochre and ultramarine blue are complementary, as are green and carmine (when the latter is toned down) and also blue and red; so that if I had mixed them in equal proportions and had also made excessive use of white, I should have achieved a "perfectly" grey picture.

One must take great care. See Fig. 91 for a graphic illustration of this major problem.[1]

The reader may, therefore, conclude that all this description of complementary colours has been given just for the sake of a fruitless argument. This is by no means the case; let us see, once more, what Van Gogh has to say on this subject:

1. See the book in this series entitled *How to Paint*, which contains a detailed discussion of the problems involved in the use and misuse of black and white, and gives guiding principles and graphic illustrations regarding the way to achieve "clean" colours.

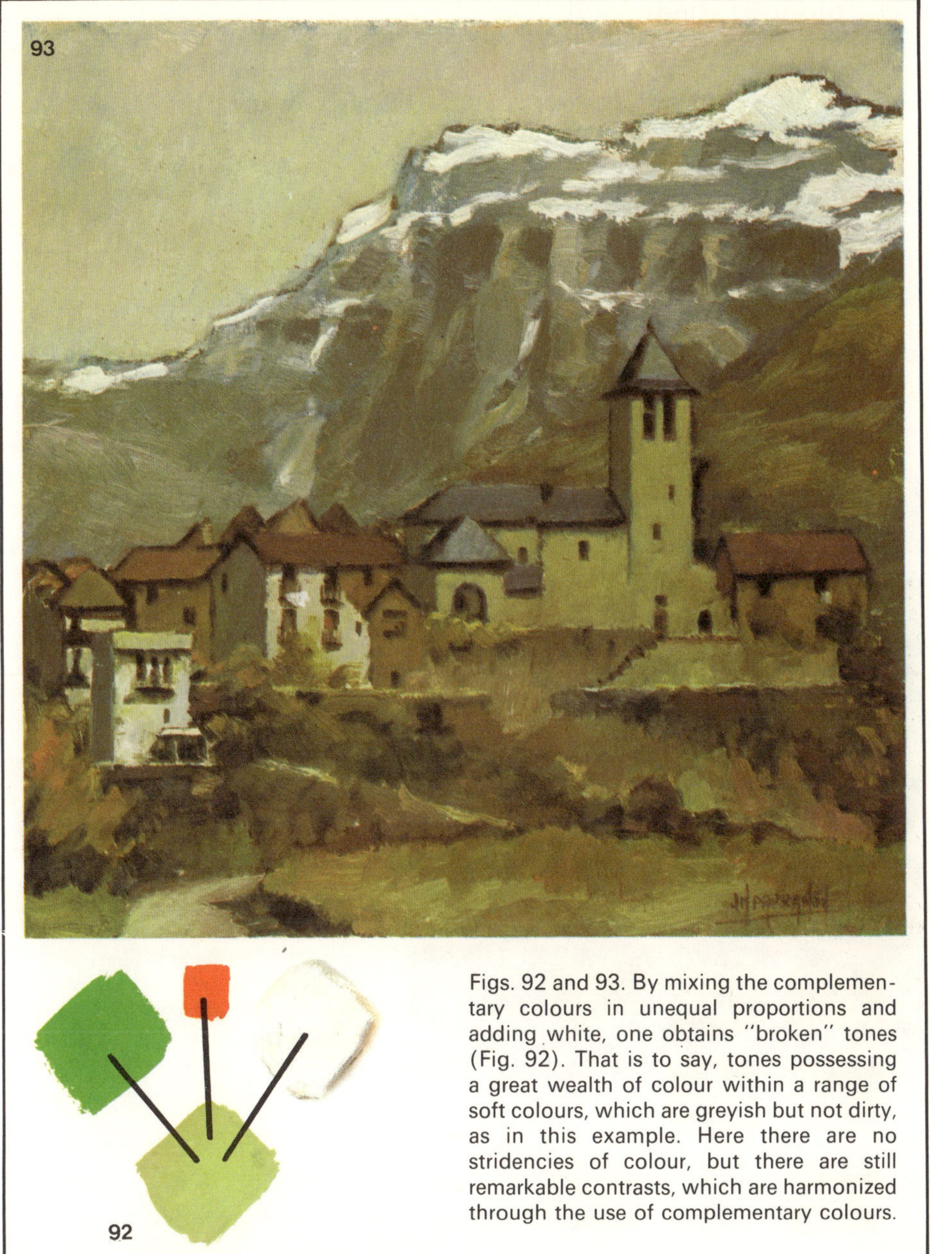

Figs. 92 and 93. By mixing the complementary colours in unequal proportions and adding white, one obtains "broken" tones (Fig. 92). That is to say, tones possessing a great wealth of colour within a range of soft colours, which are greyish but not dirty, as in this example. Here there are no stridencies of colour, but there are still remarkable contrasts, which are harmonized through the use of complementary colours.

"However, if two complementary colours are mixed in unequal proportions — for example, eight parts of green to two of purple — the colours are only partially destroyed and a broken tone is obtained, with a predominance of colour that does not prevent the perfect harmony of the two colours." (Figs. 92 and 93.)

Figure 93 shows the excellent range of colours obtained by the mixture in unequal proportions of colours which are mutually complementary. Note the rich variety of greyish shades and tones, which can be obtained through the intelligent use of the complementary colours, not simply to paint particular colours but also to paint an entire subject with this range of harmonies enjoying predominance.

The colour of shadows

The first thing that occurs to the inexperienced amateur, when he comes to paint the colour of shadows, is to add black or dark grey to the local colour (or colour proper) of the subject. The effect is one of darkness, greyness and dirtiness, but not of shadow, because black and, for similar reasons, grey or dark grey, are the negation of light. And in the shadows, even the darkest ones, there is light. As regards this problem, and a long time ago, the great achievement of Rembrandt, Velázquez and Goya was their depiction of chiaroscuro, which Prinet has defined as "the art of conducting light and making its presence felt in all parts of the picture, even the darkest parts".

What, then, is the colour of shadow?

The bright palette used by the Impressionists had its origin in the desire to replace, when painting shadow, "pitch" (a type of dark colour used until the 18th century) with the colour blue. Monet used to say to his friends:

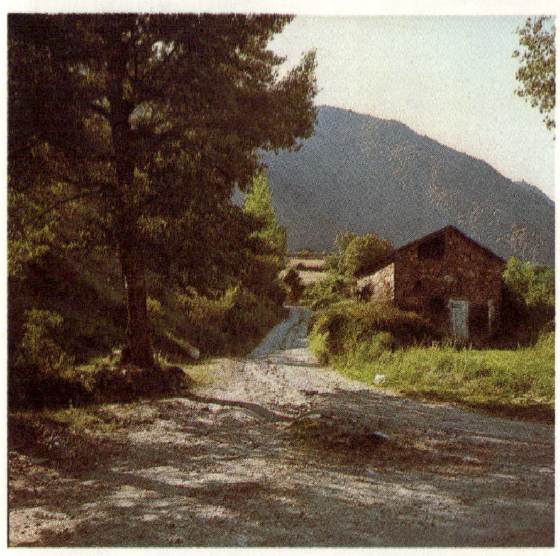

Fig. 94. This photograph is a good example of the presence of the colour blue in shadows. Moreover, in this case the dominant blue colour is accentuated by the fact that the photograph was taken in mountainous country, where the atmosphere is purer and the blue more evident.

"When night falls, the entire landscape turns blue". Or, in other words, as the light diminishes the influence of the colour blue increases (Fig. 94).

Blue is, therefore, the most important colour in any shaded area.

The second colour consists of the colour complementary to the actual colour of the subject. If we paint in blue a faraway mountain, the colours of the shadow will include red, which is complementary to blue.

The third and last colour concerned is the actual colour of the subject, but in a darker tone. In the case of this mountain, the "tonal" colour can be produced by using blue mixed with a very small amount of burnt sienna or natural sienna.

The following are the colours of shadows:
Blue + The colour complementary to the actual colour
+ The tonal colour

This is not as complicated as it sounds. Some pictorial examples may help to clarify this problem:

Fig. 95. Observe this picture in colour, which includes a tree (natural colour: green), throwing its shadow across a recently mown wheatfield (natural colour: yellow-ochre), with a mountain in the background (natural colour: blue).

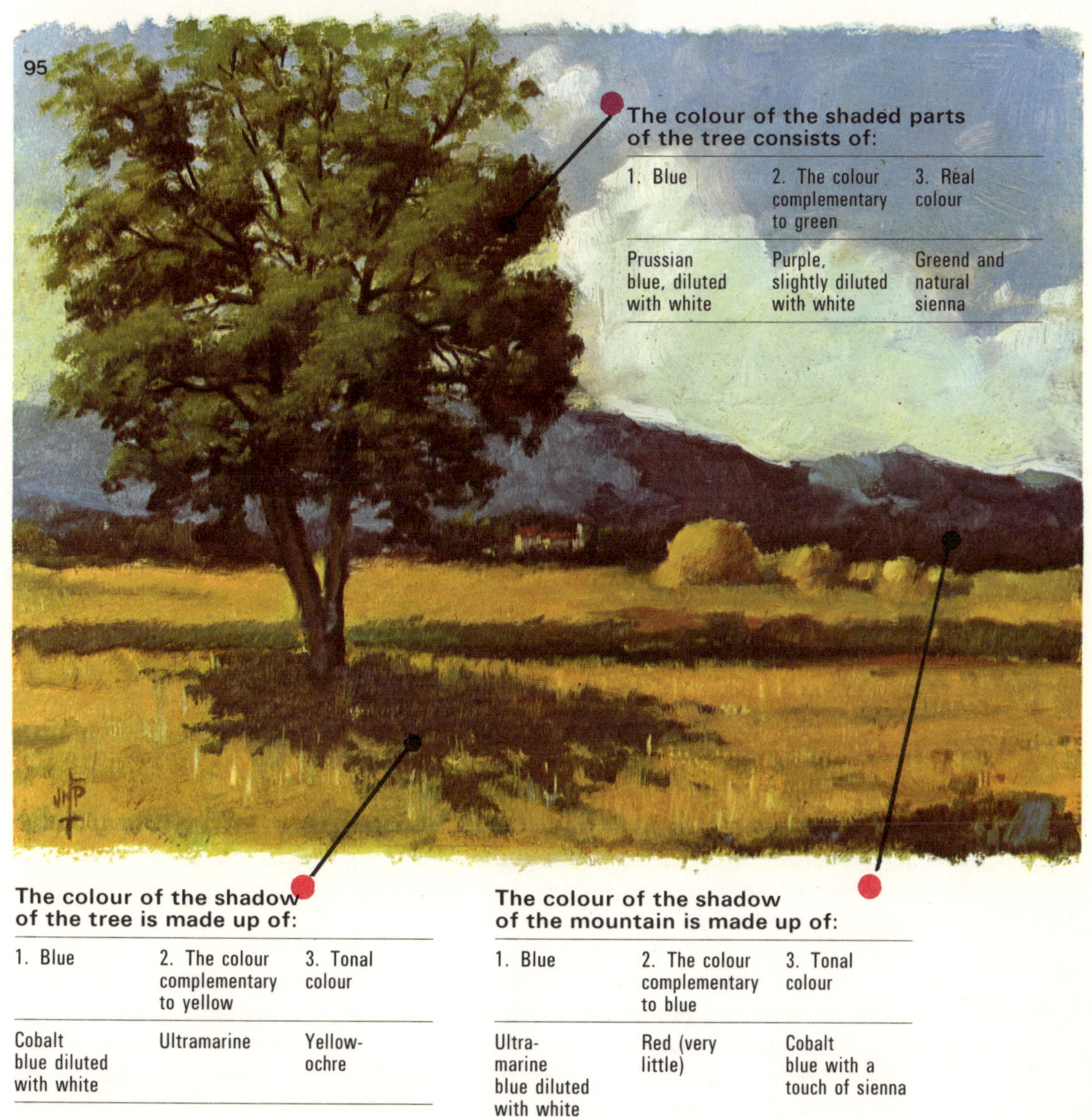

The colour of the shaded parts of the tree consists of:

1. Blue	2. The colour complementary to green	3. Real colour
Prussian blue, diluted with white	Purple, slightly diluted with white	Greend and natural sienna

The colour of the shadow of the tree is made up of:

1. Blue	2. The colour complementary to yellow	3. Tonal colour
Cobalt blue diluted with white	Ultramarine	Yellow-ochre

The colour of the shadow of the mountain is made up of:

1. Blue	2. The colour complementary to blue	3. Tonal colour
Ultra-marine blue diluted with white	Red (very little)	Cobalt blue with a touch of sienna

The three blues on the palette

We have seen in the previous illustration how we have been painting with the three blues: Prussian blue, cobalt blue and ultramarine blue. Why are there three blues? What is the difference between them, and when should each one be used?

This is an important consideration in landscape painting if one bears in mind the difference in tone between these three blues:

Fig. 96. Prussian blue has a greenish hue; it is the most luminous of the three blues and includes a very wide range of shades. It is a strident blue.

Fig. 97. Cobalt blue is equally luminous, but less strident. It is a "pastel" shade of blue, eminently suitable for painting transparent shadows. It is the "bluest" of the three blues.

Fig. 98. Ultramarine blue has a violet-coloured and more greyish hue, especially when it is mixed with yellow, red and sienna.

It is not possible to recommend the use of one blue rather than another for each case, since the choice of the appropriate blue depends on several factors, the most important of which is the harmonization of the colours which go to make up the landscape.

The harmonization of colours

The harmonization of colours involves the various laws which make it possible to assess the measure of agreement of colour with other colours and of various colours with each other: for this purpose, the artist must bear in mind the luminous tendency of the landscape and paint it in accordance with this tendency.

The first of these laws is that this harmony is derived, in principle, from Nature itself, in which there exists a luminous tendency which relates some colours to others and the range of colours as a whole. In bright sunlight and in mid-summer, between four and six in the afternoon, in the case of an urban landscape, the luminous tendency is warm; that is to say, it is composed of yellows, orange-like colours, ochres and reds. On a sunny day in winter, between nine and eleven in the morning and in the open country (and, to an even greater extent, in mountainous country), the luminous tendency is blue. On a cloudy day, in level country (and, even more so, in the city) the tendency is grey, and includes "broken" colours and tones produced by the mixture in unequal proportions of complementary colours (Fig. 93).

So far, the problem appears simple; one merely has to identify the luminous tendency and then interpret it, extracting the greatest possible advantage from it, and painting with one of the three tendencies mentioned above: 1, reddish-yellow; 2, blue-green; and 3, with "broken" grey tones produced by mixing complementary colours. Unfortunately, however, what often happens is that the luminous tendency is not so obviously identifiable as in the three examples mentioned above. In that case one must make a decision, one must interpret, selecting one of the three ranges of colours described above, since these are, broadly speaking, those most commonly used in landscape painting.

The range of warm colours

"Range" means a succession of colours in precise order, and the term "warm" is applied, by association of ideas, to the colour red and its derivatives. It stretches, within the chromatic circle, from yellow-green to violet (Fig. 99). However, to paint with a range of warm colours does not, of course, mean painting with these colours alone but painting with all the colours while making the warm ones dominant.

The range of cold colours

This term is applied to blue and its derivatives, embracing the greens,

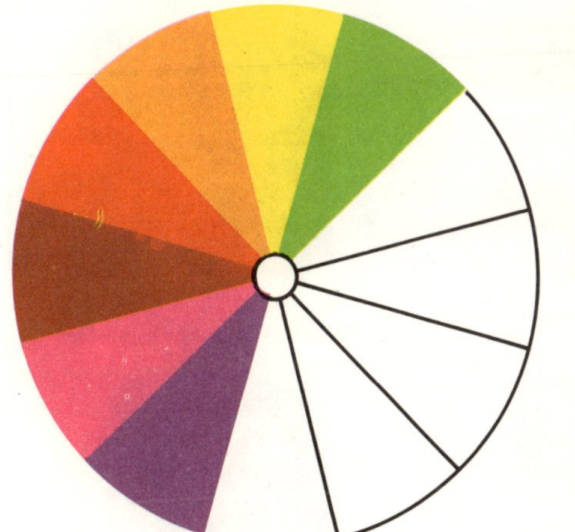

Fig. 99. Range of warm colours, consisting of bright green, yellow, orange, red, carmine, purple and violet.

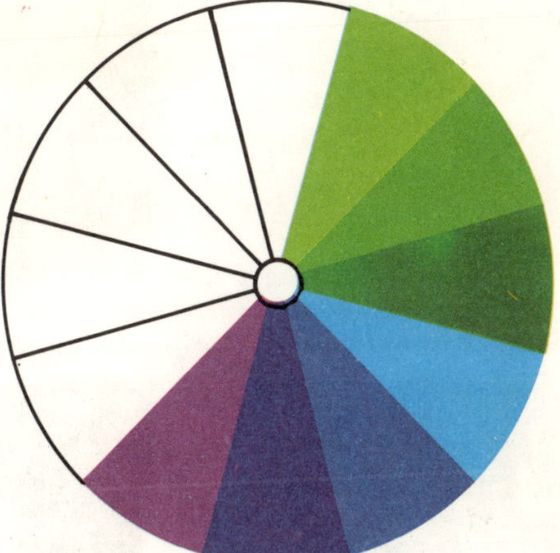

Fig. 100. Range of cold colours, consisting of bright green, green, emerald green, luminous (Prussian) blue, cobalt blue, deep (ultramarine) blue and violet.

blues and violets of the chromatic circle (Fig. 100). As in the previous example, its application requires the use of blues and greens in all colours, including the warm ones.

The range of complementary colours

This is probably the most difficult to achieve. It is, basically, the product of the mixture in unequal proportions of the complementary colours, as explained in Figs. 91, 92 and 93. As in the other ranges, all colours are used, but the artist tries constantly to obtain broken shades and tones, and colours which, though vivid, are not so strident as the yellows, reds and blues just as they come out of the tube.

Fig. 101. Oil-paints normally used by the landscape painter

(Samples by courtesy of Pelikan)

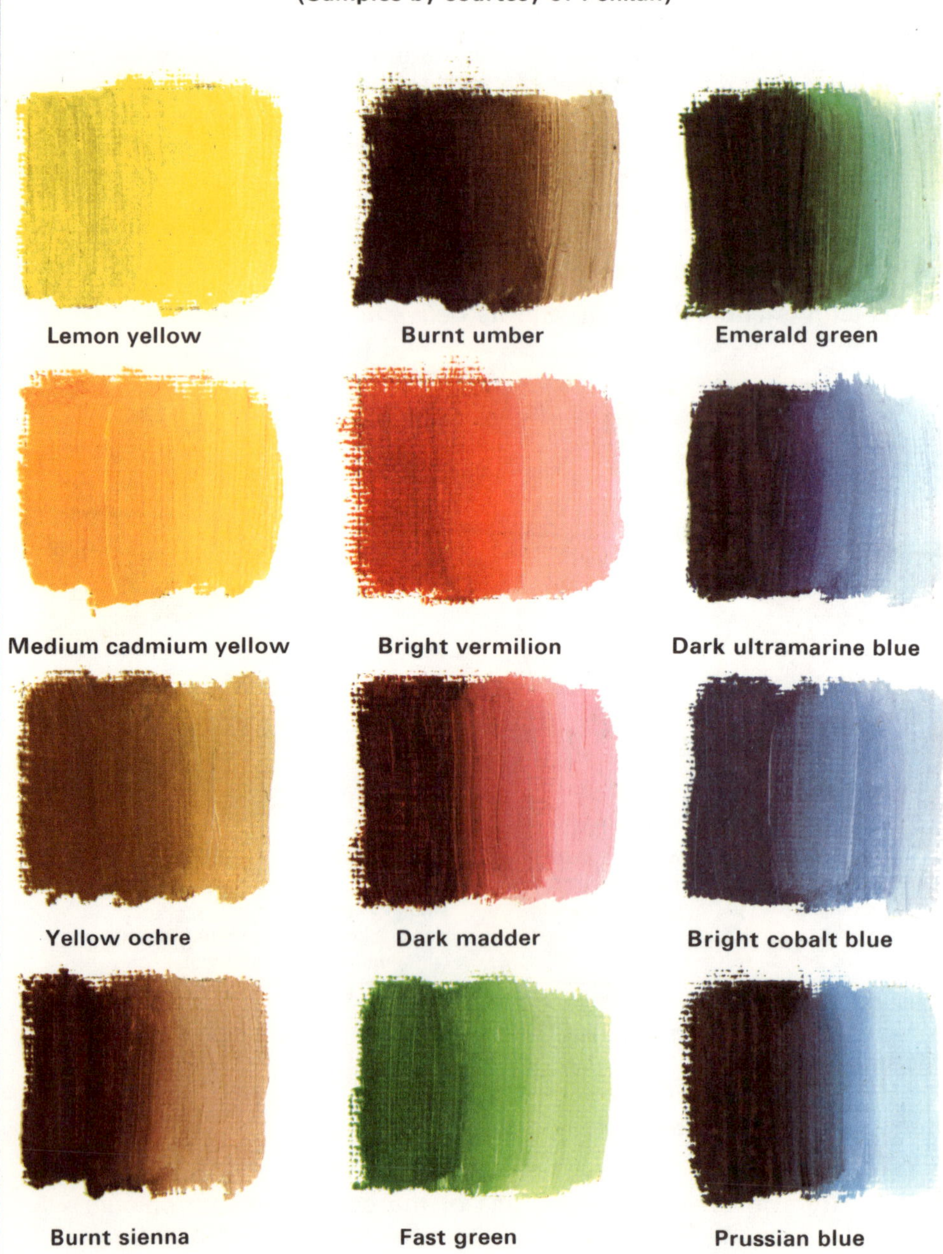

Titanium white and ivory black should be added to this list.

Materials and equipment for landscape painting in oils

It is important to use good-quality oil paints. The best-known makes are Rembrandt, Academie, Reeves, Lefranc, Pelikan, etc. Get to know your colours too, deciding on a particular range and trying to avoid changing it, at least until you have acquired sufficient experience to make up your own mind on what suits you best.

The following is a typical range of colours used by the landscape painter (Fig. 101 on facing page):

Selection of oil paints for landscape painting

* Lemon yellow	* Burnt sienna
Medium cadmium yellow	Emerald green
Yellow ochre	Dark ultramarine blue
* Fast green	Bright cobalt blue
Burnt umber	Prussian blue
Bright vermilion	Titanium white
Dark madder	* Ivory black

If you wish to reduce this range, you can eliminate lemon yellow, burnt sienna, fast green and ivory black. However, it is really advisable to work with the complete range.

Oil paints are sold in metal tubes with screw-on tops, in four or five sizes, as follows:

1. I would refer the reader to the book in this series entitled *Oils*, which contains a detailed description of the materials and equipment needed, and how to use them.

Measures and contents of tubes of oil paint

Tube No.	Length of tube	Contents of tube
2	6 cm	9-20 grams
6	9 cm	30-45 grams
7	10.5 cm	35-55 grams
10	15 cm	100-200 grams
13	20 cm	450-750 grams

Bearing in mind that white is the colour most frequently used, it is advisable to acquire a large tube of this colour.

Brushes for oil painting

These should, if possible, be of so-called pig-bristle (a hard, bone-coloured hair) although in some cases sable brushes (soft, light-brown hair) are used. Indeed, when one has to paint a line or stroke superimposed on another colour — slender branches, blades of grass, the small spots of colour colour made by the flowers in a field, etc. — and this has to be done in a patch which has already been painted, then the brush made of sable, with paint slightly diluted with turpentine, makes it possible to paint above the underlying coat, and there is hardly any mixing with the colour below. This is achieved thanks to the softness of the brush which does not scratch the recently painted surface. In addition to this property, this brush is essential for painting small shapes.

Brushes used for oil painting are made with three kinds of tip: round, straight-edged, and in the shape of a cat's tongue — filbert brushes, as they are called (Fig. 102).

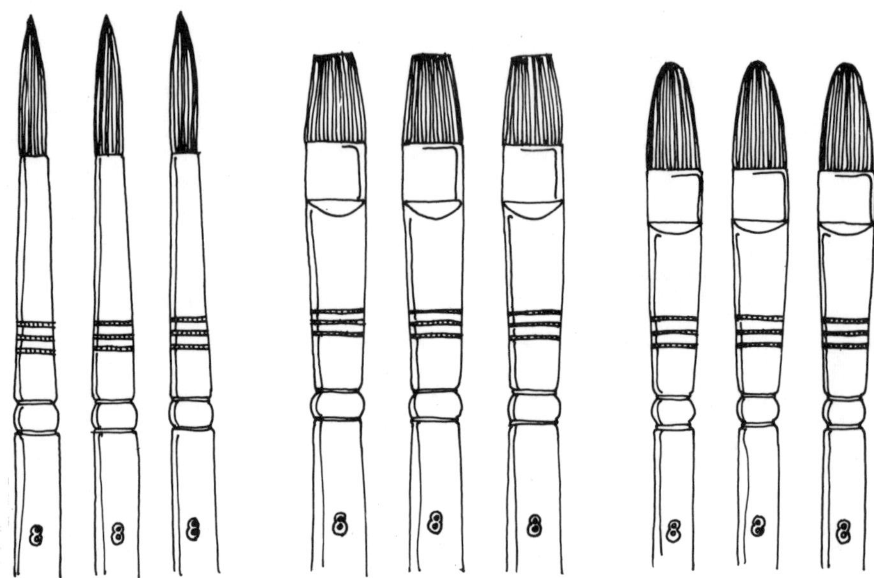

Fig. 102. Bristle brushes for oil painting (actual size). The total length of the brush is 26-30 cm.

Note, in Fig. 102, the number of each brush, which indicates the thickness of the head: these sizes are expressed in even numbers from 1 to 22 (1, 2, 4, 6, 8, 10, etc).

The following is a normal range of brushes for landscape painting:

Range of brushes normally used for landscape painting

Two round brushes, bristle, No. 4
Two round brushes, sable, No. 6
Two flat brushes, bristle, No. 6
Three flat brushes, bristle, No. 8
One "cat's tongue" brush, bristle, No. 8
Two flat brushes, bristle, No. 12
One flat brush, bristle, No. 14
One "cat's tongue" brush, bristle, No. 14
One flat brush, bristle, No. 20

The choice of flat or filbert brushes is optional. Personally, I prefer flat brushes because I think they apply the strokes of paint more vigorously.

Palette knives

Palette knives are used for three principal purposes: painting directly with them, instead of with brushes; cleaning a recently painted area, in order to rectify some error; and cleaning the palette, when one has finished painting.

See Fig. 103, for the different forms of palette knife, always bearing in mind that for the first and second purposes mentioned above — painting and erasing with the palette knife — it is preferable to use a palette knife shaped like a stoneamason's trowel, this type being extremely flexible, whereas for cleaning the palette it is best to use the type which is shaped like a knife and is less pliable.

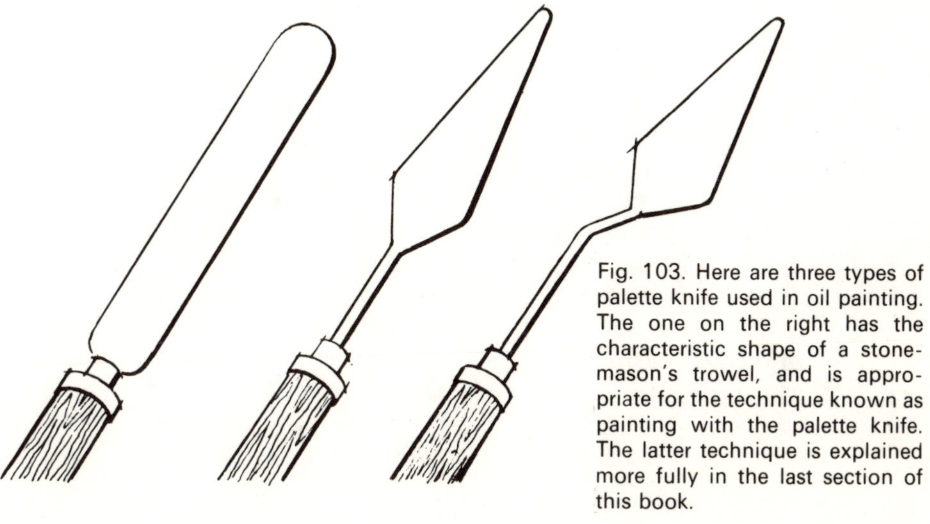

Fig. 103. Here are three types of palette knife used in oil painting. The one on the right has the characteristic shape of a stonemason's trowel, and is appropriate for the technique known as painting with the palette knife. The latter technique is explained more fully in the last section of this book.

Supports for landscape painting in oils

The supports most frequently used for landscape painting in oils are canvasses, panels, cardboard or thick drawing paper.

Canvasses are made of linen or hemp and are manufactured in different types, of varying thickness. The quality selected affects the grain of the warp and the thickness of the threads of the finished canvas. In canvasses of higher quality, the warp is more compact and the grain slightly more pronounced. Canvasses are produced in units of 0.70 by 2 metres, and are also sold mounted on wooden stretchers. The latter consist of a wooden framework, with small wedges at the four vertices which make it possible to stretch out the canvas properly.

Canvasses, and also panels and cardboard, are sold with a primer or coat of paint applied, usually white, on one side only; this primer consists of glue mixed with distemper, casein or gypsum, which makes possible a greater degree of adherence and of conservation of the colours of oil paints. Some firms sell canvasses with a primer grey or sienna in colour, instead of white. This provides the artist with an initial background which, for certain subjects, may be appropriate.

Canvasses, panels and cardboard are classified according to size by a number which determines the proportion and the thematic definition made necessary by the picture itself. This system of classification embraces the topics of figures, landscapes and seascapes; the framework for painting figures is than that used for painting landscapes squares inshape and is seascapes (Fig. 104). This system of measures and proportions is internationally standardized, so that a No. 12 landscape canvas stretcher, for example, measures 61×46 cm throughout the world. The following is the table of measurements:

International table of measurements, in centimetres, for canvas-stretchers for oil painting

No.	Figures	Landscape	Seascape
4	33 × 24	33 × 22	33 × 19
5	35 × 27	35 × 24	35 × 22
6	41 × 33	41 × 27	41 × 24
8	46 × 38	46 × 33	46 × 27
10	55 × 46	55 × 38	55 × 33
12	61 × 50	61 × 46	61 × 38
15	65 × 54	65 × 50	65 × 46
20	73 × 60	73 × 54	73 × 50
25	81 × 65	81 × 60	81 × 54
30	92 × 73	92 × 65	92 × 60
40	100 × 81	100 × 73	100 × 65
50	116 × 89	116 × 81	116 × 73
60	130 × 97	130 × 89	130 × 81
80	146 × 114	146 × 97	146 × 90
100	162 × 130	162 × 114	162 × 97
120	195 × 130	195 × 114	195 × 97

Wood (or hardboard) panels usually have a primer of glue and gypsum, offering a smooth and matt surface, and corresponding in size to Nos. 1 to 8 in the table above.

Cardboard is medium-grain and is sold wrapped, in the same sizes as wood panels.

Ordinary thick cardboard, of good quality, prepared by oneself with simply a thin coat of oil paint, is an excellent support. An additional characteristic is that it makes possible an absolutely matt finished painting (which can, of course, be varnished when the picture is finished).

Lastly, drawing paper, thick, of good quality and thoroughly glued (Canson paper, for example) is perfectly suitable for painting preliminary outlines and sketches.

Personally, I would advise the reader to acquire canvases on stretchers for pictures of a size greater than No. 5 (35×24 cm, landscapes) and wood panels and cardboard for smaller pictures.

The palette

As will be seen in the following pages, for landscape painting in oils one uses a carrying case in the form of a small suitcase, inside which are, among other things, one's palette for painting. The latter must, therefore, be made of wood and rectangular (see Fig. 105).

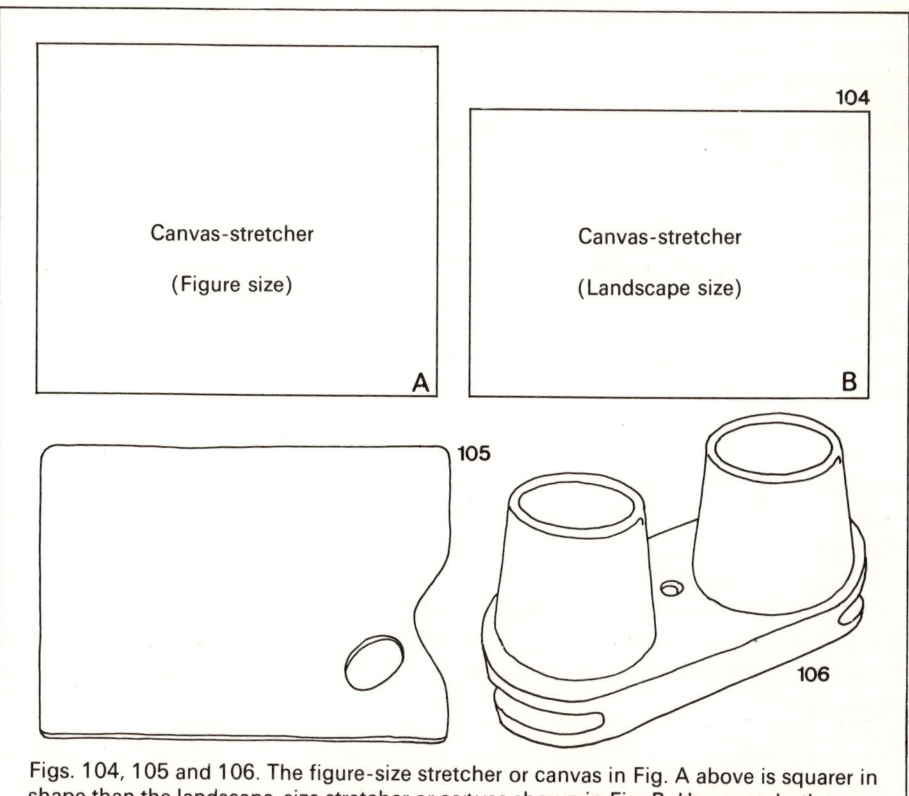

Figs. 104, 105 and 106. The figure-size stretcher or canvas in Fig. A above is squarer in shape than the landscape-size stretcher or canvas shown in Fig. B. However, both types are used for the painting of landscapes or figures. This illustration also includes a traditional type of wooden palette (Fig. 105) and a sketch of oil-containers to be attached to the palette (Fig. 106).

Thinners

Thinners normally used in oil painting are essence of turpentine (refined turpentine) and linseed oil. Essence of turpentine gives colours a matt quality, whereas linseed oil tends to make them more vivid. Moreover, when one uses essence of turpentine the colours dry more quickly, and for this reason it is the most appropriate for the rapid painting of landscapes.

Personally, I use this thinner almost exclusively, although it is quite common for the artist to use a mixture of essence of turpentine and linseed oil in equal parts.

Both products are sold in small bottles, which can be carried in the carrying case mentioned above. I would, however, advise the reader to acquire a slightly bigger bottle of turpentine, both because it is used more often and it is also useful for cleaning brushes and, occasionally, one's hands.

Dipper cup

A dipper cup, as it is known, is a small utensil with two cavities to hold thinners: the base is in the shape of a pair of pincers, which makes it possible to attach to the container to the palette (see Fig. 106).

Old rags and sundry utensils

It is essential to have a supply of old rags to clean brushes, wipe one's hands, erase a part of the painting and, when one has finished painting, to clean the palette. A couple of black crayons and a spray-gun filled with fixing liquid may also be needed.

Carrying case

Fig. 107 shows the normal type of carrying case used when painting landscapes in oil. The closed box measures 39×30 cm — the depth being 7.5 cm — and is made of white wood varnished with wax. It has the appearance, as can be seen, of a small suitcase (A). On opening it, the first thing to be seen is the palette attached to the framework of the box by small metal hinges (B). Inside the top, as can be observed, there are two strips which can be inclined forward, each with an internal groove which makes it possible to insert a hardboard or piece of cardboard for painting, size No. 5 (C). As can be seen, this contrivance makes it possible to make a sketch, with the top of the box serving as an inclined easel, capable of holding the cardboard. At the same time, the lid of the box with the picture inside can be closed (first turning the board the other way round) without any danger of smudging or otherwise injuring the painting (D).

On taking out the palette, it can be seen that the box itself is divided into five or six compartments for carrying tubes of paint, brushes, palette knives and black crayon, dipper cups, thinners and old rags (these last should be folded and then placed over the various compartments, before putting the palette on top).

Open-air easel

The type of open-air easel most frequently used consists of a wooden tripod, with folding legs which make it possible to reduce its size and make it easier to carry about. It is important that this should be properly constructed and finished, and have the following properties: a) lightness; b) strength; c)

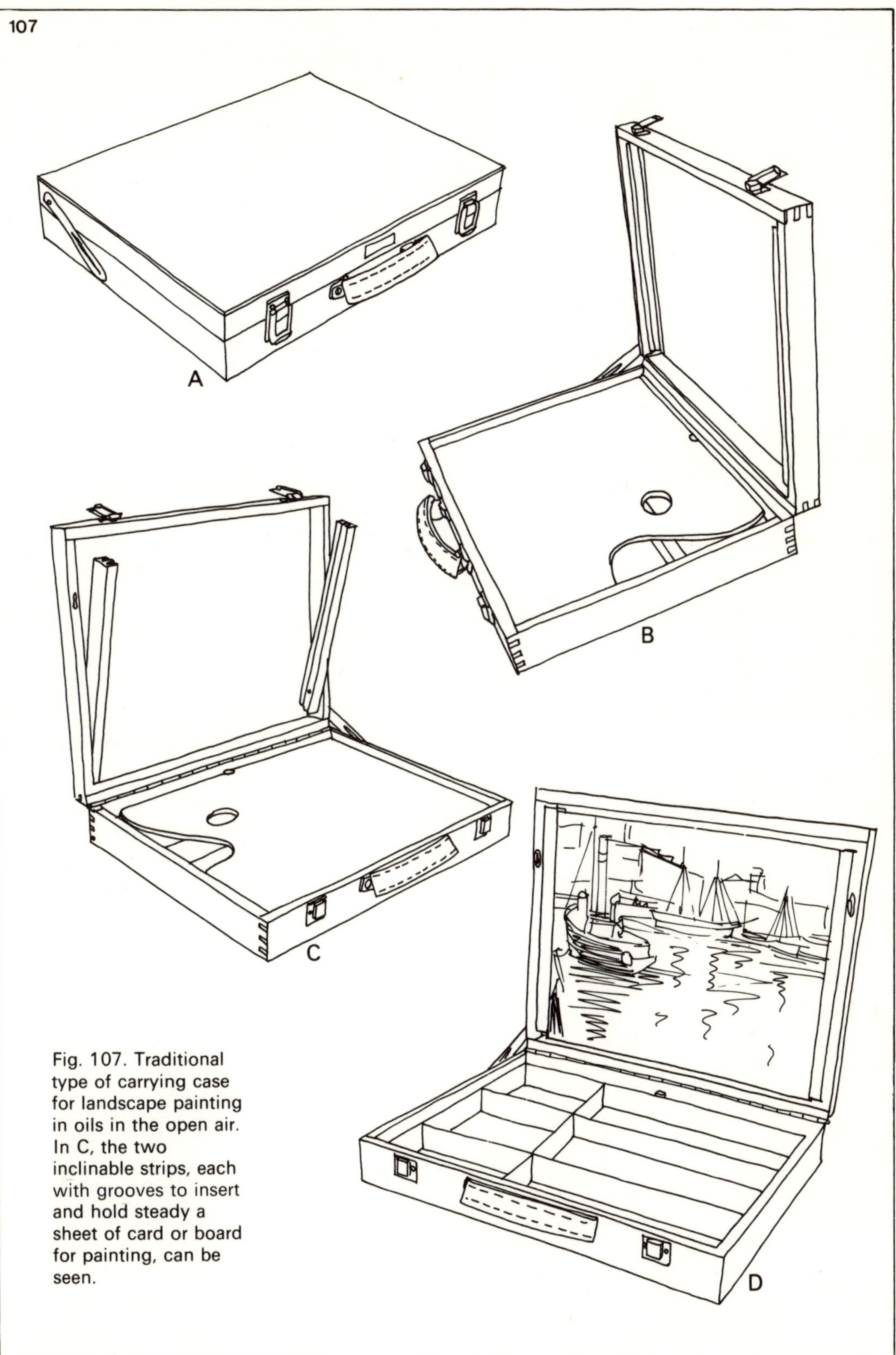

Fig. 107. Traditional type of carrying case for landscape painting in oils in the open air. In C, the two inclinable strips, each with grooves to insert and hold steady a sheet of card or board for painting, can be seen.

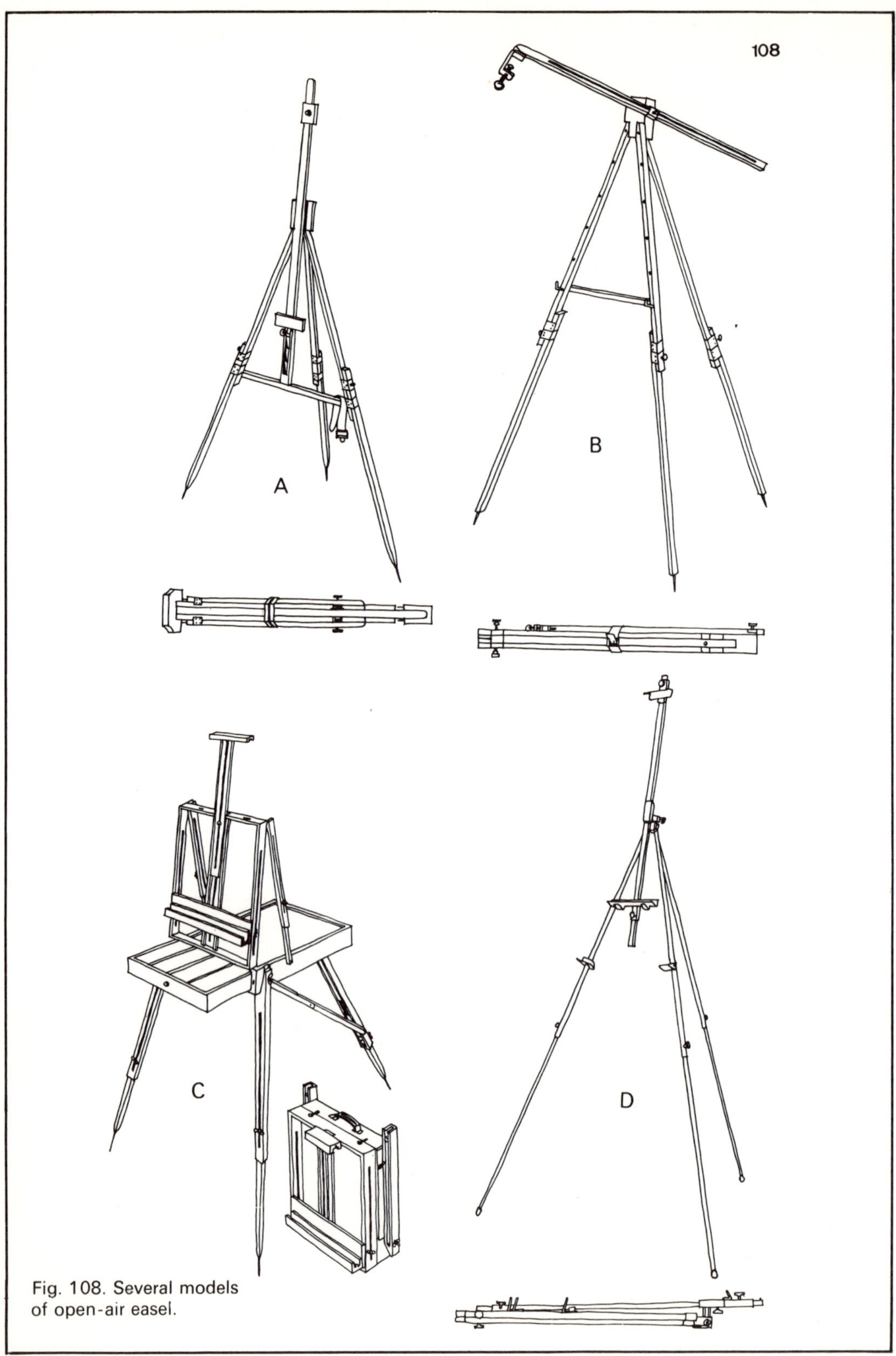

Fig. 108. Several models of open-air easel.

sufficient height; d) be equipped to maintain the height of the picture and hold the upper part of it, so keeping it steady. Figure 108, models A and B, shows the most usual design, the former being simpler, and the latter larger, more solid and sophisticated. Model C (bottom left), in which the carrying case and the easel are all in one piece, is firm, convenient and stable. Despite its design, which is apparently complicated, it is easily set up and is very compact once folded. (This is the type I myself use.) Last comes Model D (bottom right), which has only recently come onto the market. Its design is similar to that of Model B, except that it is constructed of metal and is very firm and stable, even though there are one or two defects as regards balance in the devices for holding the canvas steady.

The stool

Whether one paints sitting or standing is, in my opinion, a question of habit, although it is true that, occasionally, as a result of the viewpoint selected or the proximity of the foreground, the effects of perspective, etc., one simply has to paint standing up. However, since painting for two or three hours at a stretch is really tiring — both mentally and physically — I would recommend the reader to take with him, not a stool, but a folding chair (of the type made of canvas and metal tubing) as light, stable and compact as possible.

The stretcher-carrier

This is a simple and practical piece of equipment which comes in two parts and is used for carrying canvases already painted: the most usual type is illustrated in Fig. 109. As can be seen, in order to protect the painted canvas another of the same dimensions should be carried.

As a simpler form of stretcher-carrier, painters also use a set of four nails, with points at each end and a sort of button or washer inserted into the centre of each one: these are used to nail together the painted canvases, keeping them rigidly separated and avoiding damage to each picture. This is a sound solution, since it serves the same purpose as the traditional stretcher-carrier and takes up very little space (see Fig. 109).

109

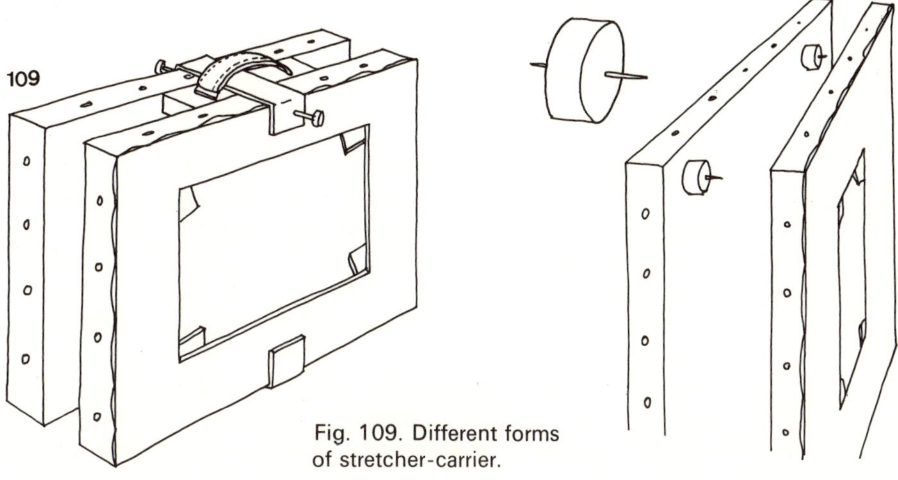

Fig. 109. Different forms of stretcher-carrier.

Twenty-four practical ideas and suggestions

As a supplement to the suggestions provided, regarding materials and equipment for landscape painting in oils, I shall now give some practical advice and suggestions which I hope will be useful for the reader's progress as a landscape painter.

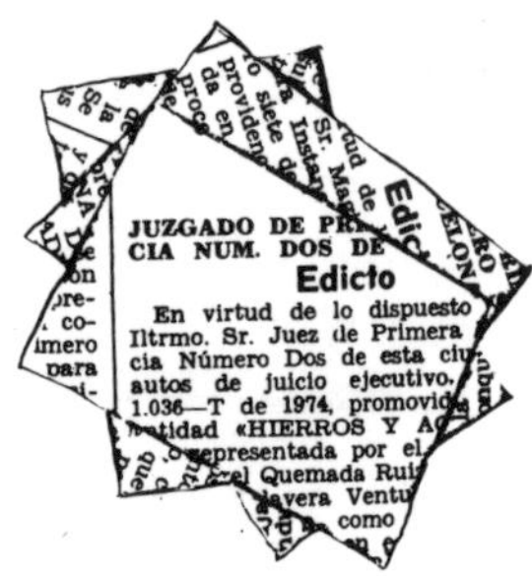

1 Old rags... and scraps of newspaper. For oil painting, as has already been stated, one needs some old rags. However, in addition to old rags I advise the painter to take with him scraps of newspaper cut to specific dimensions (a half or quarter of a sheet) with which he can drain off and clean brushes, palette, etc., throwing away the scraps of newspaper and keeping the rags for cases where they are essential. (Warning: remember that when you throw away pieces of newspaper covered with oil paint in a wood or on dry grass, you may cause a fire.)

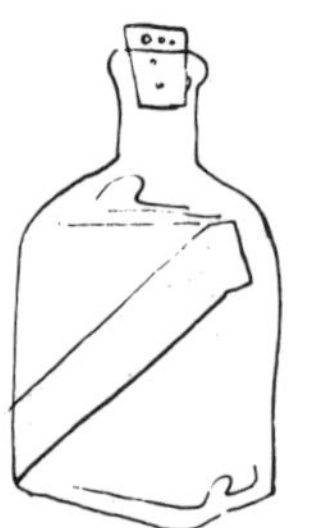

2 Use ordinary turpentine for cleaning. I advise you to include in your equipment a bottle of at least a quarter-litre capacity of ordinary turpentine to clean your hands, your clothes, the brushes and palette when you have finished work. Stains on clothes can be easily cleaned by rubbing with a clean cloth, soaked in ordinary turpentine, while the paint is still wet. Once it has dried, this operation is much more difficult.

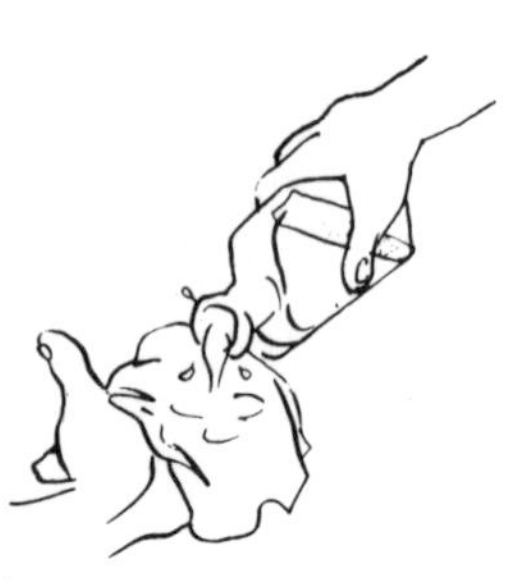

3 Lastly, clean your hands. This bottle of ordinary turpentine must, of course, be outside the carrying case. When you have finished painting for the day, put everything away in its right place — case, easel, the picture in the stretcher-carrier, etc., — and, last of all, wipe your hands with turpentine, to avoid leaving paint-stains on yourself again. Do this in the following way: open your left hand and put a clean rag in it. Squirt turpentine over the rag and then, with the rag soaked in turpentine, rub your hands together as if you were drying them (see illustration).

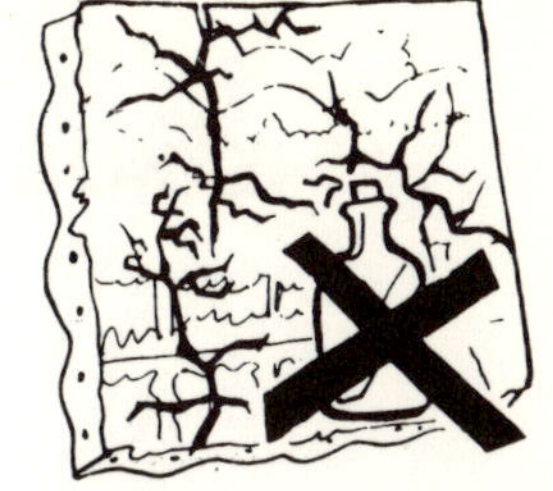

4 However, do not paint with ordinary turpentine. On no account do this. Ordinary turpentine can change the drying process of the paint and affect its conservation. If you use ordinary turpentine as a thinner, you run the risk of the paint cracking after a time. As a thinner, use only turpentine that has been refined and prepared for painting, ie essence of turpentine, which is to be found in all shops selling artists' materials.

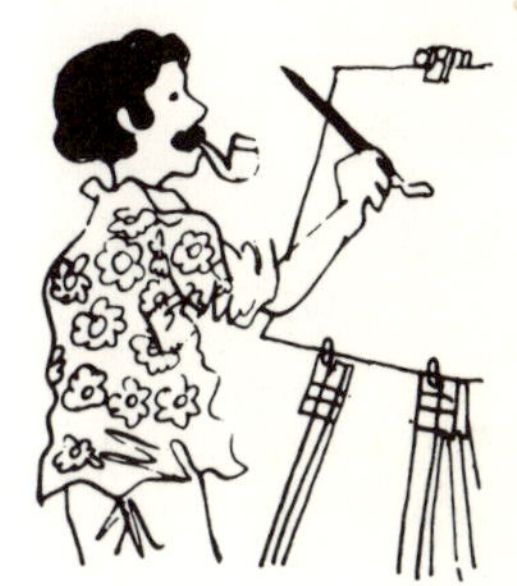

5 Do not use a dressing-gown. Wear old clothes. Many professional artists paint in the studio wearing a dressing-gown or smock: in this way they feel freer and less worried about getting paint on their clothes. To go out into the open air to paint wearing a dressing-gown does not exactly look very appropriate, but one can wear an old shirt in summer and an old sweater in winter... This will not provoke protests from the family, and one will feel more at ease.

6 Cleaning the brushes. This can be done with turpentine but there is the risk of the hairs of the brush coming apart, and the brush eventually looking like a worn-out broom. The best materials are soap and water. This is the procedure: the first step is to get the remains of the paint off the brush by means of an old rag soaked in turpentine. When there is practically none left, rub the brush-head in a lather made of ordinary soap, as if painting, and then rub the brush-head on the palm of your hand (again, as if painting), backwards and forwards and also with a circular motion, but always without twisting or disarranging the hairs of the brush. The lather resulting from this operation is the colour of the paint which was on the brush; this indicates that the latter is still not clean. Rinse the brush out with water and repeat the operation a further two or three times until the lather is white and the brush clean. The brush is dried with a rag, and then left in a jar with the brush-head upwards.

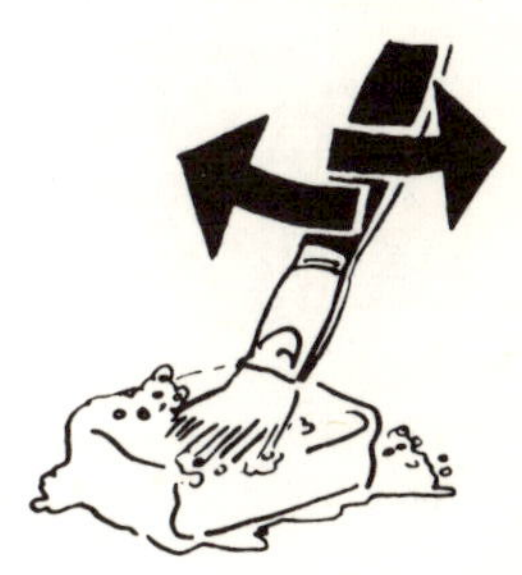

7 A way to leave the cleaning of brushes until later. First of all, it must be emphasized that brushes must always be cleaned while the paint is still wet, and to carry out this operation once the paint has dried is extremely laborious and inevitably spoils the brush. It must also be admitted that this business of cleaning brushes is the most tedious task involved in the painter's occupation. Hence, occasionally one comes back from a day's painting and... leaves it until the next day (this can, to a certain extent, be done). Well, to leave it until the next day — and even the day after — put the brushes in a shallow bowl, covered in water. This way, they will be all right for two or three days; then, of course, they *must* be cleaned.

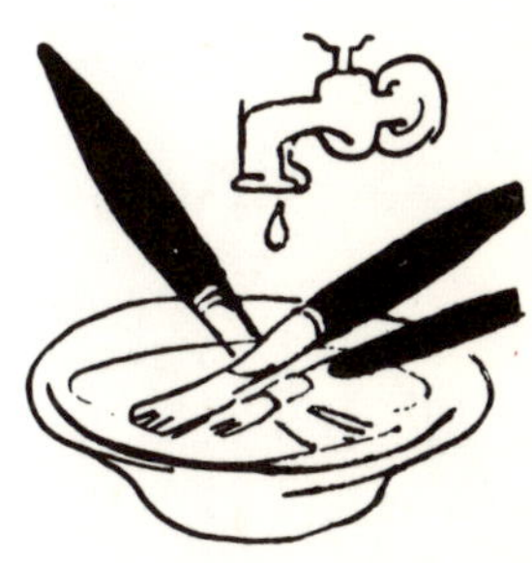

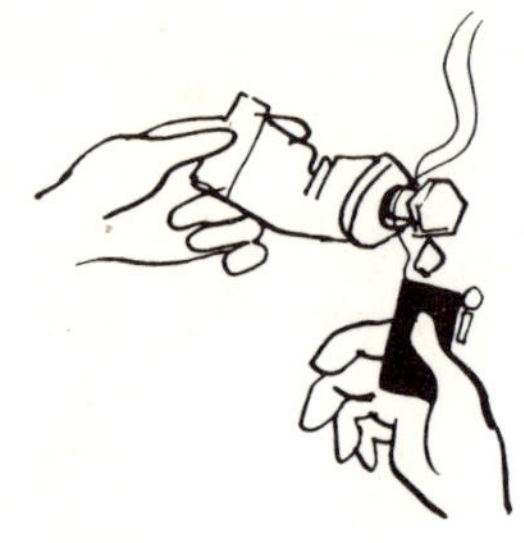

8 When the cap of the paint-tube does not work. The metal screw-top cap of the tube of oil-paint often gets stuck because it has not been screwed on properly and the paint has dried. The solution is not to try to force it open — this can crumple and even break the tube — but simply to light a match or cigarette-lighter and warm the cap in the flame; then, take hold of the cap with a rag, so as not to get burnt, and the cap will unscrew easily.

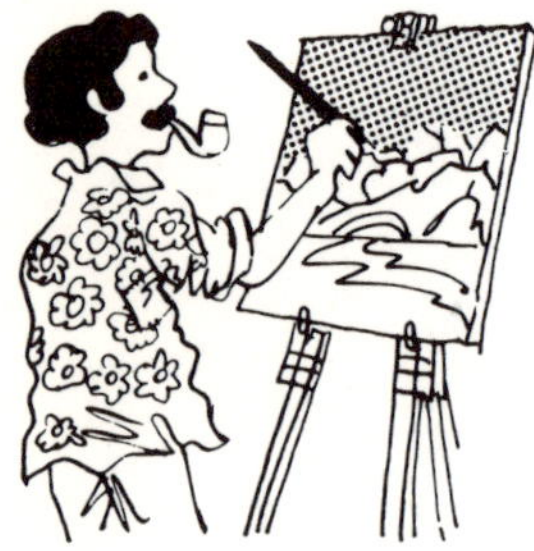

9 What to do with old canvases. Do *not* throw them away. Paint them with a coat of ordinary paint: grey, beige or bright sienna in colour, and you will have a canvas with a coloured background which may prove extremely useful. Moreover, if the canvas previously bore a painting which turned out badly, its surface will still show the clots and ridges of that earlier painting, and, when you paint on it again, you will obtain an impression of thick impasto, in vivid colours, worthy of Van Gogh himself!

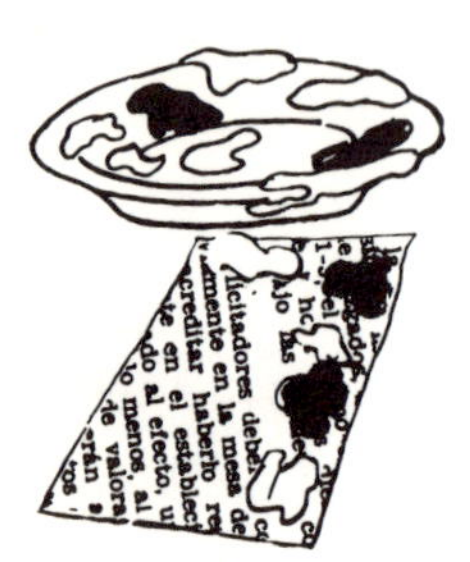

10 Picasso's palette. I have pointed out above that, for landscape painting, a wooden palette of rectangular shape is used. It is worth knowing, however, that in practice any surface can be used as a palette. Picasso, as he explained to Geneviève Laporte, never used a palette — he used a newspaper instead. "My palette is a newspaper". Matisse used a plate as a palette. So, if you ever forget to put your usual palette in the carrying case (I have sometimes done this) remember Picasso and use as a palette the first object that comes to hand.

11 You need a palette knife. At least one. It is advisable to take with you, along with brushes, a couple of palette knives (one in the shape of a stone-mason's trowel, and the other knife-shaped) to correct or paint particular areas of the picture. This is unless you wish to paint entirely with the palette knife. In any case it is essential to have a knife-shaped palette knife to clean the palette, whether in the course of the session or afterwards.

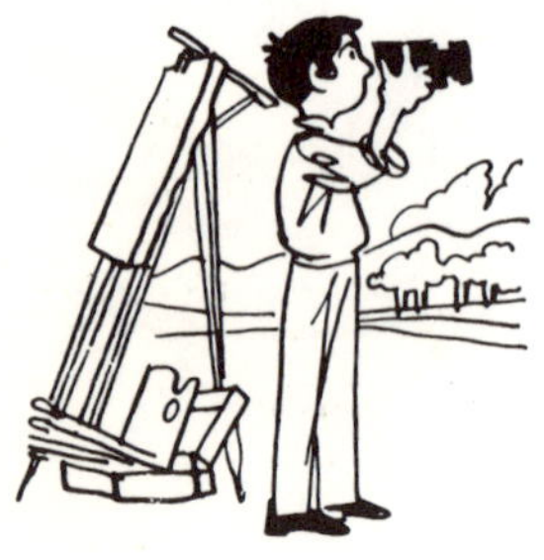

12 The camera: an extremely useful piece of equipment. I have mentioned this before, but I emphasize once again the advisability of taking a camera when you go painting. Apart from the possibility of taking photographs of various subjects on the way out and the way back, of studying and practising composition, the establishment of the framework of a picture, the selection of a viewpoint and so on, you will have the opportunity of taking a photograph of the scene which you are painting. This will enable you to compare the picture with the real landscape, retouch it, put finishing touches, etc. The photographs must, of course, be in colour.

13 Listen to music while you are painting. If you have a cassette-recorder or portable radio, consider taking it with you, so that you can listen to music while you are painting. This is something that many professional painters do in their studios. So why not do it when painting in the open air?

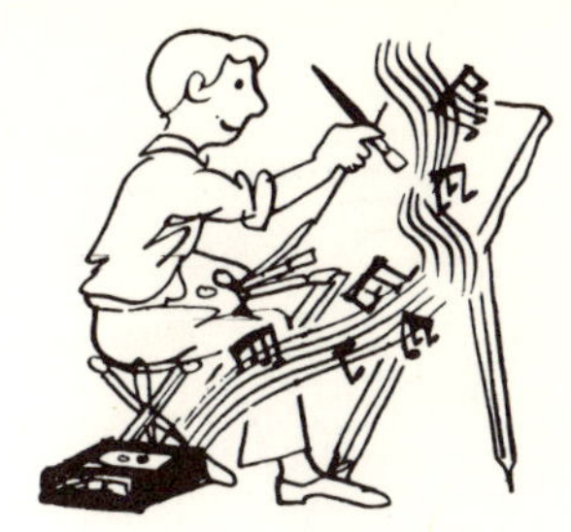

14 And take some chilled beer with you, even if you are in the heart of the country. This is, of course, only a minor problem. But at times one is out there in the country, painting, and it is summer and the sun is shining; the painting session may last two hours, or three and... a fellow gets thirsty. The solution is to take along one of those small insulated containers, a sort of waterproof bag which holds three or four bottles and a few ice-cubes from the refrigerator. This will be enough to slake your thirst with a cold drink while painting.

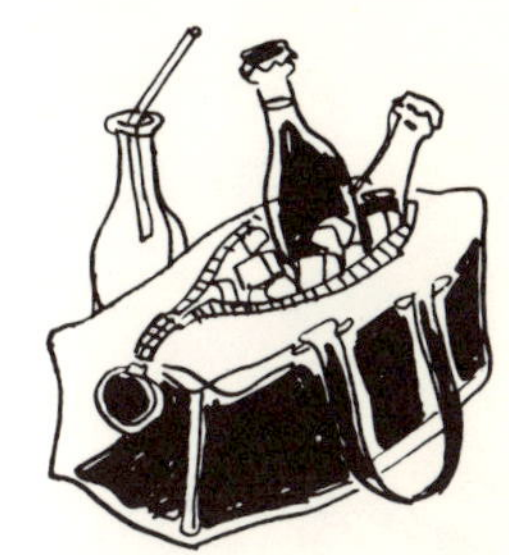

15 Also, a length of thin string. Yes, this is sometimes needed to solve small problems: the carrying case that does not close properly; the secondary pieces of equipment that one does not know how to carry all together, because one of its joints is not working, or the easel itself is broken, or it can't be folded up because the strap has been damaged; and so on.

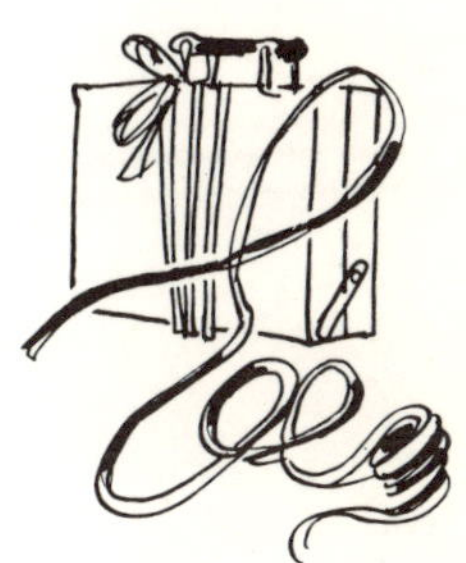

16 When the easel becomes unstable in a high wind. The canvas mounted on the easel is like the sail of a ship: when the wind shifts slightly, both easel and canvas lose stability. In that case (and here is another use for that length of string) it is advisable to find a fair-sized stone and, tying the string round it, hang it from the centre of the top of the easel, as shown in the illustration. However, if the wind becomes very strong, it would be better to fold up the easel, the canvas, put things away in the carrying case and leave painting for another day.

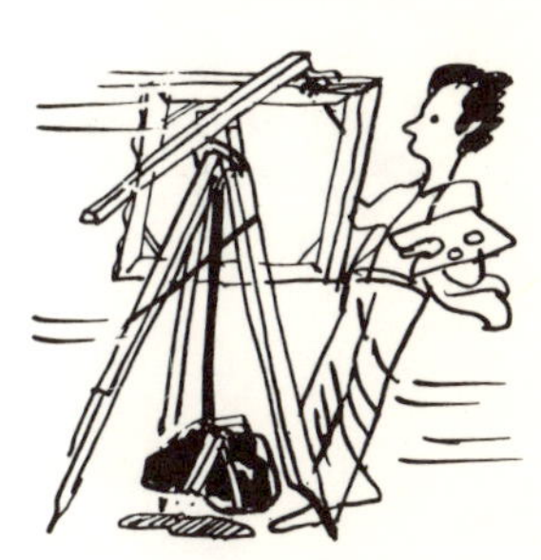

17 Traditional method for establishing the framework of a picture. This serves, also, to study composition. It consists of a frame of cardboard covered with black paper, with an aperture of about 14×10 cm, and a thickness of about 5 cm. By holding this this up in front of the subject, a careful study of the best framework for the subject can be made.

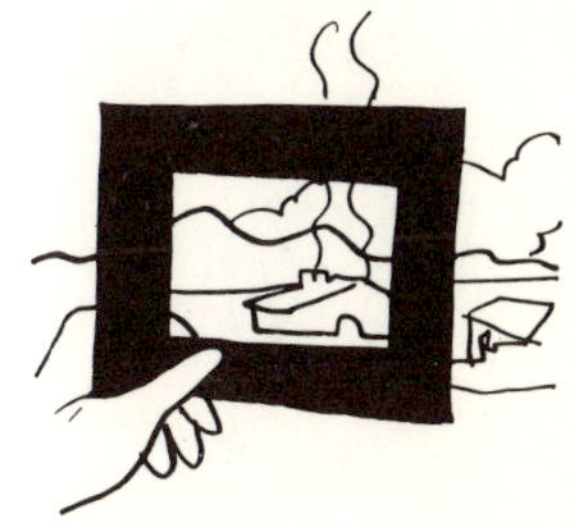

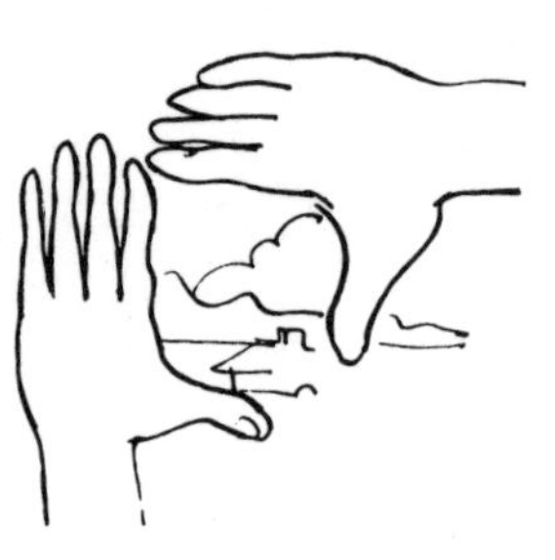

18 The same thing can be done using the hands or four paint-brushes. As a substitute for the previous method, you can use your hands, placing them in the position shown in the illustration, or use four paint-brushes, forming a rectangle with them. Occasionally, when you have acquired some experience, it is enough to use two brushes forming a right angle. Sometimes, you can "see" the framework without the help of brushes, or a cardboard frame, with the naked eye. At times, however, if there is any doubt, it is worthwhile establishing the framework by one of the procedures described.

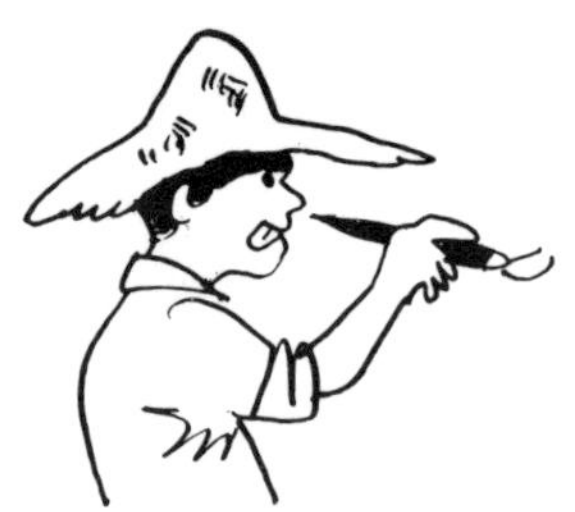

19 Acquire a broad-brimmed hat for hot days. And also a car in working order, you might add, with all those odds and ends to carry... But the hat is very often absolutely essential — one of those straw hats, whether a peasant's hat or a smart one, as long as it is cool. One of these, I repeat, prevents the chance of your being severely sunburnt when painting in the open country on a hot summer's day. The Impressionists always took their hats with them.

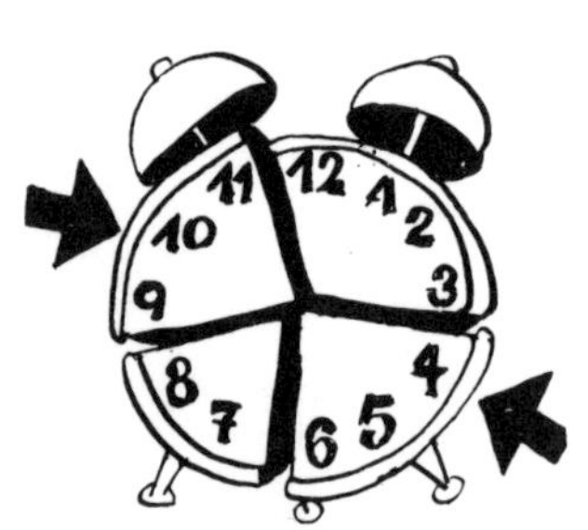

20 The best times for painting in the open air. If it is a cloudy day, any time will do. However, when the sky is clear and the sun is shining brightly, the best times are from 9 to 11 in the morning and from 4 to 6 in the afternoon (in summer until 7). Bearing in mind what has been said above with regard to the "chromatist" style, the hours in the middle of the day are equally suitable, perhaps even better: provided that one works under shade. In bright sunlight, and at one or two o'clock in the afternoon on a sunny day, there is a problem which will be described in the following paragraph.

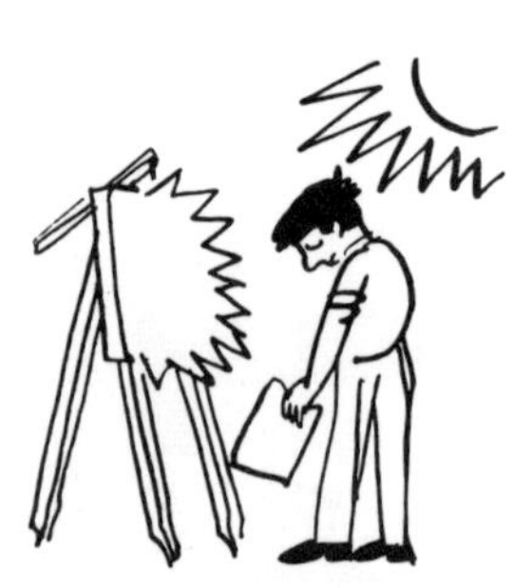

21 The problem of dazzling. There is a famous picture by Manet called *Monet painting on the Seine*, where Monet can be seen on the deck of a boat painting in bright sunlight, but beneath a parasol. There is another of Renoir, painting under an umbrella or a large sunshade. The point is that when the sun is at its height the colours on the canvas have a dazzling effect (especially the white of the canvas itself) and the artist unwittingly employs a range of somewhat darker colours which, when the picture is later hung in a room with normal lighting, appear positively murky. Hence, it is not advisable to paint in bright sunlight, when an excess of light falls on the canvas modifying one's concepts of colour and contrast. One should either paint in the shade or leave it for another day.

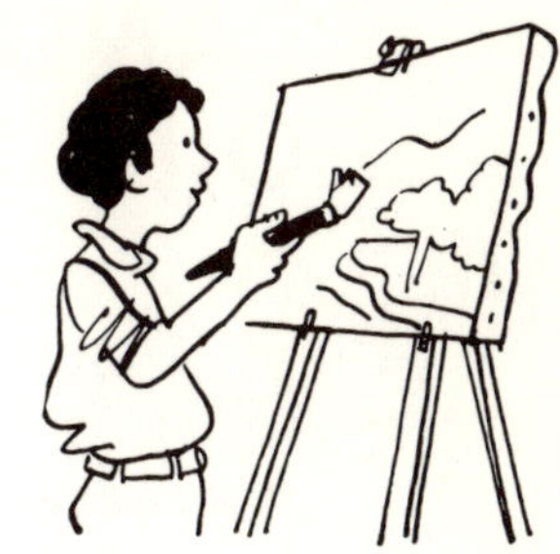

22 Half-close your eyes in order to "see" better. If you look at the subject with your eyes half-closed, this has the effect of eliminating the minor details and allowing you to see the main masses of shape and colour. This is essential if you are to grasp, from the very first, the validity of the subject as a topic to be painted (when, with eyes half-closed, you see many large patches of colour, it means that the subject has excessive dispersion and variety) and it is advisable to do it while painting, in order to "keep the details under control" as Ingres used to put it, and see, above all other things, the large bodies, the patches of colour — there should be only a few — which determine the effective composition of a subject.

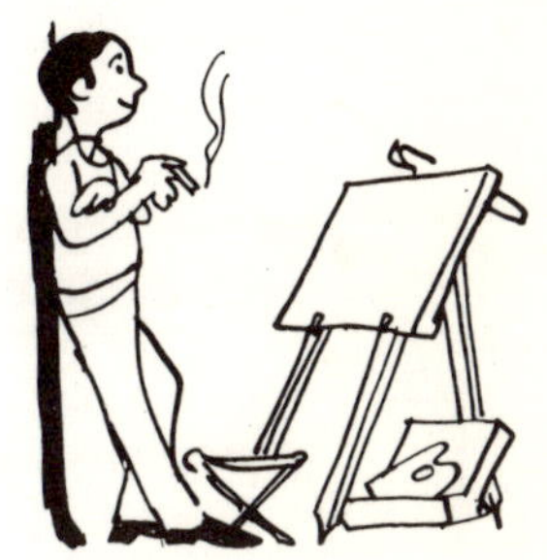

23 Do not go on, and on, and on painting. Do as the oarsmen do: they put the oar-blade into the water, row as hard as they can, moving the boat forward... and then they rest. Get up from time to time, stop looking at the picture, smoke a cigarette, clean your brushes and palette... relax and come back later, and try to see where you have succeeded and where you have gone wrong. And, when you come back, try and look at the picture as a whole. And when you are painting, too, look at it as a whole.

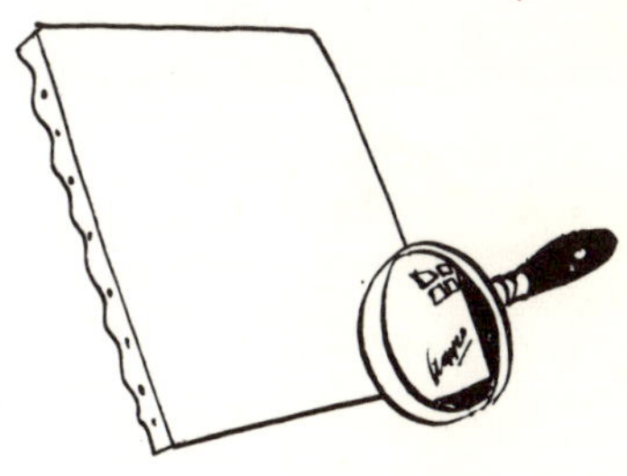

24 Sign the picture like a professional artist. Firstly, sign with a quiet colour. Do not sign in a vivid red or blue, as inexperienced amateurs usually do. Secondly, make your signature a discreet size. Thirdly, sign in some inconspicuous place: in a corner of the picture. Just reflect that, if the picture is good, the spectator will look for your signature and find it. Whereas, if it is bad, why advertise blatantly "I painted this picture"?

LANDSCAPE PAINTING IN OILS IN PRACTICE (I)

A practical study of specific aspects

I believe it is now possible to deal with practical questions, beginning by carrying out a series of exercises in which we will examine specific aspects of landscape painting. We will discuss the sky and clouds, providing illustrations of the various problems posed by these. And we shall see what happens in the case of the colour of the earth, fields, roads and mountains. We will draw and paint trees, and then rocks and sea water, complete with boats. Finally, we shall examine the problem of the figure incorporated into the landscape.

The sky in landscape painting

The sky is an important part of the picture: at times, it may well occupy over half the picture. There have been, and there are, painters who specialize in painting the sky, and most landscape painters begin by painting the sky — Sisley, one of the Impressionists, said, "I always begin my pictures by painting the sky". The colour of the sky and its degree of light usually affect the harmonization of colours in the picture as a whole. There is no doubt that the sky is extremely important.

I recommend you to go out into the country one day just to paint skies: clear skies, cloudy skies, at sunrise, in the mid-afternoon, when, with a few cumulus clouds about, really fantastic effects are produced. The theme or subject of the picture can then be the sky itself, with a narrow strip of earth or mountains at the bottom — this is a subject which has already been painted but is still of value, especially when one is practising landscape painting.

When painting a smooth and completely clear sky, the first thing to be appreciated is that, in general, the colour of the sky is more intense higher up than down on the horizon, where it tends to become brighter. Another principle to be borne in mind is that, in the upper part of the sky, the blue tends to have a tinge of carmine or red: that is to say, it is closer to ultramarine blue, whereas lower down, as one approaches the horizon, the blue loses its intensity and acquires a slightly yellowish hue.

The sky even when it is absolutely clear — and even when it is not — must not be painted as a perfectly harmonized blend. Such a sky would be something unreal, mechanical and would have the appearance of a metallic background. On the contrary. One has to create in it a vibration of light and colour, mixing with and above the blue or general colour other blues and colours with slightly different hues. One must paint with different types of brush-stroke, alternating bold strokes with brief touches, to break up the pattern of uniformity.

Lastly, it must be remembered that the colour of the sky is not always necessarily blue: it may be blue with a yellowish, pink or violet tinge... and it may be definitely pink, yellowish, greenish, etc. In this connection, bear in mind that you can choose a range of warm or cold colours, with the possibility of emphasizing the range offered by the actual subject, or of inventing a completely new range, taking as your starting-point the colour of the sky (see Figs. 134-136).

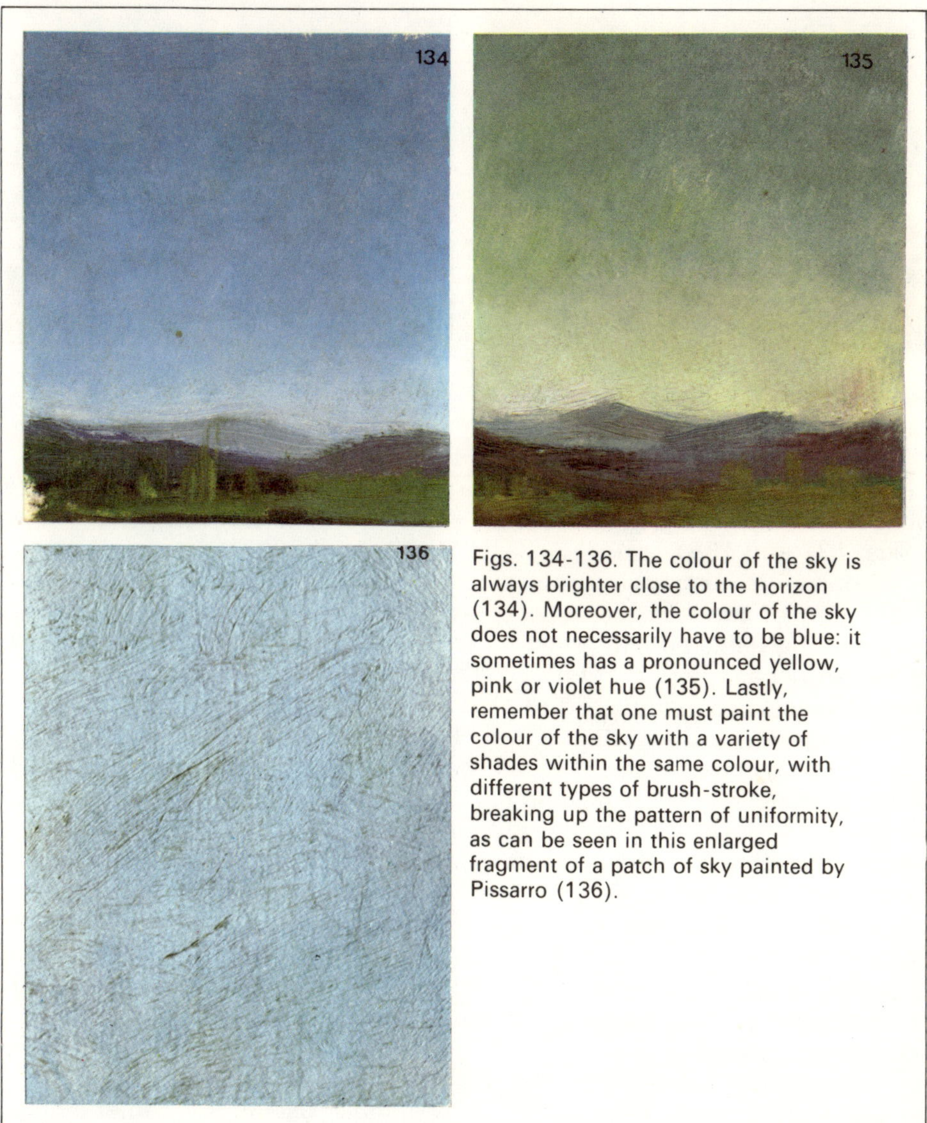

Figs. 134-136. The colour of the sky is always brighter close to the horizon (134). Moreover, the colour of the sky does not necessarily have to be blue: it sometimes has a pronounced yellow, pink or violet hue (135). Lastly, remember that one must paint the colour of the sky with a variety of shades within the same colour, with different types of brush-stroke, breaking up the pattern of uniformity, as can be seen in this enlarged fragment of a patch of sky painted by Pissarro (136).

Cloudy skies

The above principles can be applied generally, as regards clear skies and cloudy skies, since a cloudy sky is, essentially, nothing more than a "background of blue, pink or greenish colour — dark above, and bright lower down — upon which clouds appear". Consequently, when painting a

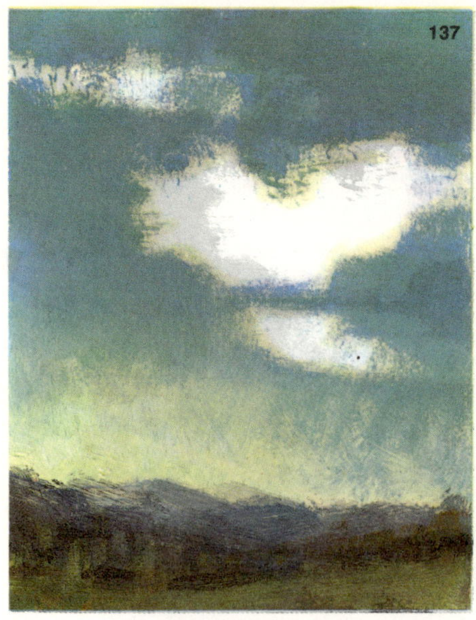

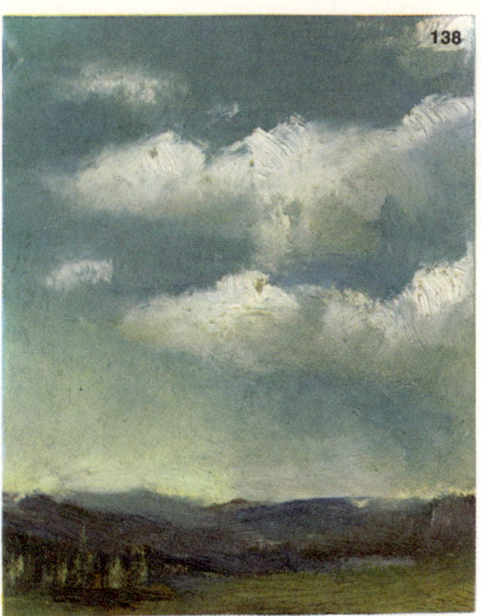

cloudy sky, begin by painting a background "curtain", leaving blank the spaces corresponding to the clouds, and painting and shaping these later (Figs. 137 and 138).

Clouds are simply a problem of draughtsmanship and of correct evaluation of tones. Such aspects as shapes, contrasts, varying shades, shadow and reflected light must be studied and constantly borne in mind. When proper attention is not paid to these factors, you tend to paint floating lumps of cotton-wool instead of clouds.

I suggest you draw clouds. Use Ingres paper (specially designed for drawing with charcoal and in pastel shades) blue in colour, and a small stick of white pastel or crayon, making use of a blurred pattern previously rubbed with some strokes of charcoal crayon. Use also an india-rubber to bring out white patches and outline and draw areas of half-light. Lastly, if it is not possible to draw direct from Nature, use good photographs. Then bear in mind, when you come to do the drawing, that a cloud is like a great floating body lit by the sun, and that the sunlight reaches that body from only one direction, and so produces certain specific illuminated areas, filled with brilliant light and contrasting with the darker background of the sky, and some areas in shadow within which, on the side opposite to the light, there are patches of reflected light (Fig. 139A).

Do this drawing exercise: it is extremely useful and entertaining. Then, when the moment comes to paint, bear in mind that normally clouds are white in colour in their sunlit parts — a brilliant white, which may need the use of the palette knife to achieve patches that are quite smooth and flat, and can reflect more light and more whiteness — whereas the shady parts are grey. (I am speaking here of clouds such as cumulus, against a blue sky, on a sunny day, and in the middle of the day.) In these conditions, the shadowy-grey of the clouds is brighter than the blue tone of the sky (Fig. 139B).

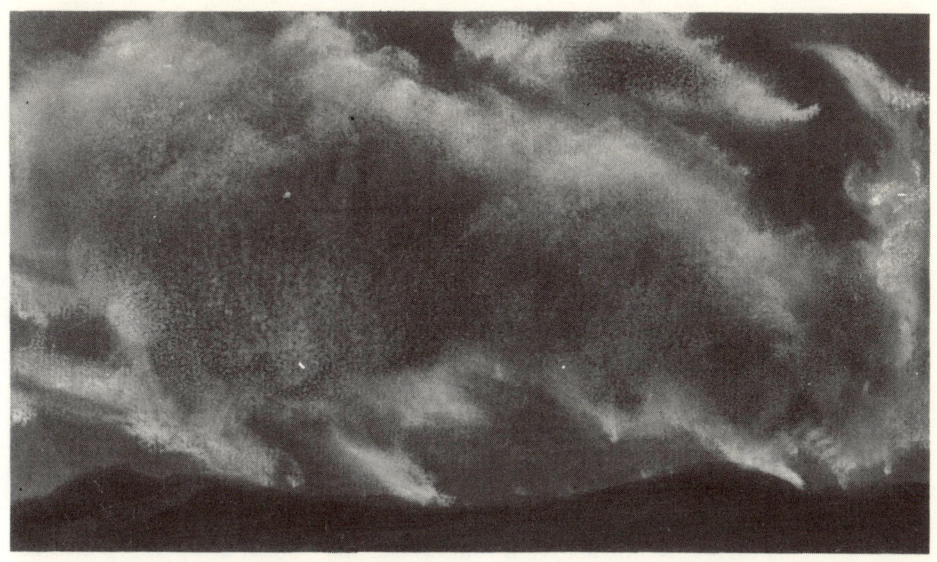

Fig. 139 A.

This general principle does not, of course, apply to overcast days, with a cloudy sky foreshadowing rain. In this case, the colour of the clouds may be a very deep grey: darker than the blue or grey tone of the sky.

Lastly, it must be emphasized that the problems of evaluation of tones are the same when the sky has a yellowish, pink or other hue.

Sunlit areas: these sometimes require the use of the palette knife or the fingers. They may have a yellowish tinge.

Areas in shadow: very light grey, mixed with the same blue as that of the sky.

Areas of reflected light: a lighter grey, with a very slight bluish or yellowish hue.

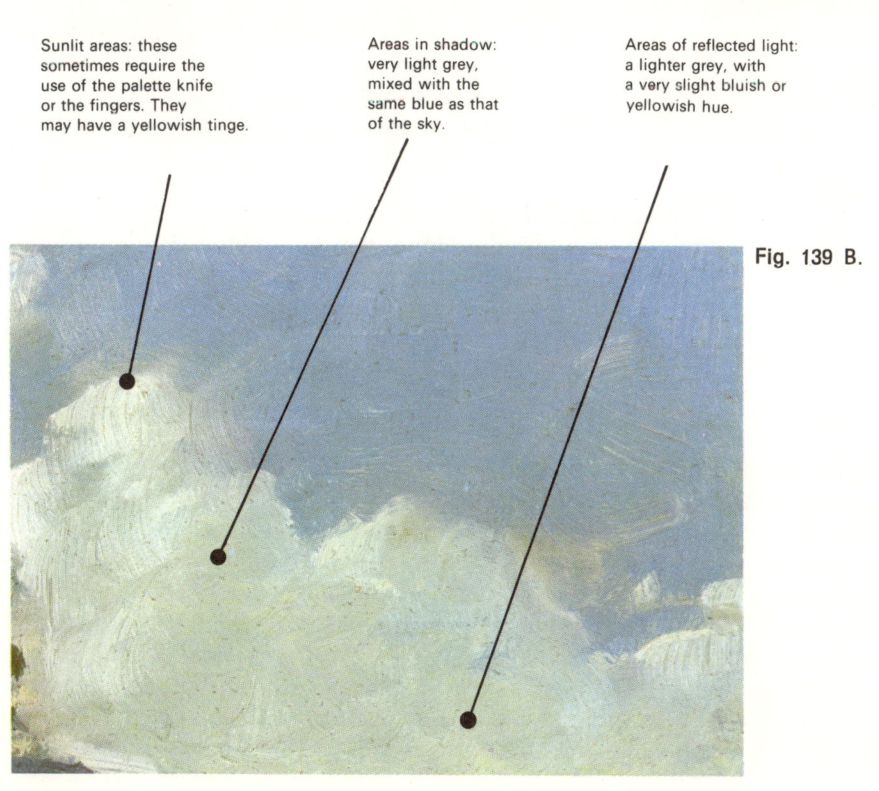

Fig. 139 B.

The earth

The colour of the earth in fields, roads and mountains presents varying colours and tones, according to the landscape, the season of the year and the weather. There are, however, certain common aspects.

The colour of earth is, in general, dark in the case of cultivated fields, lighter in the case of uncultivated or fallow fields, and lighter still in the case of tracks and pathways. The reason is obvious: cultivated earth is earth which has been turned over, with clods of varying size, dampened by irrigation and possessing a structure which encourages shadow and presents a darker tone. The earth of tracks and pathways, on the other hand, is a dry, smooth and trodden earth, which reflects more light and therefore has a lighter tone. For the same reason, the colour and the shadows of turned earth tend more towards sienna, red and carmine, whereas that of tracks and pathways is yellower in the sunlit parts, and bluer in the shaded parts (see illustration in adjoining Fig. 140).

However, the colour is never uniform. This generalization is true of fields, tracks and meadows, whatever their real colour may be. It is a principle to be constantly borne in mind: it is necessary to mix with the real colour slight variants, and differing shades, and paint with — or on top of — the basic colour, by means of touching and retouching which diversifies the general colour. Try to observe these small differences of colour in the model itself. They really are there!

Be careful with the direction of the brush stroke. it should always, or nearly always, be horizontal. A field or a track painted with vertical brush strokes will give the impression of a field of grass, with turf or with newly-mown dry wheat.

Be careful, too, with "productivity". Some amateurs make up a blend of paints resembling the earth and then simply paint and paint — displaying extraordinary "productivity" — all the patches of earth that appear in the subject. For goodness' sake, do not fall into that trap. Don't be over-eager.

> In the whole of Nature, no two colours of earth are identical. Make an effort to discern the differences between them: to make the differences as pronounced as possible, and put time and effort into painting them in different colours or hues.

Mountains and hills, as the reader already knows, when they are in the background, lose their vivid colours and become blue, violet-tinged or grey.

When dealing with mountains or hills in the middle distance, which present a wide variety of patches of earth, rock, vegetation, woods, trees, etc., that is to say, with a considerable variety of shapes and colours, the best advice is the following: bear in mind the principles described above, and do not get impatient. Do not improvise. It may seem that this is hardly worth saying, but I really have seen too many landscapes done badly because of the artist's fatal desire to finish early and the disastrous mistake of painting without remembering what the subject is "saying".

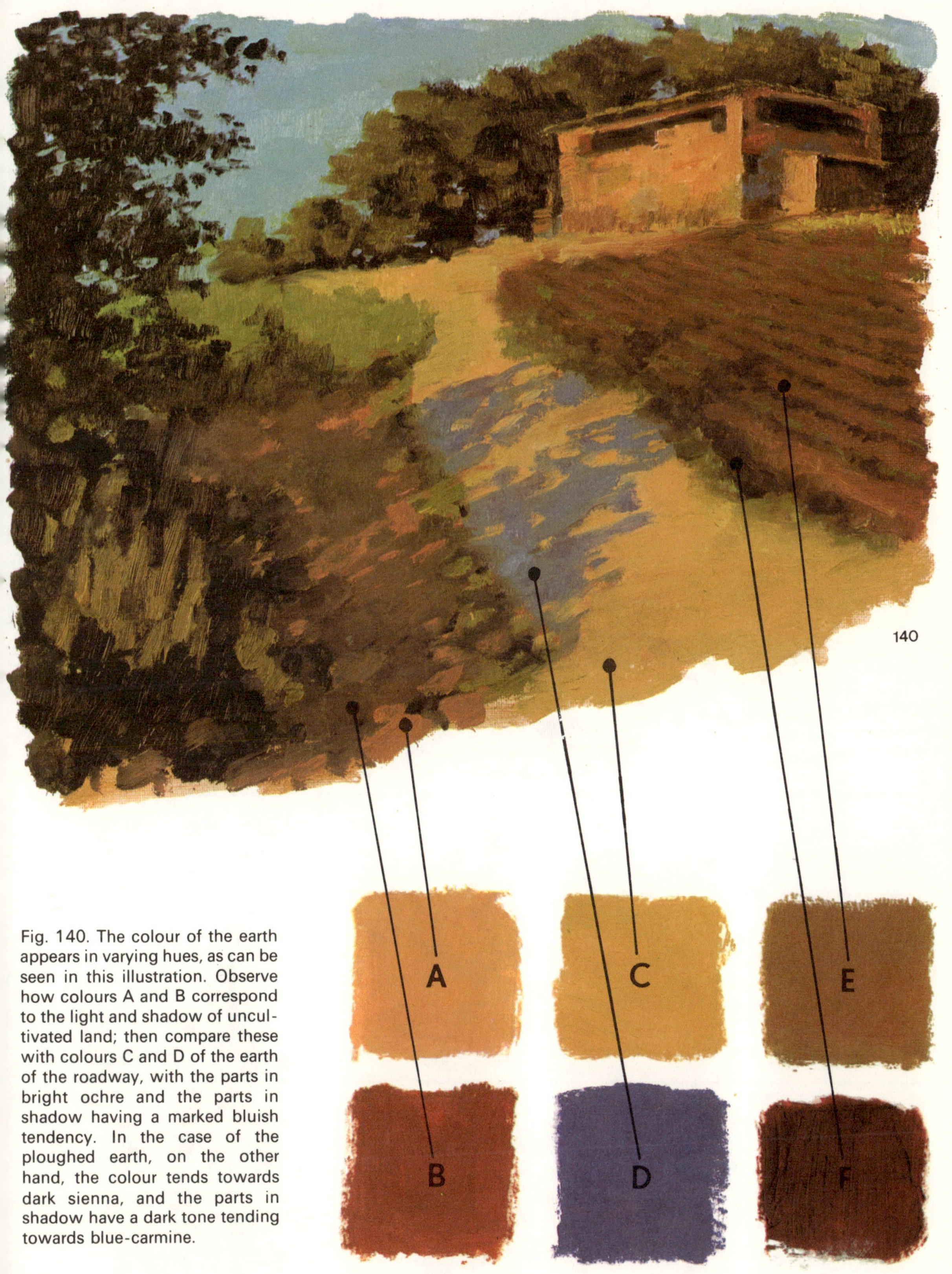

Fig. 140. The colour of the earth appears in varying hues, as can be seen in this illustration. Observe how colours A and B correspond to the light and shadow of uncultivated land; then compare these with colours C and D of the earth of the roadway, with the parts in bright ochre and the parts in shadow having a marked bluish tendency. In the case of the ploughed earth, on the other hand, the colour tends towards dark sienna, and the parts in shadow have a dark tone tending towards blue-carmine.

Trees, shrubs and thickets

I cannot emphasize too strongly that shapes and colours cannot simply be improvised. They cannot be painted from memory on a "hit-or-miss" basis. And the same is true of trees. it may seem that to paint a tree, with all its branches, leaves and sprigs, is a very difficult task, but this is not the case: it is more laborious, it requires more work, and one needs to concentrate more on what the subject "explains" — but that is all. There are some tricks of the trade, but the best trick consists of "drawing it all patiently", as Michaelangelo advised centuries ago.

The reader must submit himself to the discipline of spending a long time drawing trees, shrubs and thickets, as Van Gogh did continuously, in order to be able, as he was, to paint them synthesizing and summarizing in a few brush-strokes the entire structure of branches and leaves. The beginner should draw bare trees, with just the scaffolding of the bare branches, then groups of branches and leaves, and then branches covered with leaves, if he is really going to learn to paint trees. As an example of this, I reproduce some of my own drawings and sketches, done in pencil from nature (Figs. 141 to 144).

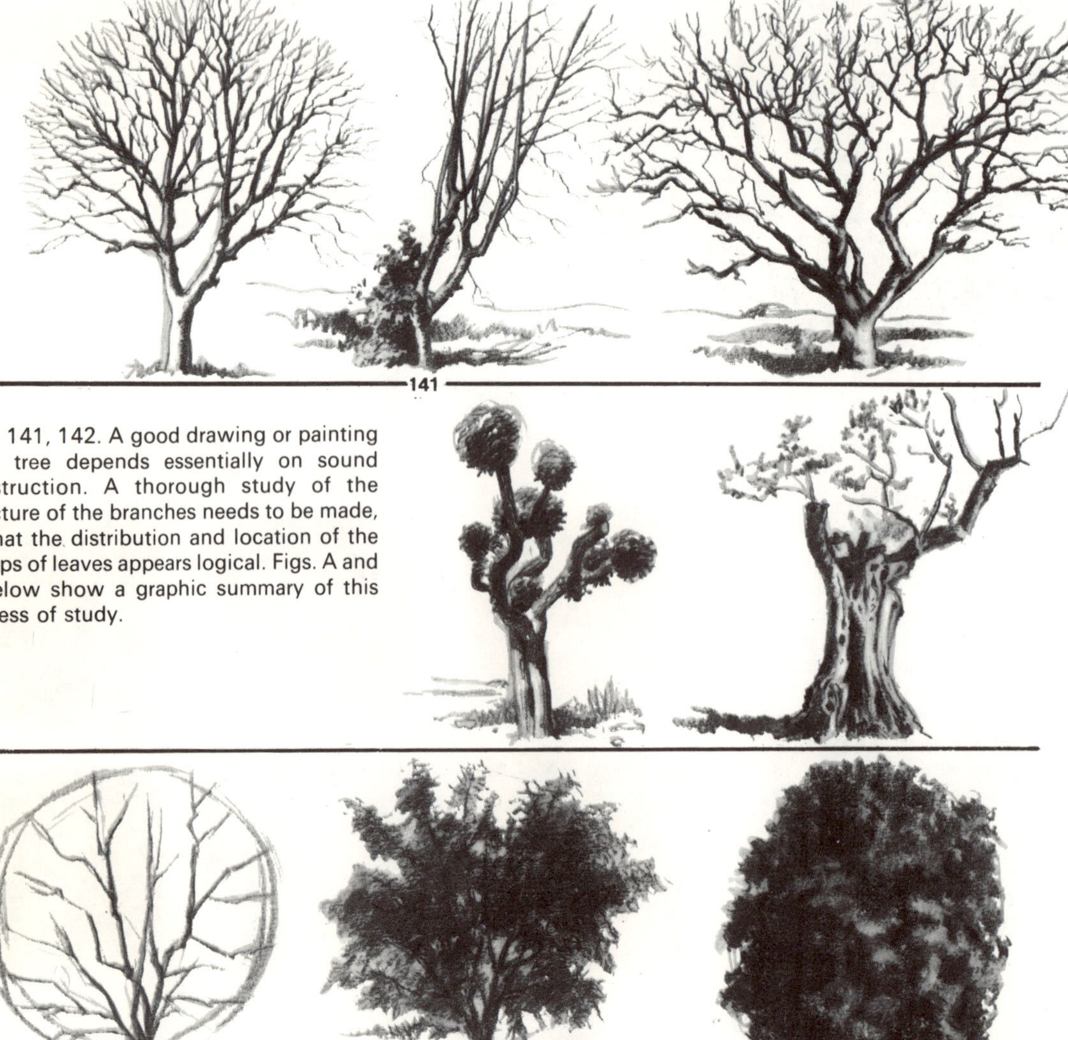

Figs. 141, 142. A good drawing or painting of a tree depends essentially on sound construction. A thorough study of the structure of the branches needs to be made, so that the distribution and location of the groups of leaves appears logical. Figs. A and B below show a graphic summary of this process of study.

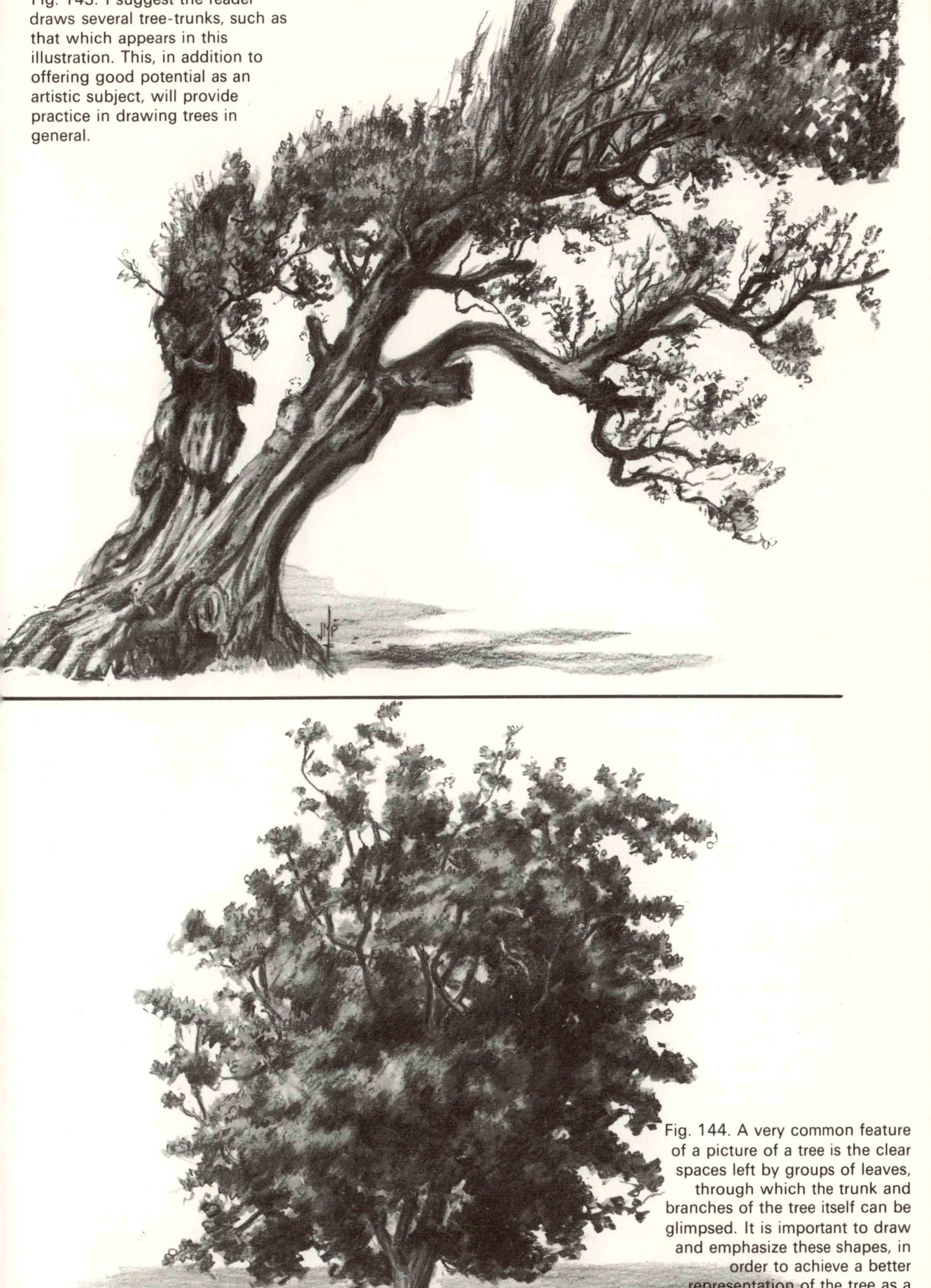

Fig. 143. I suggest the reader draws several tree-trunks, such as that which appears in this illustration. This, in addition to offering good potential as an artistic subject, will provide practice in drawing trees in general.

Fig. 144. A very common feature of a picture of a tree is the clear spaces left by groups of leaves, through which the trunk and branches of the tree itself can be glimpsed. It is important to draw and emphasize these shapes, in order to achieve a better representation of the tree as a graphic concept.

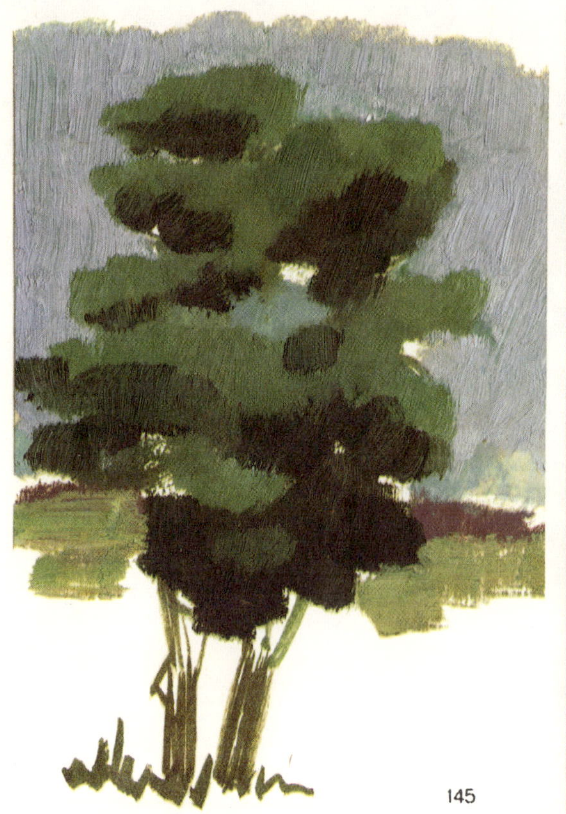

145

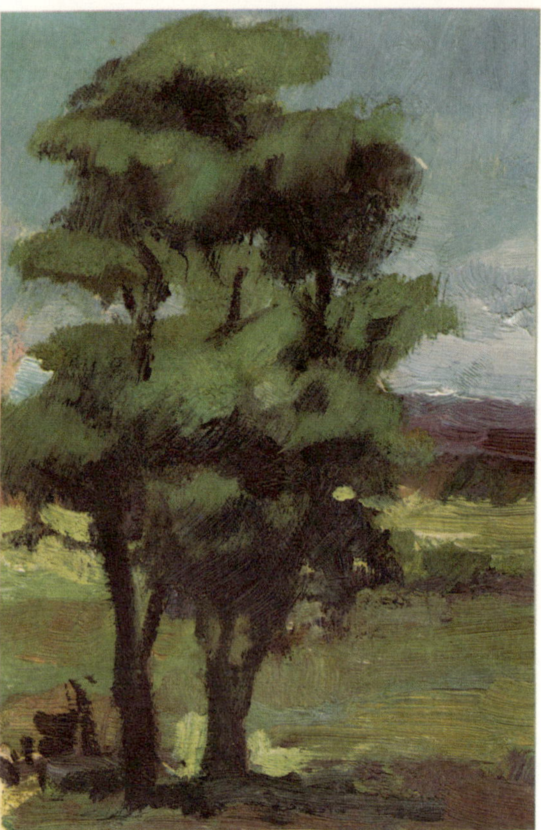

And what should one paint? This, in principle, is an easier problem, as can be gathered from the following examples:

See, for example, in Fig. 145 above, a summary of the process to be followed to paint one of these trees a certain distance away from the viewer, which makes it necessary to have less sharply-defined outlines: just patches of colour, without any detailed depiction of small branches and leaves, as we have seen in the sketches reproduced on the previous pages.

Next comes the more detailed process: the painting of a tree situated in the foreground, where the shapes and colours of the subject need to be defined in greater detail. This process is more laborious, but no more difficult.

How to paint a tree

Let us suppose that you have already drawn the tree, in charcoal crayon, most conscientiously, with light and shadow, trunks and branches, groups of leaves, etc.; this drawing, even though it will later be covered by the first coat of oil paint, will serve as a framework of reference: a preliminary study which will familiarize you, the artist, with the problems of volume, contrast and construction.

This, then, is the process to be followed:

1. The sky and the dark parts

The first task is to cover with paint diluted in turpentine the colour of the sky, extending the paint into the areas or patches corresponding to groups of

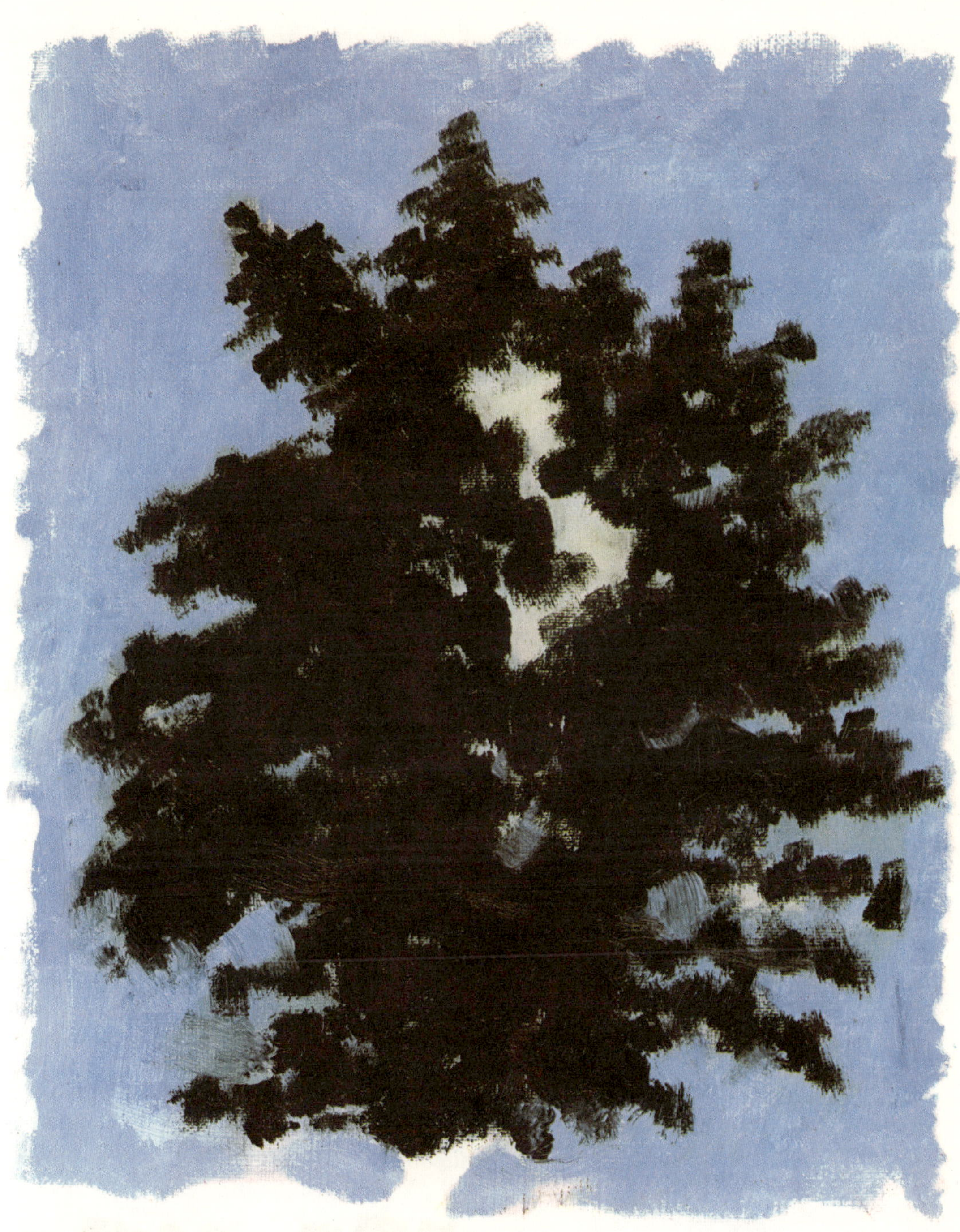

146

leaves of the tree: that is to say, "entering" (colouring with brush-strokes) the parts that have been drawn. Make up the colour of the sky, for the moment, with ultramarine blue and white. Then mix, with plenty of turpentine (when referring to turpentine I mean, of course, the special essence of turpentine for oil-painting already mentioned)... mix the colours Prussian blue and burnt umber, which will give a dark green, almost black, colour. If the tree as a whole has a bright green appearance then mix this first colour with more Prussian blue. If the tree has a darker green aspect (ochre or reddish) make the mixture predominantly of burnt umber colour.

Paint the general structure of the tree with this dark colour, leaving free of paint only the very sunlit parts and the "loopholes" through which the sky can be seen. It does not matter if this is carried to excess; on the contrary, it *can* be, provided that the paint is not too thick — that is to say, thanks to the large quantity of turpentine, it dries quickly. See Fig. 146 above for the result of the first stage of this process.

2. More solid construction and estimate of volume, painting with only three colours

Examine Figs. 146A and 146B: in the former, I have painted three samples of colour: the blue of the sky and the greenish-black of the previous stage, and also a brighter green — in the centre — made up of Prussian blue, yellow, ochre and a small quantity of white. See, in Fig. 146B, the state of the tree on completion of this second phase: notice the part played by this third green colour, and note that I have been working with all the three colours together, using the green-black colour for the painting and creation of the silhouette of the leaves against the blue background of the sky, using the bright green for the sunlit parts of the tree, and trying also to construct shapes, groups of leaves, etc.; and, lastly, using the blue to make holes in the spaces through which the sky can be seen.

After this second stage, of course, the colours are now thicker, without turpentine, so that they cover what is underneath when we paint over the dark colour.

3. Securing the colours and putting the finishing touches (Fig. 146 C p. 93)

We must now proceed more slowly. Try to examine and perceive the volumes, the play of light and shade, the colours, and the differences between luminous greens, medium greens and shady greens. Paint and "draw" at the same time, always in thick colours, which cover the surface. In general, paint with bright colours over darker colours, noticing where and how the bright leaves stand out against dark backgrounds: paint in bold strokes, constantly putting a new and clean colour on the brush, so that the colour on the brush does not lose its initial hue by being applied on other colours which are still wet. Do not "comb" the colours with the brush. On the contrary leave them on the canvas with the brush full of paint, so avoiding an excess of blends which will blur the shape, the subject itself. Bear in mind that leaves are flat: they are patches of flat colour, superimposed on other lighter or darker colours, which are also flat.

146 A

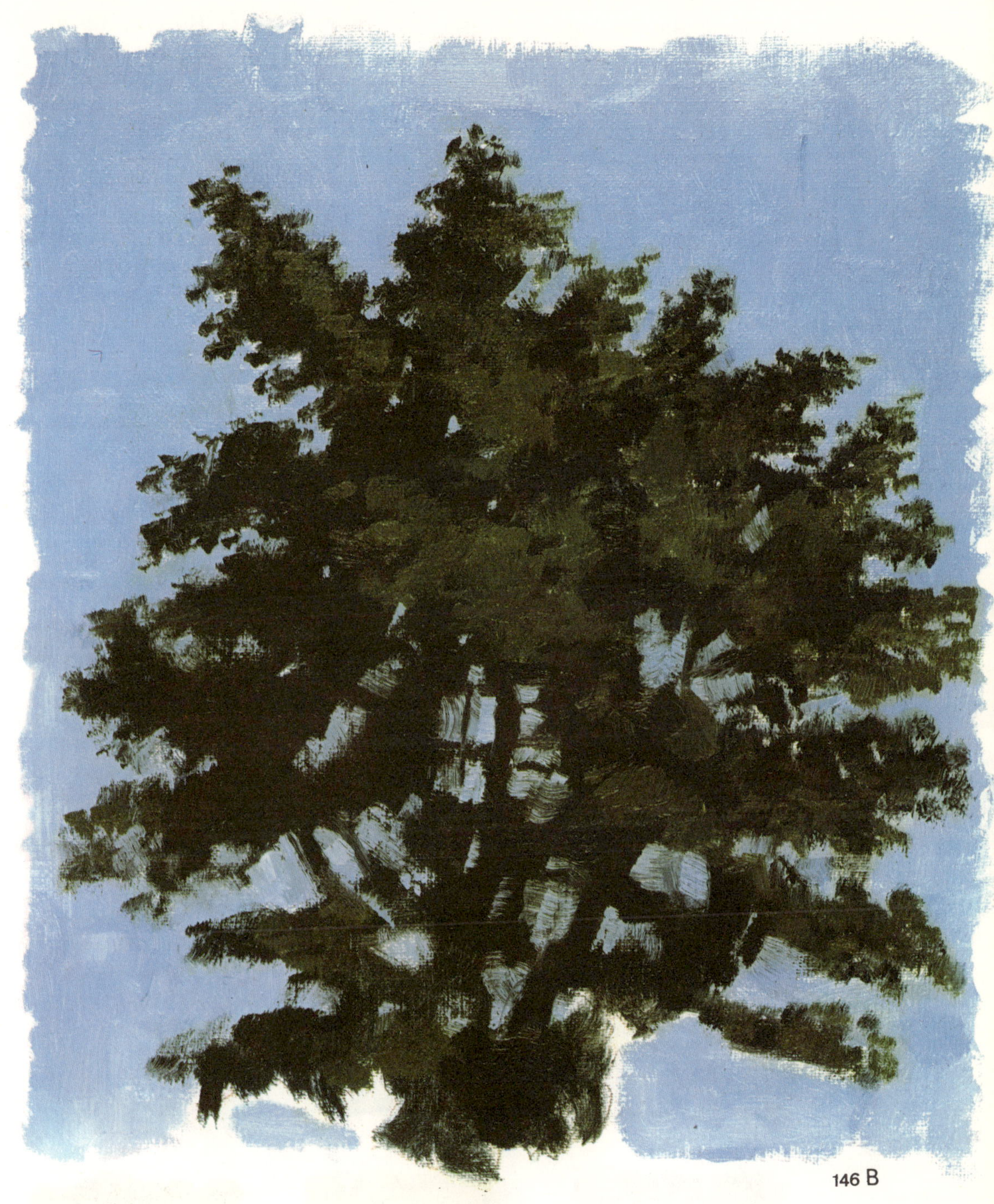

Fig. 146 B. As this illustration shows, the problems of volume and construction encountered in the first stage of painting can be solved very simply: in this case by using just the three colours at the foot of the previous page.

Work on the sky, thickening and modifying the colour. Now, to the initial mixture composed of ultramarine blue and white, a little Prussian blue and a touch of yellow can be added. Using the same colour as for the sky, the spaces which can be seen through the tree can be painted (see Fig. 146C). Note that these blue patches have been painted over the dark background of the parts left in shadow, so that with these brush-strokes in blue, superimposed on the background, it is possible to delineate and draw the thick and thin branches of the tree.

Paint with the two colours, the darker colour and the blue of the sky to establish outlines, to construct leaves and make them stand out, and to make "loopholes". Last of all, paint the more luminous patches of leaves.

Half-close your eyes, in order to visualize better the scheme of colours as a whole, and so harmonize the colours into a coherent range.

Moreover, the colours must, of course, be diversified: do not settle for two or three shades of green and just go on painting with them until the picture is finished. Try to see all the shades and colours of the tree. Make an effort to accentuate them. See, in Fig. 147 below, some examples of colours which I myself have used in the course of painting this tree.

Fig. 147. Here are some samples of colours which I myself have made up while painting the tree shown in Fig. 146: six different shades of green, one sienna, a mid-blue and a sea blue. Some of these shades, for example sienna and mid-blue, cannot, perhaps, be directly appreciated but they were used as constituents of mixtures laid on the paint itself, creating shades, reflections and tones.

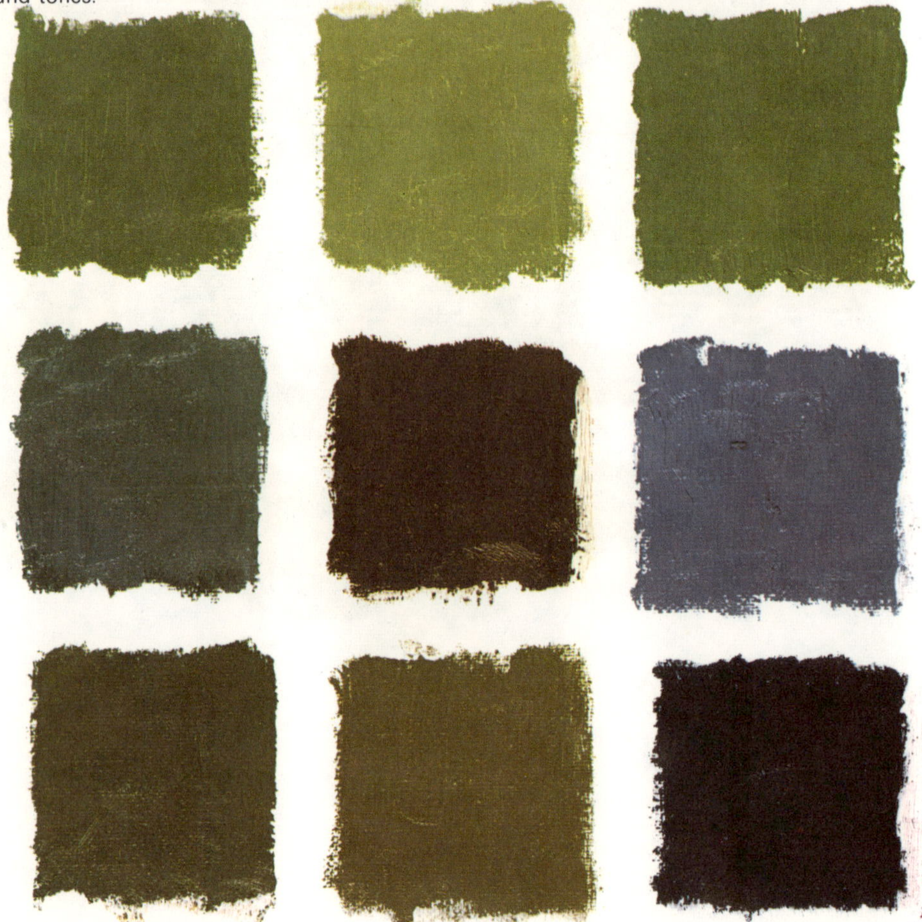

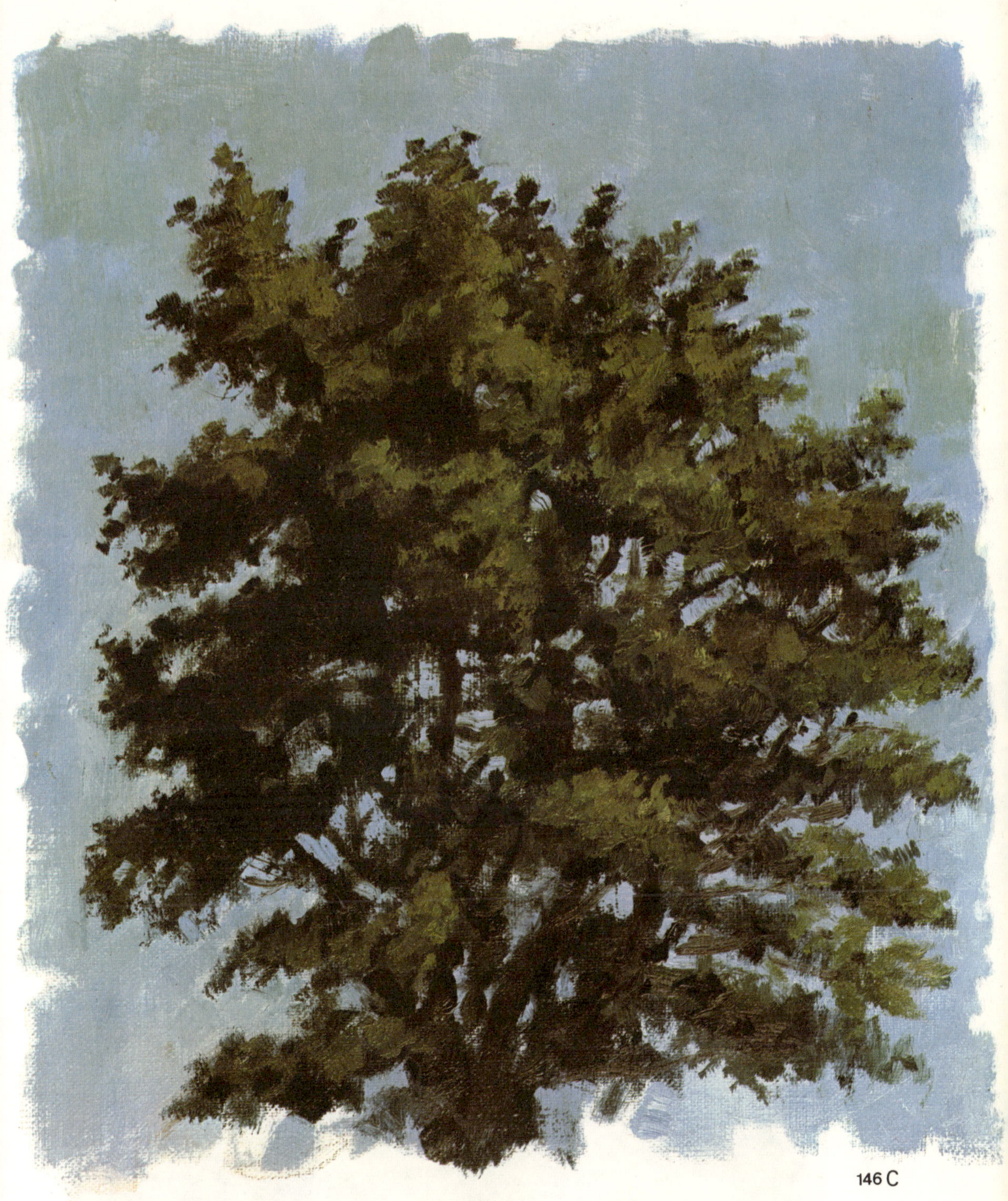

146 C

Fig. 146C. The painting of the tree, which is now finished, appears here in greater detail, in terms of construction and colour: the latter is based on the application of bright colours on darker colours. But care must be taken, at the same time, to diversify tones and shades.

The problem of painting shrubs, thickets and green fields must be solved by the same principles and hints described in the preceding paragraphs. Nevertheless, I should like to repeat an important principle first expressed by Leonardo da Vinci, and which is still valid:

Among various landscapes of similar tone, the green of the plants and trees will always be darker than that of the fields.

Look at Figs. 29 and 83 to see what is meant by this and observe that this increased vividness of tone becomes attentuated in the middle distance and the background, and serves as a point of reference for the separation of different planes of distance. See also Fig. 148 below.

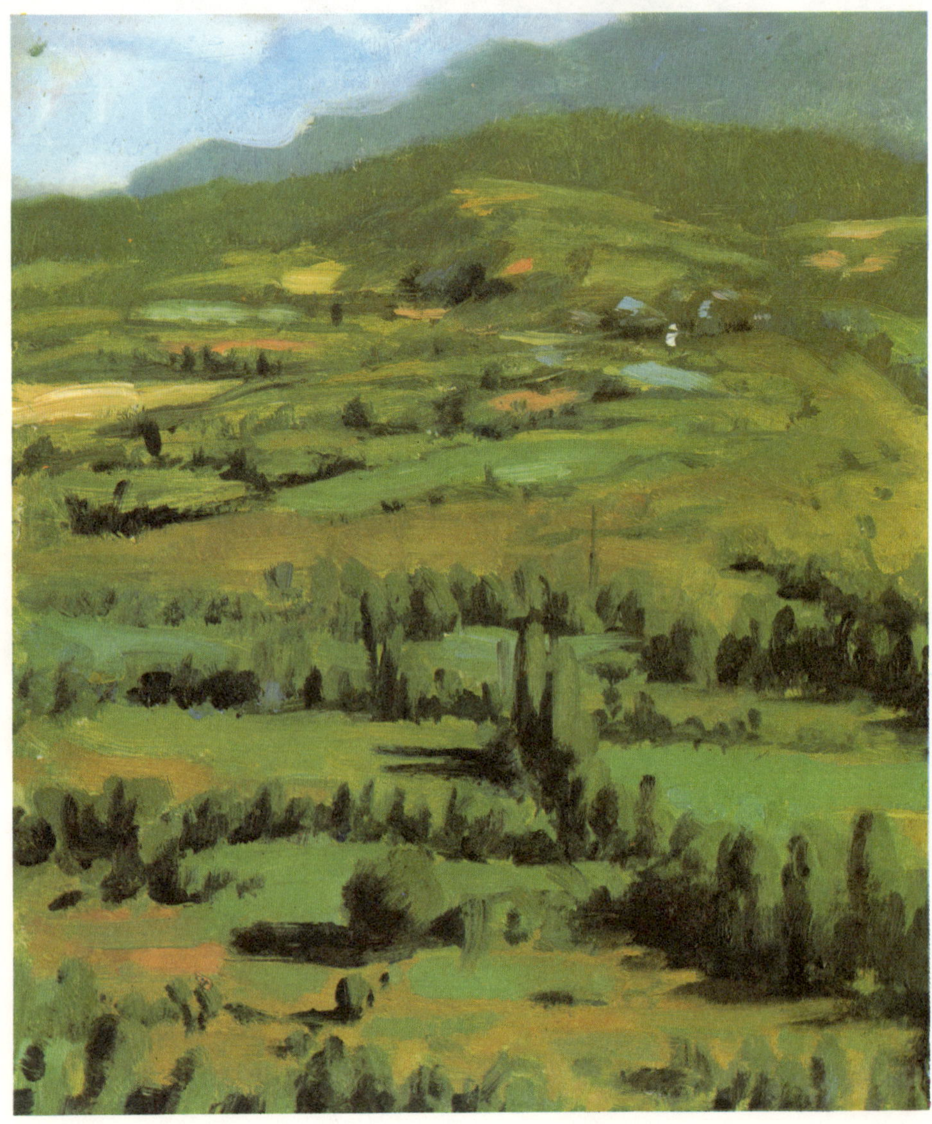

The sea

The colour of the sea, and that of lakes and deep rivers, is simply the colour reflected by the great screen of the sky. This is a fundamental rule: if there is a blue sky, there will be a blue sea; and if there is a cloudy and grey sky, there will be a grey sea.

The sea also undergoes the effects of the atmosphere between it and the viewer: its colour becomes brighter, or paler, as one approaches the horizon; the contrasts presented by the water itself — waves and foam — are sharper in the foreground. The foreground appears as sharply defined, the background as blurred.

The problem of painting the movement of the waves, the white foam breaking on the beach and on the rocks, is simply a question of practice and of knowledge of the subject. And here is the exception that proves the rule: you must paint from memory, using your powers of invention... but always with reference to the subject before you. This is because the sea is, of course, a subject which is in continual motion — the movement of the waves, the eddying of the water near the rocks, the breaking of the foam in thousands of white patches, ...this is all something which is seen and disappears and then is seen again — and each time it assumes different forms. Fortunately, however, these forms repeat themselves, and are similar. The problem is, therefore, to observe carefully for a considerable time — to observe and remember clearly — and then paint some moments — I emphasize, "some moments" — from memory, though always referring closely to the model. It is not easy, of course, but with a little practice...

The colour of the sea is, usually, blue or blue-green; however, a foreground with rocks, for example, presents an extraordinary variety of shades and colours, from black to green and bright blue, with grey reflections, flashes of white... or almost white. It is that word "almost"... One has to spend a long time looking at that part of the picture where the water forms whitecaps. It needs to be thoroughly analysed, forgetting the process of movement, and trying to perceive the precise colour of that brightness, which probably is not white at all, but more likely a very light blue, or a slightly yellowish green... and it needs to be painted with exactly this colour (which needs clean colours and clean brushes).

Rocks are, fundamentally, cubes — almost definitive geometrical shapes, with or without sharp angles: this depends on whether they are, or are not, sunken or washed by the waves. They have to be painted with different colours for each plane and within the same plane, bearing in mind that when the waves break on them, they become darker in tone. So the dark line or edge which shows high-water mark needs to be observed and noted.

Look at Fig. 149, which illustrates the points mentioned in the preceding paragraphs. Read, at the same time, the paragraphs referring to these points.

With the sea, lakes and deep rivers, the problems are similar. The problem of reflections in the water, for example, nearly always represents the mirror-image of the bodies found on earth or on the water, in slightly more vivid colours, with the shapes broken up by the to-and-fro motion of the water forming small waves... and this presents the same problem — that of studying the subject carefully, and then painting from memory.

Fig. 149. Water, rocks and sea: a few practical hints

Compare the colour of the sea, and the contrast presented by the more distant rocks, with the colour and contrast of the rocks in the middle distance and the foreground: you will see that in the former case the outlines are more blurred and the colour is in general less bright, whereas the colour of the sea is lighter in the background than in the foreground.

The level of the water in contact with the rocks shows up as a dark line at the bottom of the latter: this line is very conspicuous because it is here, at this level, that the waves break and produce white foam. This point must be borne in mind when painting rocks submerged in water.

Observe, in this small outcrop of rock in the centre, the angular shape of the rocks, which form cubes and parallelepipeds. Try to accentuate these shapes by painting boldly, perceiving and portraying real rocks, which are the effect of "dramatic" light and shade. And do not forget that, in the parts in shadow, there still come into active play colour and reflected light, which give differing shades, all within that effect termed chiaroscuro.

Observe too that, when rocks are near the water-level, they lose their sharp angles and edges as a result of the continual erosion caused by the waves breaking against them.

Note carefully the way in which the water breaks against the rock, to form this white foam... (in this part of the picture and in other parts further to the right and, in the foreground, on the left). Note that the white foam has been painted on a dark ground, by rubbing and placing — white, light blue, grey — with a few brush-strokes... carefully calculated and worked out beforehand to get exactly the right effect observed in the subject itself. This is where one has to paint from memory, remembering what one has seen. Fortunately one can repeat this process very similarly.

The colour of the water in the foreground varies from almost pitch black to green and bluish tones. It is not difficult to paint the exact colour of water as long as you forget your preconceived notions of this colour — blue, eternally blue — and paint what you see in the subject, without any distractions.

Fig. 149. Detail from the picture *Costa Brava* by Parramon (private collection).

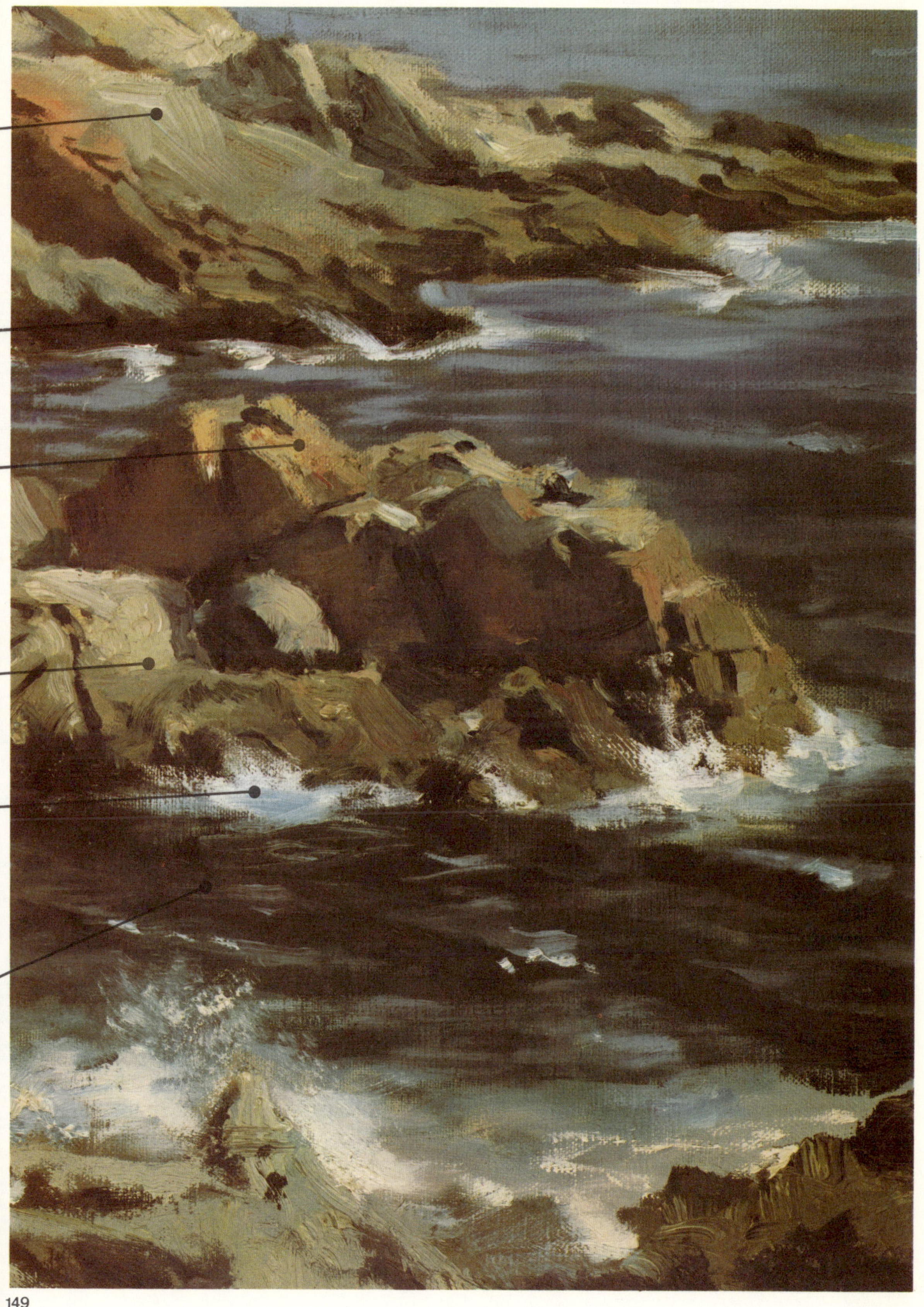

149

Ships and boats

Here the fundamental problem is that of structure: you need to make an extremely careful preliminary drawing, so as not to go astray later when it comes to painting. I would ask you to study carefully the illustrations in Fig. 150 below, together with one or two notes and hints on how to draw a boat. And I would advise you, when you are beginning, to make one of these drawings, if possible directly from the subject so that, later, you achieve a successful painting.

The colour of ships and boats is usually vivid and brilliant (especially in bright sunlight) so that it lends itself to emphasizing the contrast of light and shade, with the complementary colours playing their part. It must, however, be borne in mind that at sea and, more especially, in harbour, the accentuation of colours in the middle distance and in the background may be considerable: the concept of a marked contrast of tones and colours in the foreground, in the picture of a harbour, as compared with the background, is a typical example of the atmosphere interposing itself in a picture.

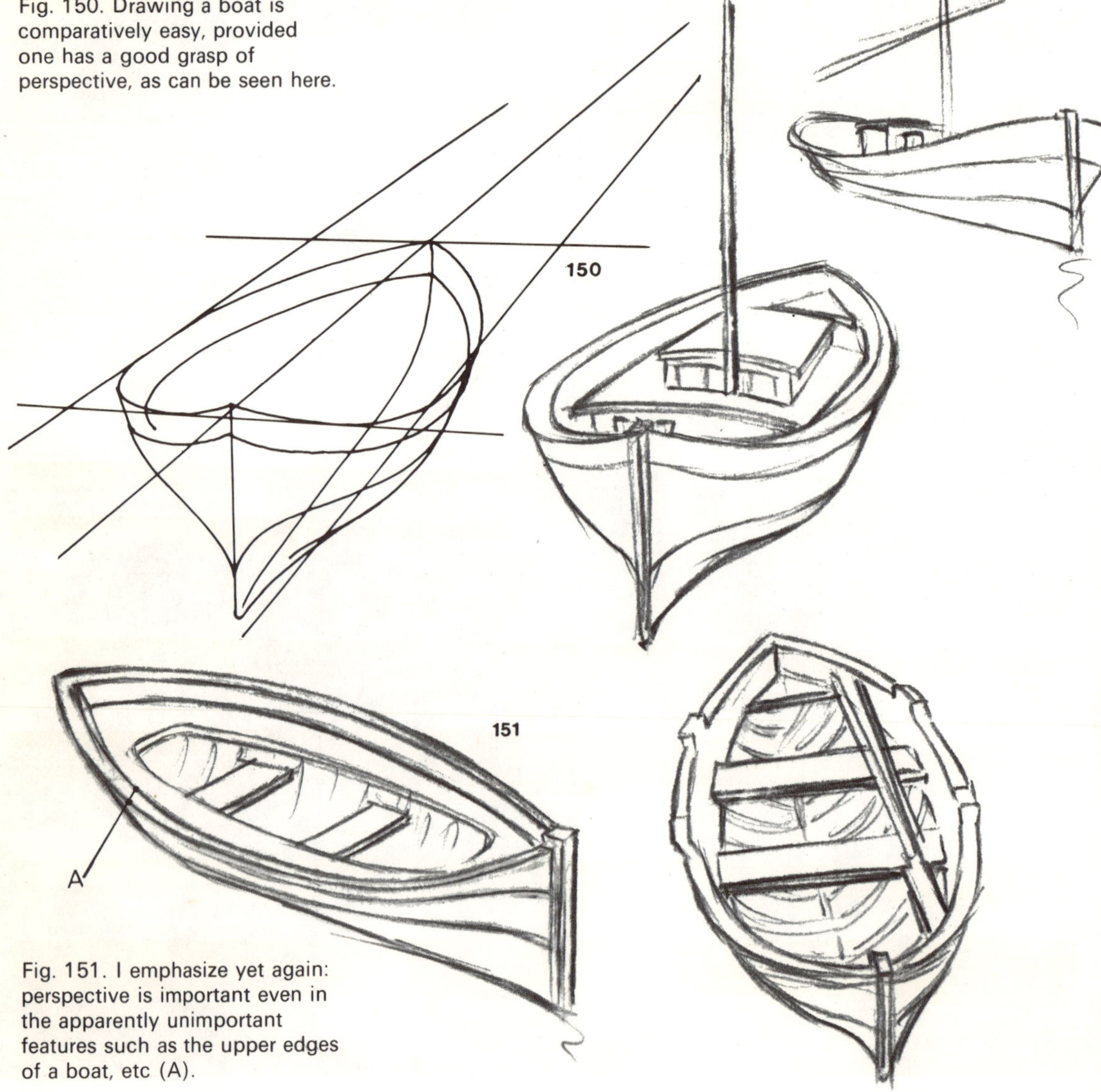

Fig. 150. Drawing a boat is comparatively easy, provided one has a good grasp of perspective, as can be seen here.

Fig. 151. I emphasize yet again: perspective is important even in the apparently unimportant features such as the upper edges of a boat, etc (A).

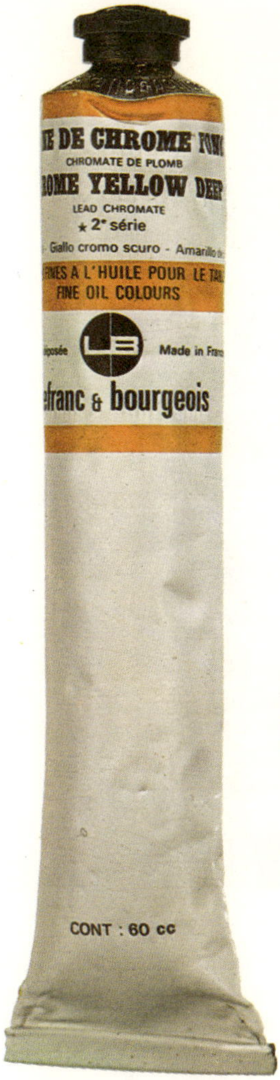

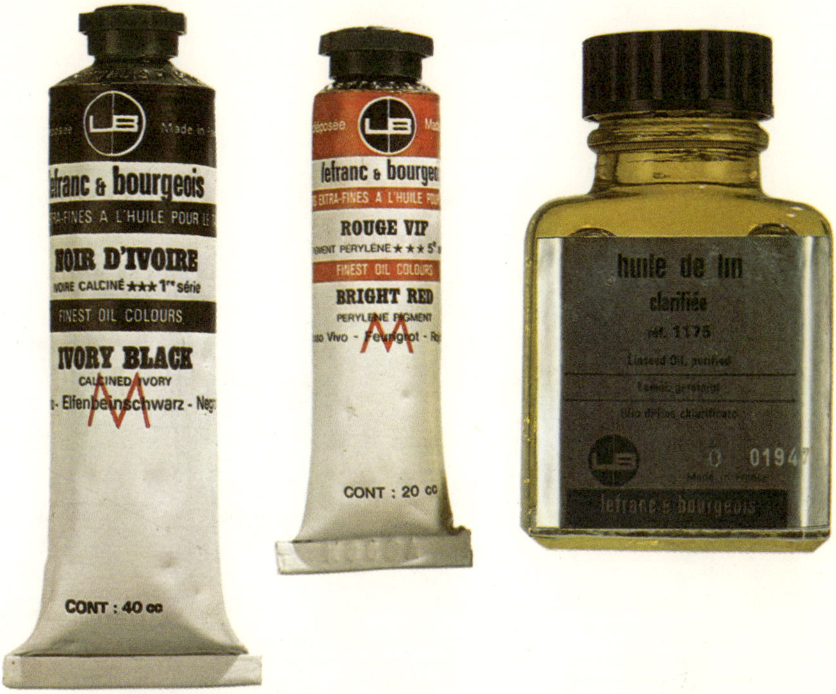

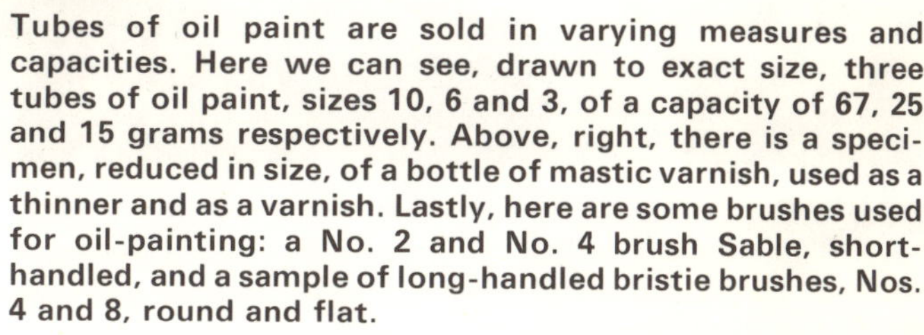

Tubes of oil paint are sold in varying measures and capacities. Here we can see, drawn to exact size, three tubes of oil paint, sizes 10, 6 and 3, of a capacity of 67, 25 and 15 grams respectively. Above, right, there is a specimen, reduced in size, of a bottle of mastic varnish, used as a thinner and as a varnish. Lastly, here are some brushes used for oil-painting: a No. 2 and No. 4 brush Sable, short-handled, and a sample of long-handled bristie brushes, Nos. 4 and 8, round and flat.

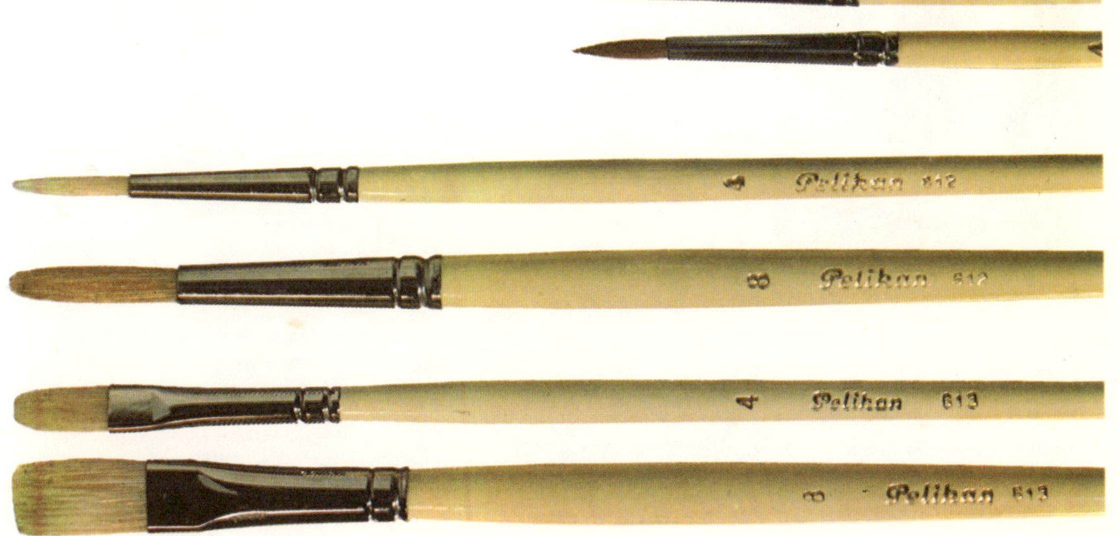

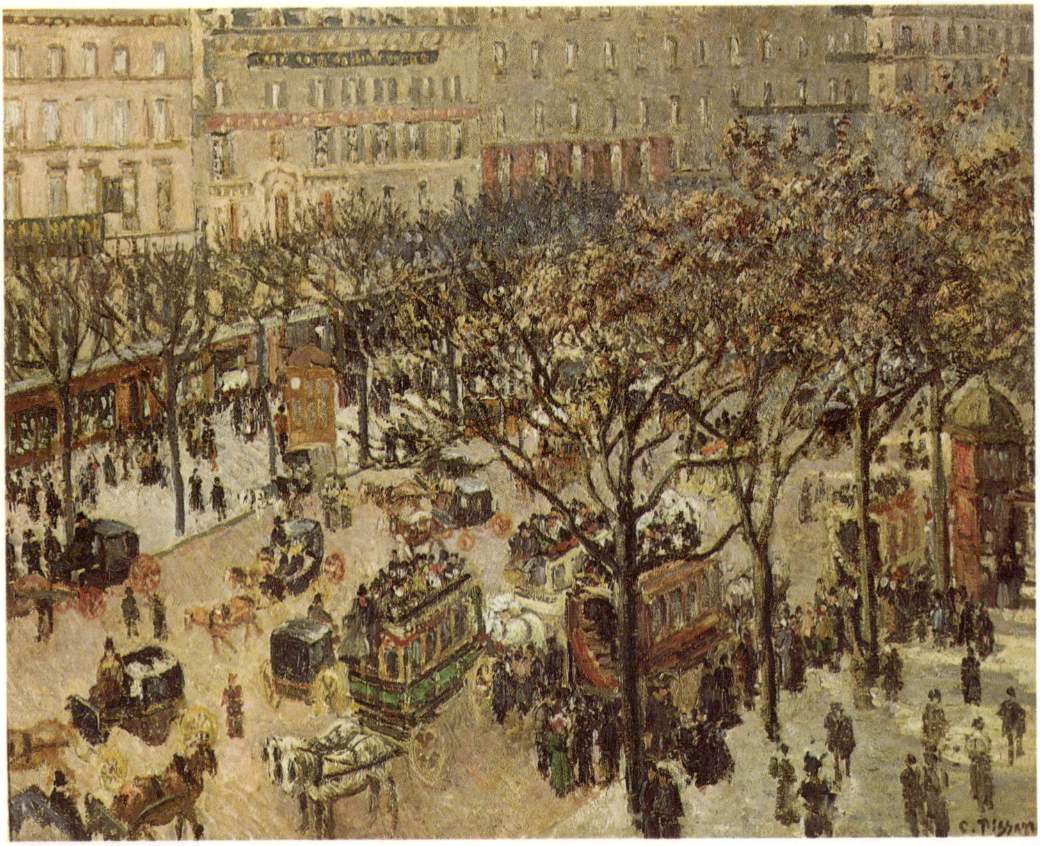

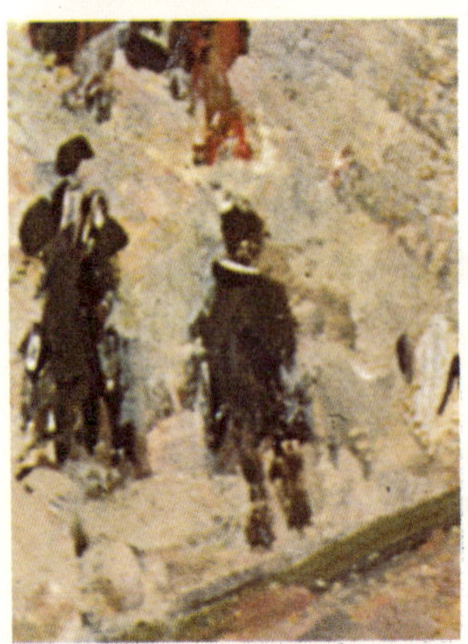

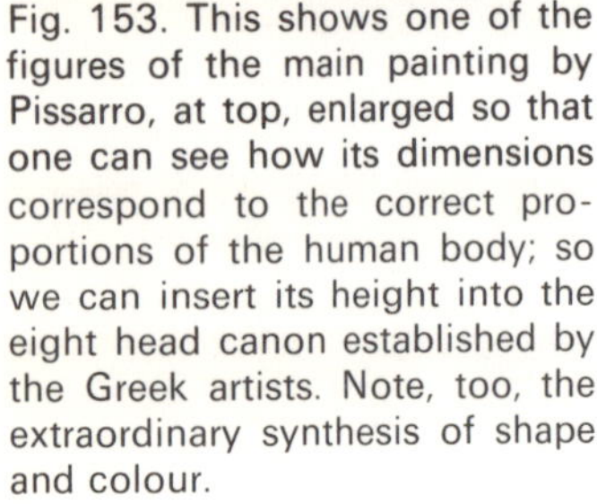

Fig. 153. This shows one of the figures of the main painting by Pissarro, at top, enlarged so that one can see how its dimensions correspond to the correct proportions of the human body; so we can insert its height into the eight head canon established by the Greek artists. Note, too, the extraordinary synthesis of shape and colour.

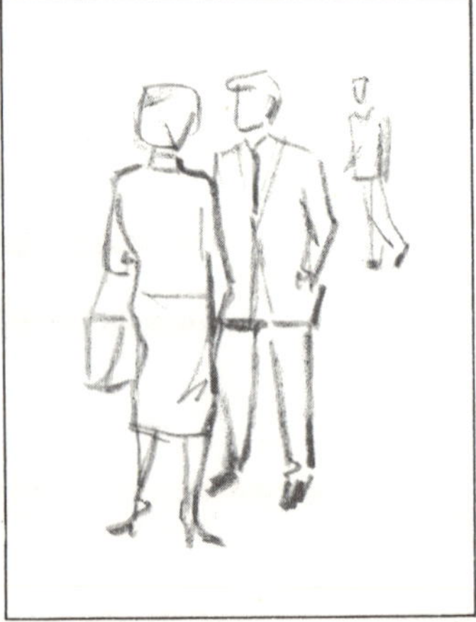

Fig. 154. There is no doubt that pissarro and the Impressionists in general were, in addition to being excellent painters, highly skilled draughtsmen; and this, without a doubt, was part of the foundation of their success. Good construction, even if only in outline — as we see in this sketch — is essential if one is to paint the picture without encountering problems.

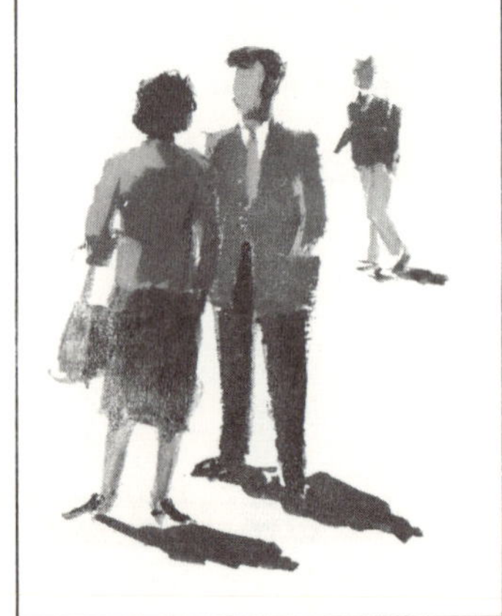

Fig. 154A. Making a number of sketches of figures, as a preliminary model, trains the artist in the knowledge and skill needed to paint his picture as a whole, because he is expressing shapes and masses in a few words — or, rather, lines. This ability to summarize the picture also cultivates the ability to perceive and express colour, so that the picture can then be painted with a minimum of explicit "language".

The figure incorporated into the landscape

If you paint a landscape in open country, a view of the coast, a village in the mountains, and so on, there is no reason to include any figures in the picture. However, if you paint the entrance to a village, or a street or square of a town, not to mention a city, you must include some human figures — walking, sitting, going about their everyday business — in addition to some vehicles.

The Impressionists — as usual with their desire to capture a scene *alive* — painted hundreds of pictures with human figures in them. Many such pictures are reproduced in this book: with small figures — just small touches of colour that lend a human tone to the subject.

What are they like? And how are they painted?

It is worthwhile asking this question, because I have seen few amateurs — or even professionals — solving this problem correctly. (Look at Figs. 152, 153 and 154 while you are reading the instructions that follow.)

The proportions are correct... so correct, indeed, that if we were to enlarge these figures to a size that made it possible to subject them to critical analysis, we would see that their heads are properly in proportion to the height of the body, the waist in the centre, and arms and legs in proportion to the overall height of the figure. We could not go so far as to say that we could apply to them the Greek principle of the eight-head, canon, but the proportions certainly are similar to this model.

The figures constitute a perfect synthesis of shape and colour in such a way that with one or two brush-strokes the head is drawn, three or four brush-strokes (including light and shade) depict and give shape to the body, a few more the skirt or trousers, etc.

They are, in short, an accurate reflection of the subject — or, rather, of an undefined subject (or various subjects) passing through the place concerned. They must be observed and studied like the waves of the sea, retaining in the memory their comings and goings or their stationary postures. So one has the opportunity of changing the colours if so desired, or situating the figure in a different place for composition purposes, using it to the best possible advantage as regards contrast, the focus of attention, the surroundings, etc.

All these considerations make it necessary for the artist to draw while he is painting and to paint slowly, with great care, carefully studying and calculating each brush-stroke. Try it. Do some preliminary studies... And do the same with the parts of the landscape that we have observed in these pages: then one will be able to say, as Van Gogh did:

"I think that doing preliminary studies is sowing, and painting pictures is reaping."

Overleaf we will embark on the adventure of actually painting a landscape or, rather, two landscapes: we shall observe, by means of illustrations and step by step, the entire process which I myself have carried to fruition, and at the same time we will study the two techniques most commonly employed for landscape painting in oils.

LANDSCAPE PAINTING IN OILS IN PRACTICE (II)

Oil-painting techniques

"Ever since I bought my first paints and artists' materials, I have been coming and going and working until I have been left utterly exhausted."
Van Gogh

According to the most complete catalogues, Van Gogh, in two years — the last two years of his life — painted over 800 landscapes and completed as many drawings. One of his biographers, Irving Stone, confirms this fantastic production when he writes: "He painted from four o'clock in the morning until night fall and he could no longer see. He painted two or three pictures in a day".

To the layman, this seems incredible. "Painting a picture in two or three hours?" he will ask. On one occasion, Van Gogh replied, to someone who had asked him this question: "Yes, I did this picture in two hours, but I have worked for years in order to be able to do it in two hours".

It is true that Van Gogh and the majority of the Impressionists began and finished their landscapes in one uninterrupted session. It was they who introduced the technique known as direct painting, in accordance with their belief that one should paint the impression of the moment, in contrast to the technique of painting by stages which had predominated for centuries in all artists' studios and workshops.

What technique did the Impressionists employ to finish a picture in two or three hours — landscapes which later were to command such astonishing prices?

The technique of direct painting

In the technique of direct painting, the artist imposes on himself the intention to paint according to a well-defined plan from the very first moment. Even Corot, who had not yet carried this idea to its ultimate conclusion, had said: "I know from experience that it is very useful to begin by sketching the picture in very simple terms, and then paint step by step, as completely as possible, following one's first intentions, so that very little remains to be done once one has covered the entire canvas". He went on to say: "I have found that all that is carried out directly turns out more natural, and more agreeable, and that when one does this one benefits from the possibility of a happy accident".

This, then, is the principle to follow:

Paint, from the first moment, with a well-defined plan in mind.

This is something that depends on your experience and degree of skill; but it also depends on the psychological attitude of the artist towards the picture.

A question of attitude

What usually happens is that you, I and everyone who paints pictures, creating and re-creating shapes, inventing and re-inventing colours, never — or hardly ever — employs his full intellectual capacity. One normally works with a certain degree of mental idleness, without full concentration, without whole-hearted commitment, knowing and taking it for granted that "there is always a second time"... to repaint, to have second thoughts, to rectify, and to go over one's work again.

However, if the artist follows the principle established by the Impressionists of "one picture at a sitting", he cannot have second thoughts! The technique of direct painting involves the adoption of an entirely different attitude: the artist must bear in mind that there will be only one opportunity for resolving any problems — painting and drawing all at the same time, painting and drawing simultaneously — to resolve, as I have said, the construction of each shape, the colour of each surface and each body. The artist must impose on himself the self-discipline of not going back over what has been done. And he must arm himself with courage, with a great courage in artistic terms, in order to be bold enough to paint with broad brush-strokes, with the brush full of paint, acting on his first impressions, committing himself fully and completely from the beginning until the end of the picture. It is, as I have said, a question of attitude, but there is also a technique to be followed, and now we are going to study and examine this technique.

The sketch: the best example of the technique of direct painting

The sketch, the small picture made as a draft — the colour sketch — painted on card or board, sometimes in less than an hour, is perhaps the most typical example of direct painting. It is also an excellent example for the examination of this question of attitude. This is because the sketch is the picture already seen and painted, the central motif which suddenly appears and which all at once invites — indeed, obliges — the artist to paint without preparation and without further ado. It is this picture — this little picture — which is painted directly, without any preliminary sketch, with the artist committing himself to it with all his senses and all his capacity..

Fig. 155 shows a colour sketch which I painted myself to illustrate this thesis.

And these are the notes which I took while I was painting this sketch:

> "No. 4 board: 33×22 cm.
>
> "I begin by applying blue-grey to the mountain in the background, on the left. Using the same colour and the same brush, I draw the outline of the cypresses, the church tower and the houses... the lines which constitute the edges of the foreground...

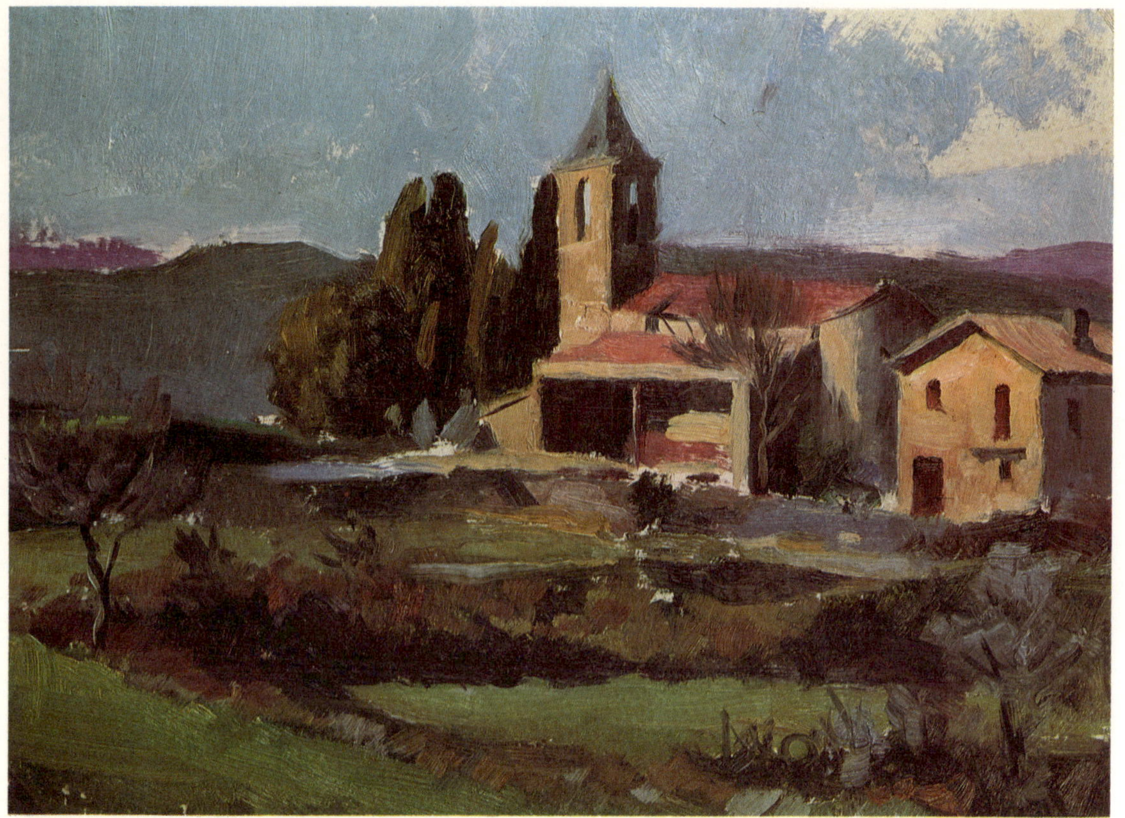

Fig. 155. Colour sketch for a landscape in oils, carried out using the technique of direct painting at a single sitting, the time taken being an hour and ten minutes. The speed of execution is made evident by the blurred outline of the shapes, and also by the fact that small parts of the canvas have been left blank and unpainted — the upper right-hand portion of the sky, for example). Of course, in a work of this nature it can be said that there is, in practice, no preliminary sketch: one begins painting straight away. (Parramon's *La Mota*, private collection.)

"With the same colour, but a bit darker, I paint the shadows of the church tower and of the house, and the shape of the mountain behind them.

"I change brush and colour: now I am painting the dark green of the cypresses, and I fill in the dark parts of the edges of the fields and meadows.

"Another brush, and green colour, for the meadows.

"Now the sky — with a new brush, and a colour made up of ultramarine blue, white and a touch of yellow.

"I blend the colour for the sunlit portions of the church tower and the houses.

"Now for the pink colour of the roofs, adding carmine and white to the luminous colour of the houses.

"Clean the brush with the blue-grey colour I first used, and blend a darker colour (emerald green, carmine, burnt sienna and ochre), to construct and paint the dark portions of the edges in the foreground.

"Emerald green and ochre for the sunlit parts of the cypresses and edges...

"Then bluish-grey for the trees and the shadows of the houses..."

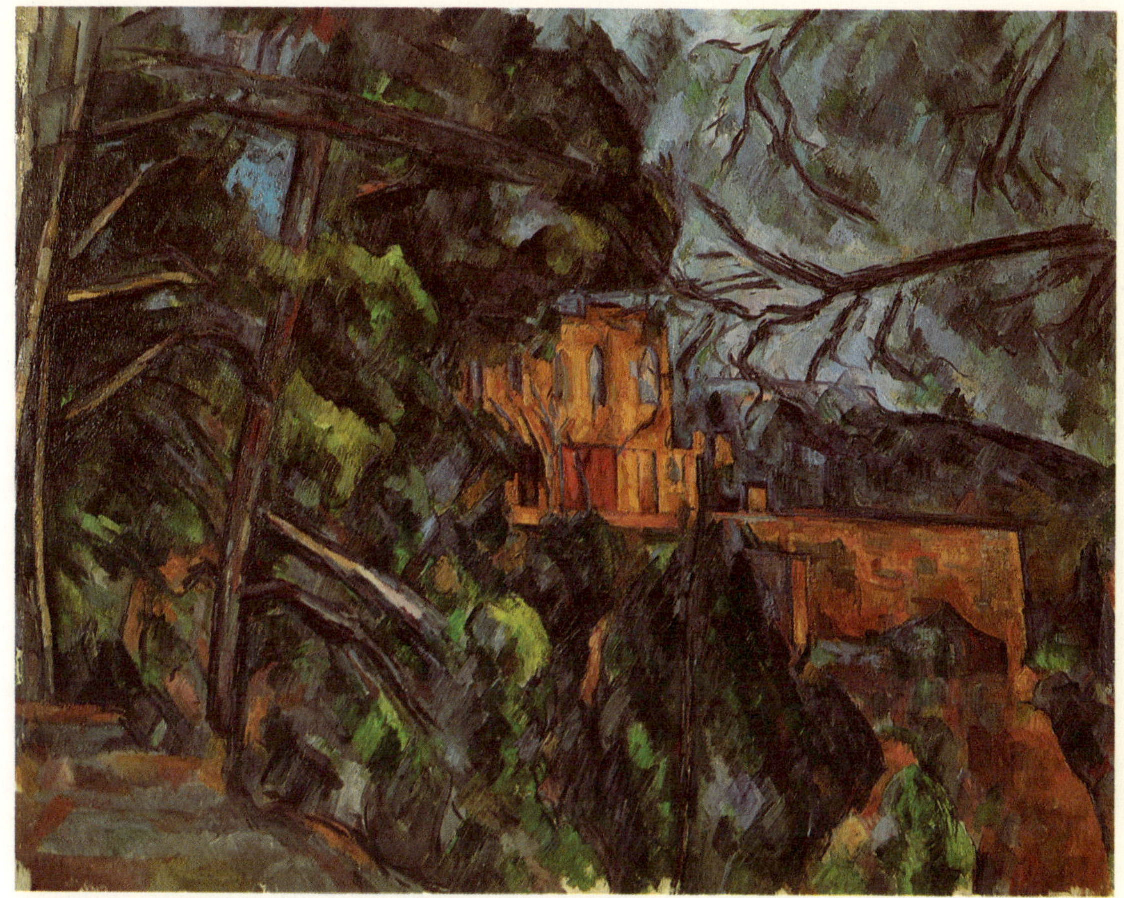

Fig. 156. Paul Cézanne's famous picture *The house of the hanged man* (of which there is a reproduction on p. 38, Fig. 59), is considered to be "the masterpiece of the first year in which the artist began painting according to the principles of the Impressionist School". It was painted in 1872. If one looks back at that picture, one can see that it is a carefully thought-out work, painted in two or more sessions. Thirty years later, Cézanne's style had developed: the search for simplicity had led him to paint pictures such as this one, completed in one sitting, in the style and with the finish of a colour sketch. (Cézanne's *The black castle*, Levy Collection, New York.)

There are no more written notes, apart from a final one saying: "Time: one hour and ten minutes".

It is not possible to give many more specific details, because one is not really following a specified procedure. One can observe, however, when reading these notes and looking at Fig. 153, that from the first brush-stroke there is an attitude of deliberate intention. For example, one begins by painting a hill and, with the same colour, one draws the outline of the shapes of the cypresses, of the church tower, the houses, and the rise and fall of the ground... and one goes on to paint, at the same time, the shadows of the church tower and the houses... all this can be done if one has an attitude of seeing everything all at once, of being in everything, of not hesitating over anything...

The reader can be assured that the Impressionists, when they reached the peak of their style, painted in this way (... except that they painted very much

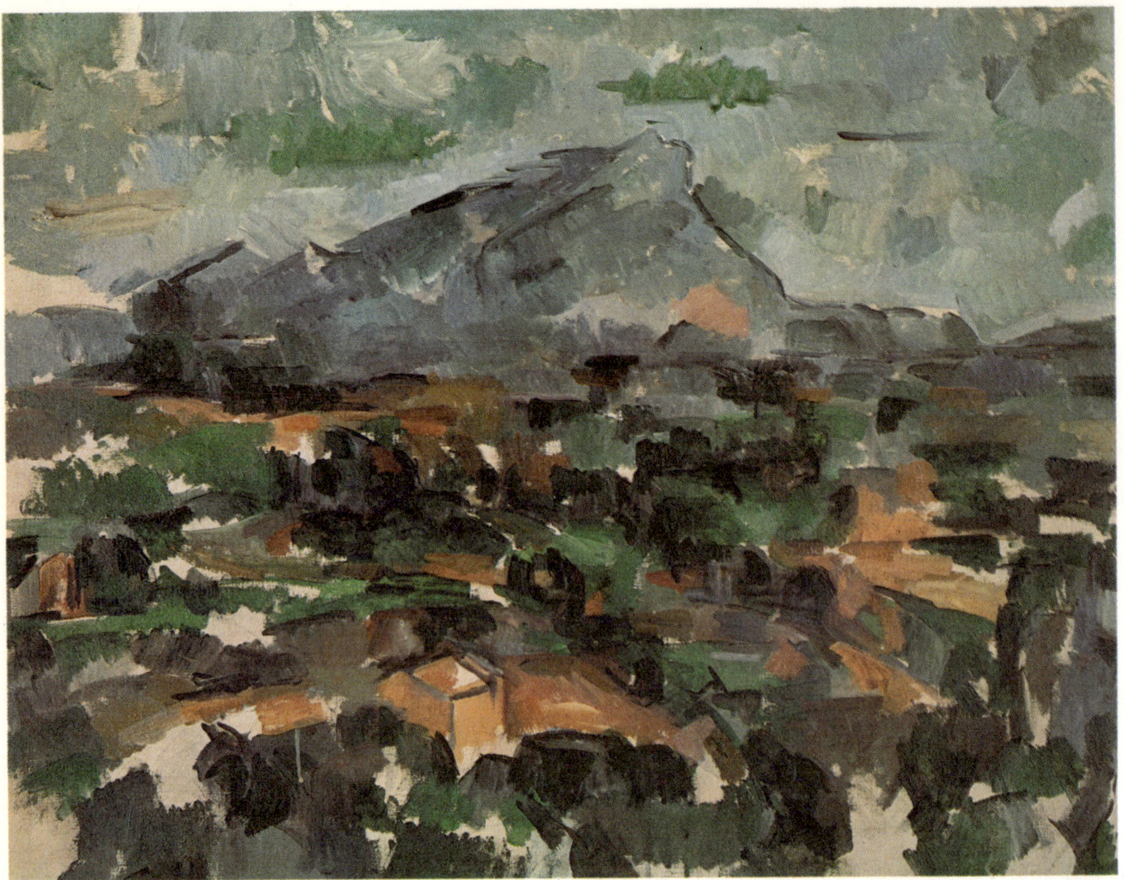

Fig. 157. This picture belongs to the early years of this century — 1901-1906. Here Cézanne has reached the fullest development of his style: his landscapes consist of a pattern of almost abstract shapes, his brush-strokes are broad and flat, and he reduces bodies, trees and houses to their basic shapes; we see here the beginnings of Cubism. Cézanne merely puts colours on the canvas: he paints a picture at a single sitting, with extraordinary speed, and he even, quite deliberately, leaves blank unpainted spaces on the canvas.

better): they concentrated their entire creative potential in a few "sessions" of frenzied effort, committing themselves passionately to the subject, to the colour, and to the picture. A good example of this "impressionist" development can be seen in the work of Cézanne who, after painting normally in one or more sittings (for example, in the case of *The house of the hanged man;* Fig. 59, p. 38), decided to complete the painting of many of his pictures in one session, as though they were mere sketches (see Fig. 156), and tended later towards an almost abstract style, painting pictures in which the summary of shapes and colours reached its most vivid expression. Indeed, in Fig. 157 (above) we can see a reproduction of his *Mont Saint-Victoire*, painted with virtually independent brush-strokes, which do not cover the entire canvas. And we can see in this synthesis an anticipation of the Cubist style, of which Cézanne was a precursor.

However, to return to our main subject, we now pass from the sketch to the picture, carefully studying the technique used by the Impressionists, employing a classic intention and style, in order to paint a picture using the technique of direct painting.

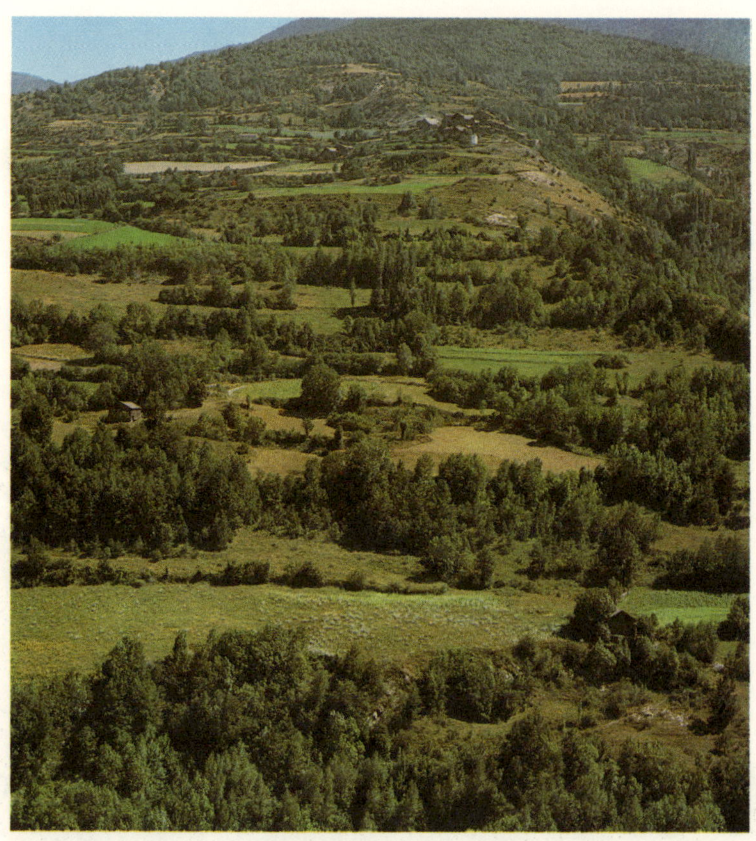

Direct painting in a single session

A few days before starting this book, I painted the picture which will serve as an illustration of these principles. I was in a small village in the eastern Pyrenees, close to the French frontier: one of those villages where the road ends, and from then on bread is bread and milk is milk and the people are called Juan, Pedro and María. While I was painting, I filled a whole tape of a cassette-recorder with factual information and momentary impressions. I was somewhat embarrassed, because the local children could not understand why, in order to paint, it was necessary to keep saying things like: "I clean the brush and add ochre to the Prussian blue". However, thanks to these phrases and others, I can now write down the following text directly, as though I were still there, actually painting for your benefit. The text reads:

"Subject chosen for this study: a mountain landscape, in the eastern Pyrenees, with a wide-ranging panorama of fields, meadows, trees and vegetation; the time is half-past-three in the afternoon.

"I set up the easel, fix the canvas (a No. 5 "figure-type" board, measuring 35×27 cm). I prepare the palette and the brushes..."

(As regards the palette and brushes, see pp. 108 and 109 for the distribution of the colours on the palette, and also how to hold the palette and brushes.)

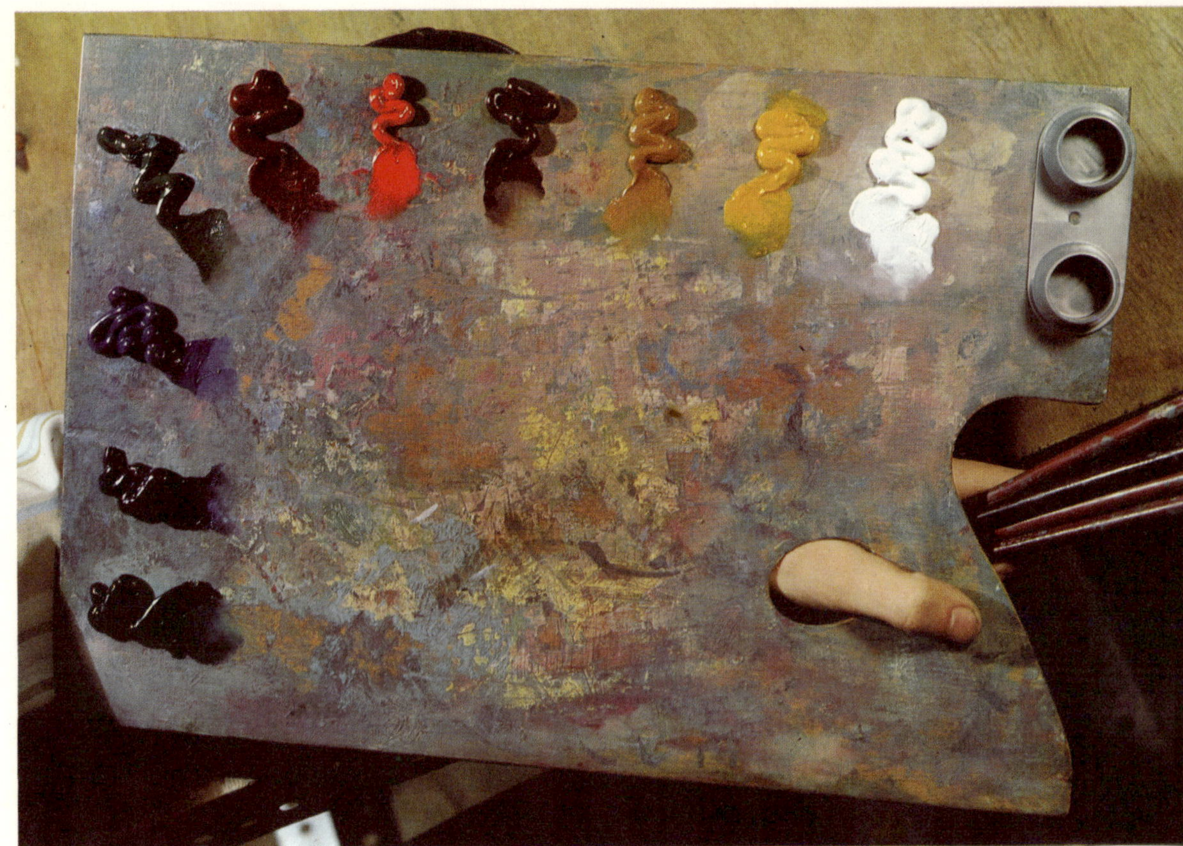

Fig. 159. Get into the habit of putting the colours on the palette in a definite order, and stick to this. Above, in the upper right-hand part of the palette, is white, followed by yellow, ochre, dark umber, vermilion, carmine, emerald green, cobalt blue, ultramarine blue and Prussian blue. This is the order used by professional artists, with the colours grouped and ordered by range.

INTERPRETATION

"The subject is magnificent; I can imagine that its great qualities can be appreciated in the colour photograph which I took this morning (Fig. 158). However, examining it closely, and imagining it as a finished painting, I think that it has a somewhat monotonous effect owing to the repetition of shapes and colours; there are a great many trees, all of similar shape and colour; the fields, too, present a very similar range of colour, especially in the upper part of the picture where the field and trees blend into a neutral mass that is blue-grey-green in colour.

"I reckon it would be better to confine myself to the part which offers greater variety, and to emphasize that variety, making the shapes of the meadows and fields more sharply defined, differentiating them in terms of colour, eliminating or bringing together the groups of trees, establishing distances between them, letting the meadows be seen more easily and to better effect...

"Now, let's see... the horizon almost at the top of the picture, two hills in the background... and then an outline of where the different strips of land begin, almost without trees, and then, in the bottom half of the picture, the various alignments of cypresses, trees and shrubs, ever more sharply defined, until we reach the foreground... a meadow in the foreground, and there we are."

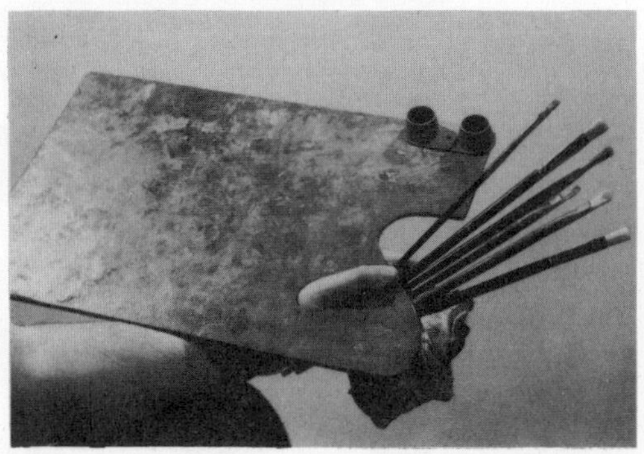

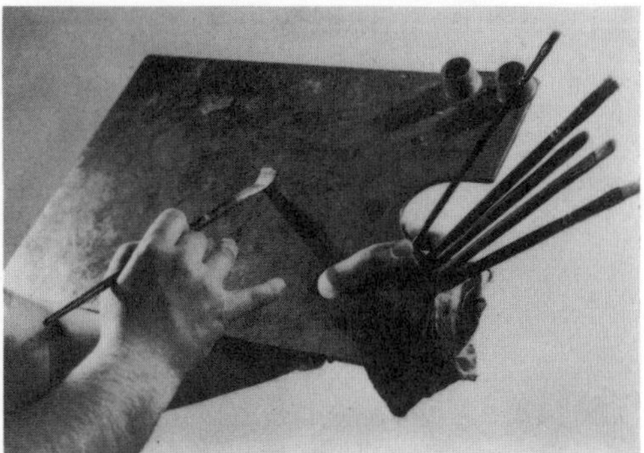

How to hold the palette and brushes

Fig. 160. In the left hand one holds the palette, a few brushes and a rag. The brushes are held by pressing them against the underside of the edge of the palette, spreading them out in the shape of a fan, to avoid their dirtying each other.

Fig. 161. In the right hand one holds the brush, as if it were a pencil, but higher up. The thumb helps to keep the palette steady, but its real support is the forearm, on which it should rest. Using the thumb as a lever, holding and supporting the palette continuously, is tiring and painful. Some artists leave the palette on the carrying case.

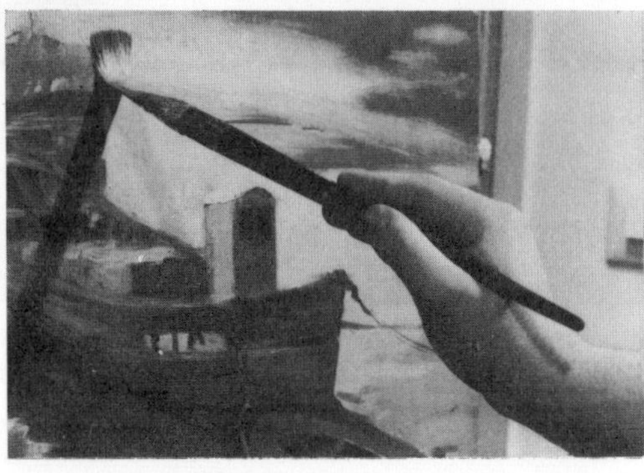

Fig. 162. This is the usual way of painting with the brush, grasping as if it were a pencil, but higher up: this makes it possible to establish a suitable distance between each brush-stroke, and gives one a broader view of the area being painted.

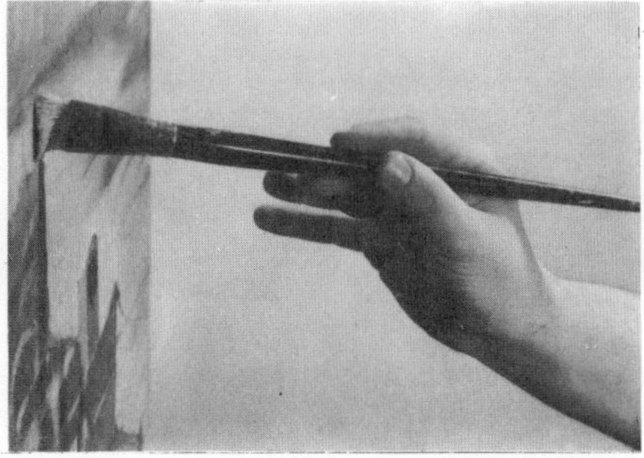

Fig. 163. Here one sees the brush being held in the same way as in the previous illustration, but here the brush-strokes are horizontal: one turns one's hand, and passes the inclined brush from left to right. It is worth-while experimenting with these basic positions.

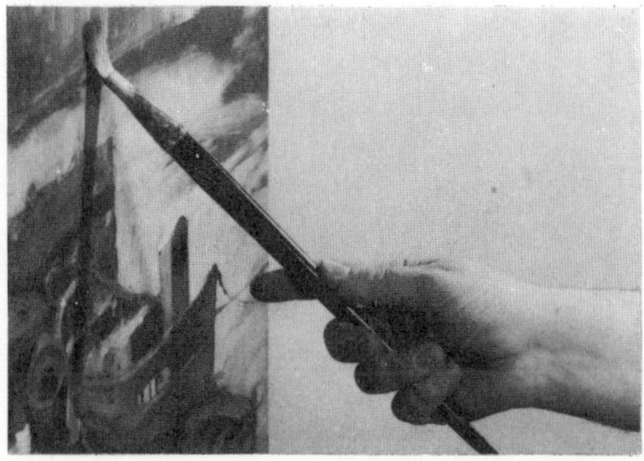

Fig. 164. This is the other way of holding the brush, with the handle in one's hand; the brush is controlled mainly by the thumb and the index finger. This makes it possible to paint with the arm fully extended, with greater freedom and ease of movement, with broad brush-strokes and a wider view of the picture.

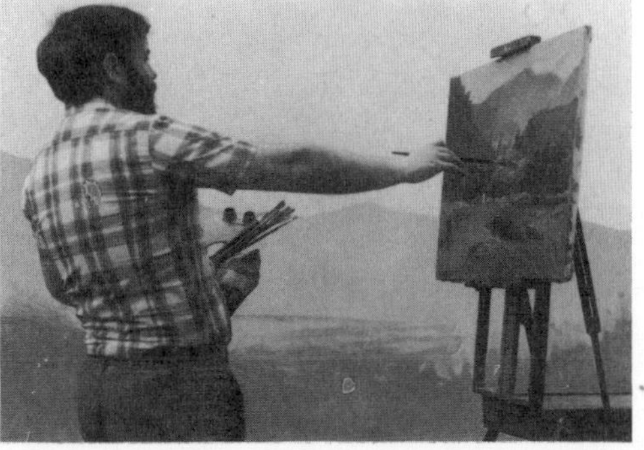

Fig. 165. Watching the way a professional artist paints, you will observe that, from time to time, he leans slightly backwards from the waist, stretches out his arm, and half-closes his eyes... This pose, which may appear affected, arises from the need to visualize and to paint from a certain distance.

Fig. 166. Compare this photograph with the reproduction of the picture in its first stage of painting, Fig. 167 opposite; you can see the differences, which are the result of the process of interpretation.

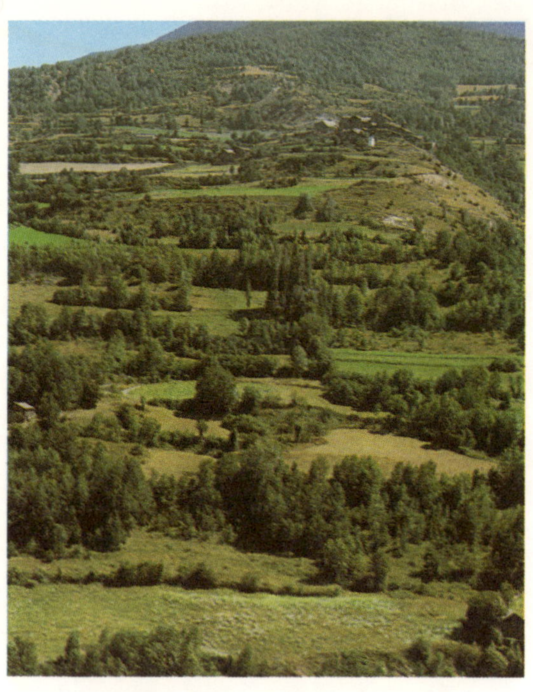

FIRST STAGE: CONSTRUCTION (Fig. 167)

"I am painting with a flat No. 4 brush and also a flat No. 6 brush; I use the edge of the former for fine brush-strokes, and use the brush flat for broad strokes. I use the latter for the bigger areas of trees and shrubs. I am using a mixture of Prussian blue and burnt umber and, occasionally, a small amount of yellow ochre. I mix these colours with a large quantity of essence of turpentine, so that they are almost liquid; this way, they dry more quickly. Sometimes I paint with my fingers, rubbing the paint in, in order to achieve those transparent tones that appear like patches of water-colour, or those "smears" that seem to consist of pastel colours (see Fig. 167).

"I work very slowly; I study the picture carefully before applying each brush-stroke, calculating the exact location of each line and each shape... Then, when the moment comes to paint, I do so without hesitation, trying not to lose my smooth rhythm and to construct the picture spontaneously."

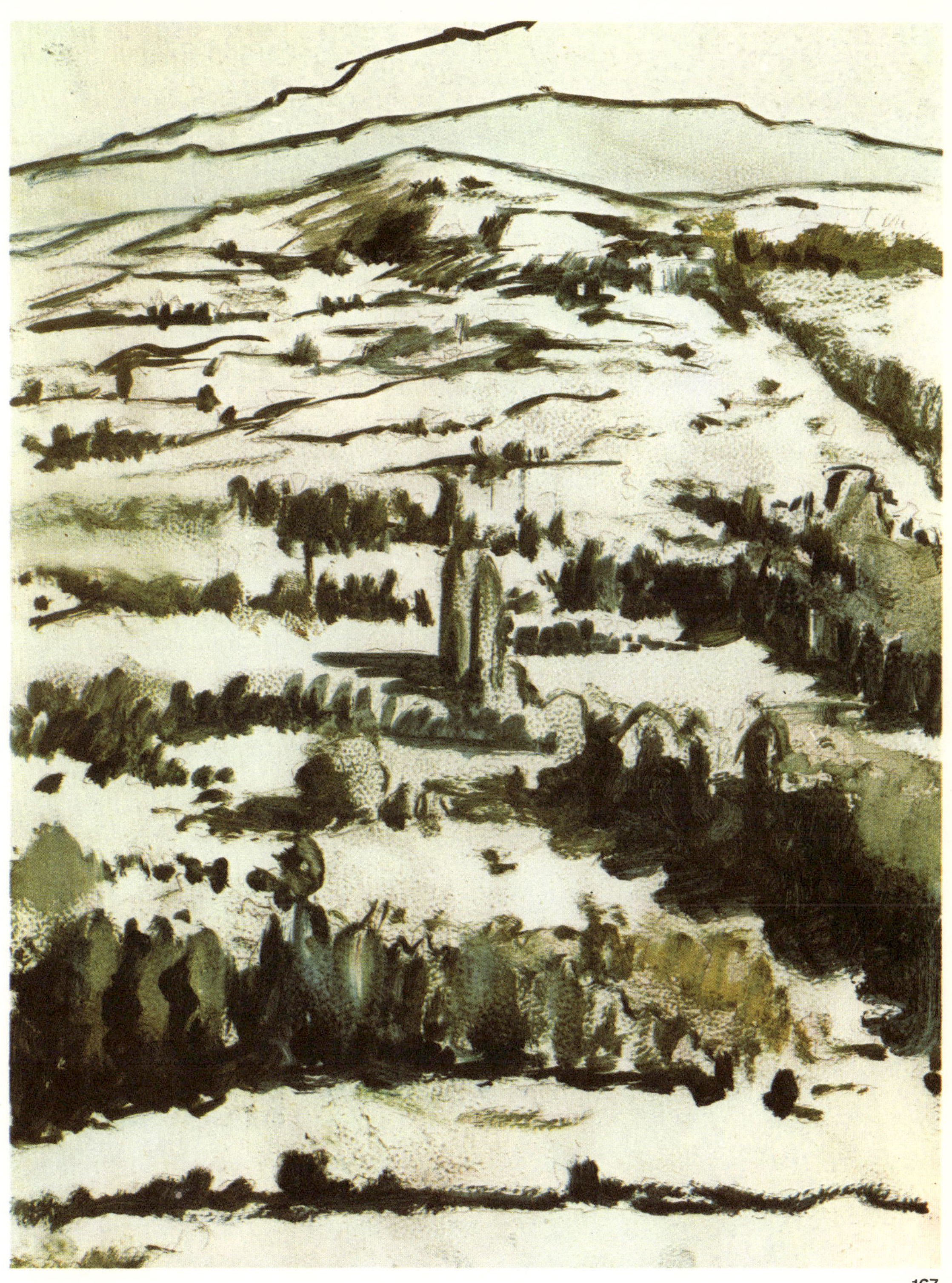

167

SECOND STAGE: FIRST ATTEMPT AT APPLICATION OF COLOUR (Fig. 168)

"It is a quarter-past-four in the afternoon. There is still plenty of light, but the range of colours is no longer greenish-blue, as it was this morning: now it has a yellow-ochre hue. I will paint with a warm range of green colours. On the palette I mix several shades of green with a tendency towards ochre-yellow-sienna, and... quickly, now! Very quickly! With fairly thin paint, and using four brushes, I soon cover the board I am using as a canvas... What I am really doing is painting background colours, and I will go back over them later (or perhaps not... it all depends on whether the tones I am using now have turned out all right). Careful, now! I must bear in mind the initial structure, the limitations and shapes of the initial construction, so that afterwards I may know whether I am on the right lines...

"It doesn't matter if, with this thin coat, I put colour on dark portions and shapes, or even cover the shadows thrown by the groups of trees. Later, when I come to paint the trees, I will make their shapes and their shadows stand out against the present colour background."

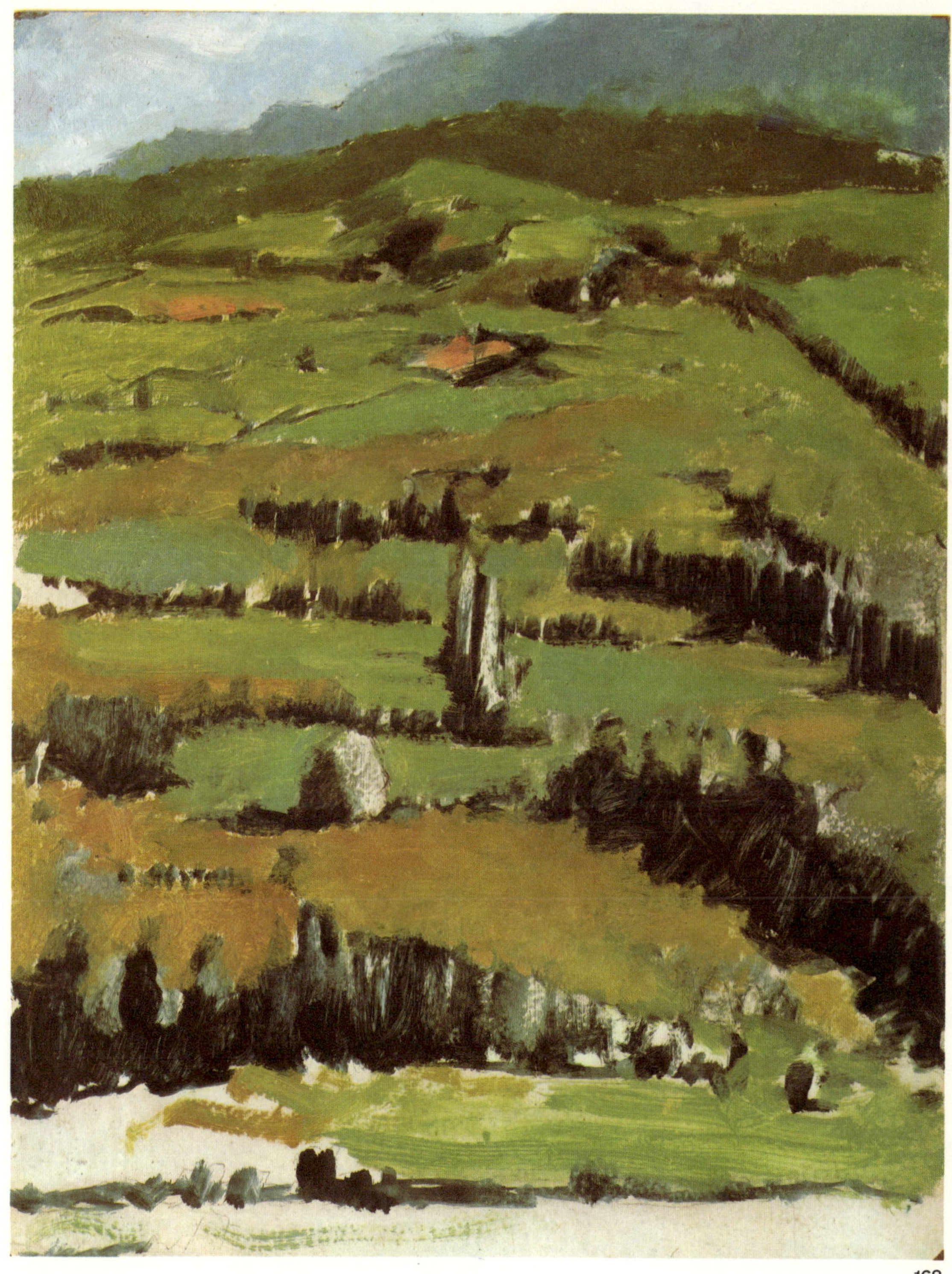

168

THIRD AND FINAL STAGE: GENERAL ADJUSTMENT OF COLOUR, AND FINISHING TOUCHES (Fig. 169)

"It is half past four, Now we need the paints mixed as a thick paste, and definitive colours, as if the picture were really beginning now.

"From the top downwards, I paint shades and colours with easy brush-strokes, with greens, ochres, browns, blue-greens and pinks... and at the same time, with other brushes, I paint the dark portions, and lines and points to represent those lines of trees and shrubs in the middle distance and the background.

"I then paint the meadows and trees in the lower half of the picture, using rather thicker brushes.

"The colours first painted, during the previous stage, serve as a background and a foundation for this final stage: they make it possible to complete, now, the initial conception of the picture.

"I really am painting in accordance with my first intention, bearing in mind four fundamental factors:

1. Paint without hesitation, "definitively". What is done, is done.

2. Synthesize (or summarize) what the subject "says".

3. Achieve diversity of colours.

4. Make sure that one is painting in the right direction (horizontal in the case of meadows and fields, vertical in the case of trees and shrubs).

"Now it's finished. It is half past five."

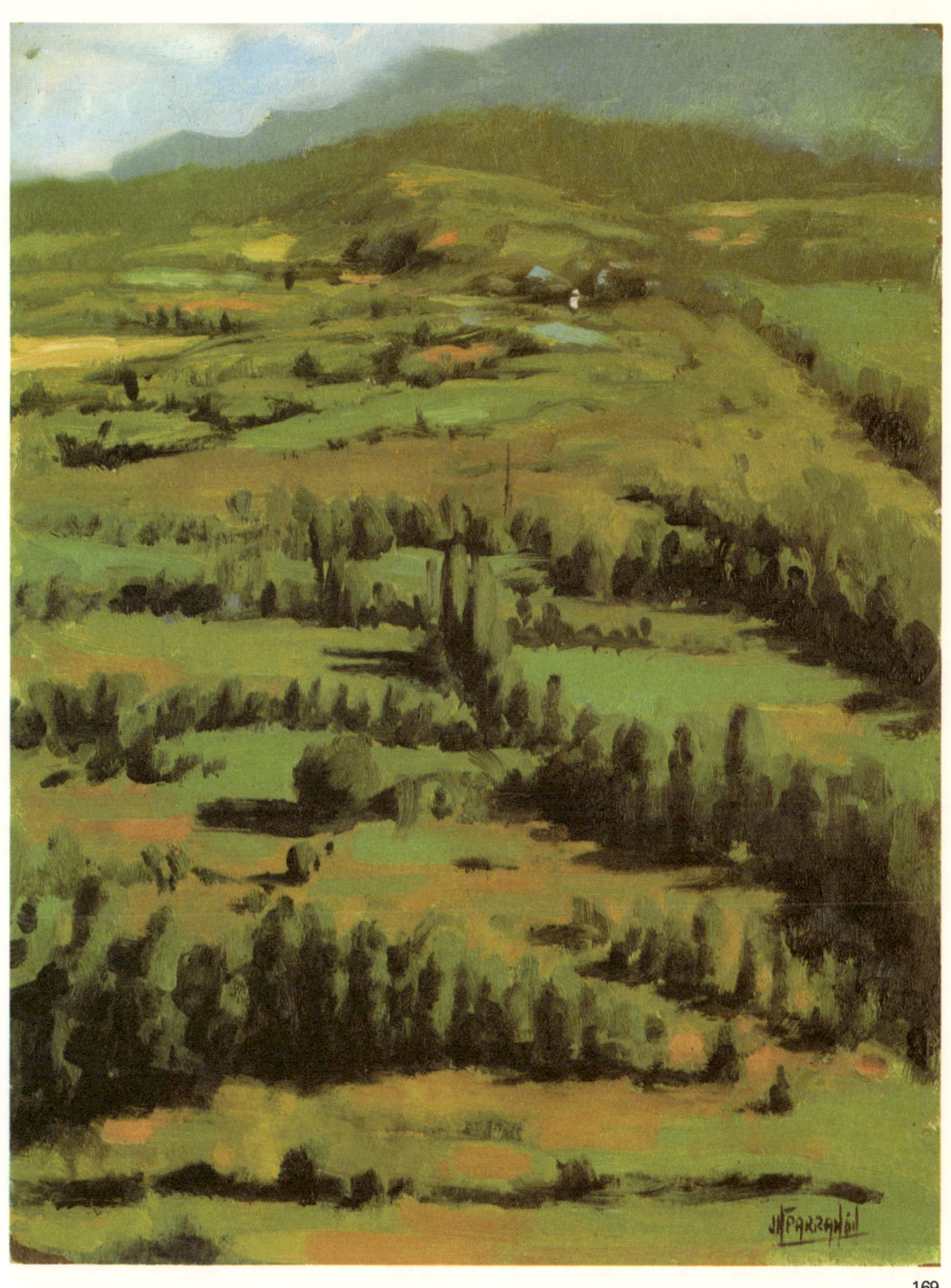

169

Direct painting in several sittings

Now we shall try to solve the problem of the second of the landscapes, in this case working with the direct method but leaving open the possibility of painting the picture in more than one sitting (or, to be more exact, in two sittings).

During the first sitting, I shall solve the problem of the drawing or construction of the landscape, first studying its composition and interpretation. As part of this first sitting, there will also be a second stage, during which I will paint with very thin colours, well diluted with turpentine, leaving the general adjustments and the finishing touches until the following day.

FIRST STAGE Composition, interpretation and construction (Fig. 170)

Fig. 170 shows how I have emphasized the line of the Golden Section, making it coincide with the outline of the small hill on which the houses and the church tower are situated. And I have placed these houses in an arbitrary, almost horizontal line. I have also changed the shape and height of the mountains in the background, giving them more importance in terms of size, that the church tower and the row of houses stand out in sharper relief against a more ample background; I have reduced the length of the small hill on the left-hand side. Moreover — and this is important — I have emphasized the horizontal lines dividing the yellow meadows in the foreground.

Lastly I drew in some fields with crops painted in straight lines which do not exist in the actual model, and I have placed the trees in the meadow wherever I wanted, in an attempt to animate and make more varied the part of the picture. Figs. 171 and 172 show a linear outline of the actual model and a sketch of my interpretation of the central motif.

It must be emphasized that this interpretation was not achieved without effort on my part. On the contrary, I have had to persist, go back on my tracks, and start afresh, in order to reach the end of this first stage. This is an advantage of using the technique of direct painting with more than one sitting, since one has more time and can work in less of a hurry. As can be seen, I have drawn this sketch with charcoal crayon, and this has made it possible to

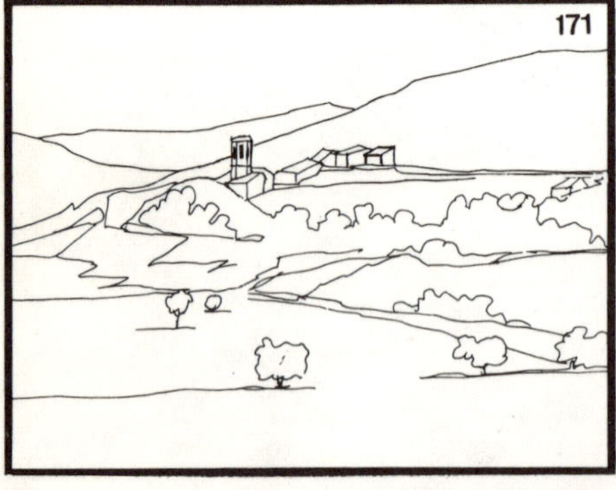

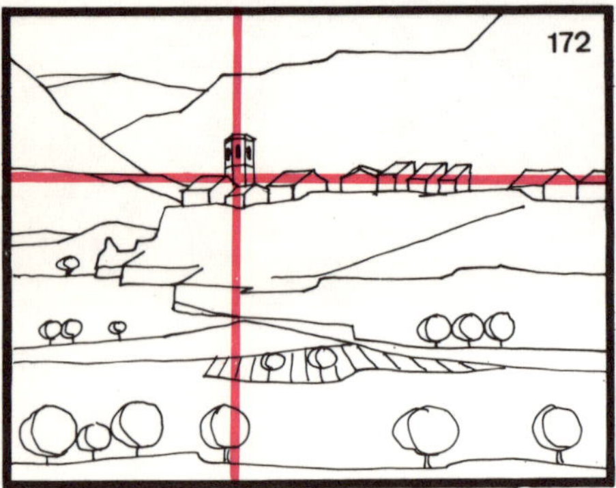

Figs. 171 and 172. Top: a sketch of the subject as it actually appeared. Below: an outline of the process of interpretation. The modifications are explained in the text.

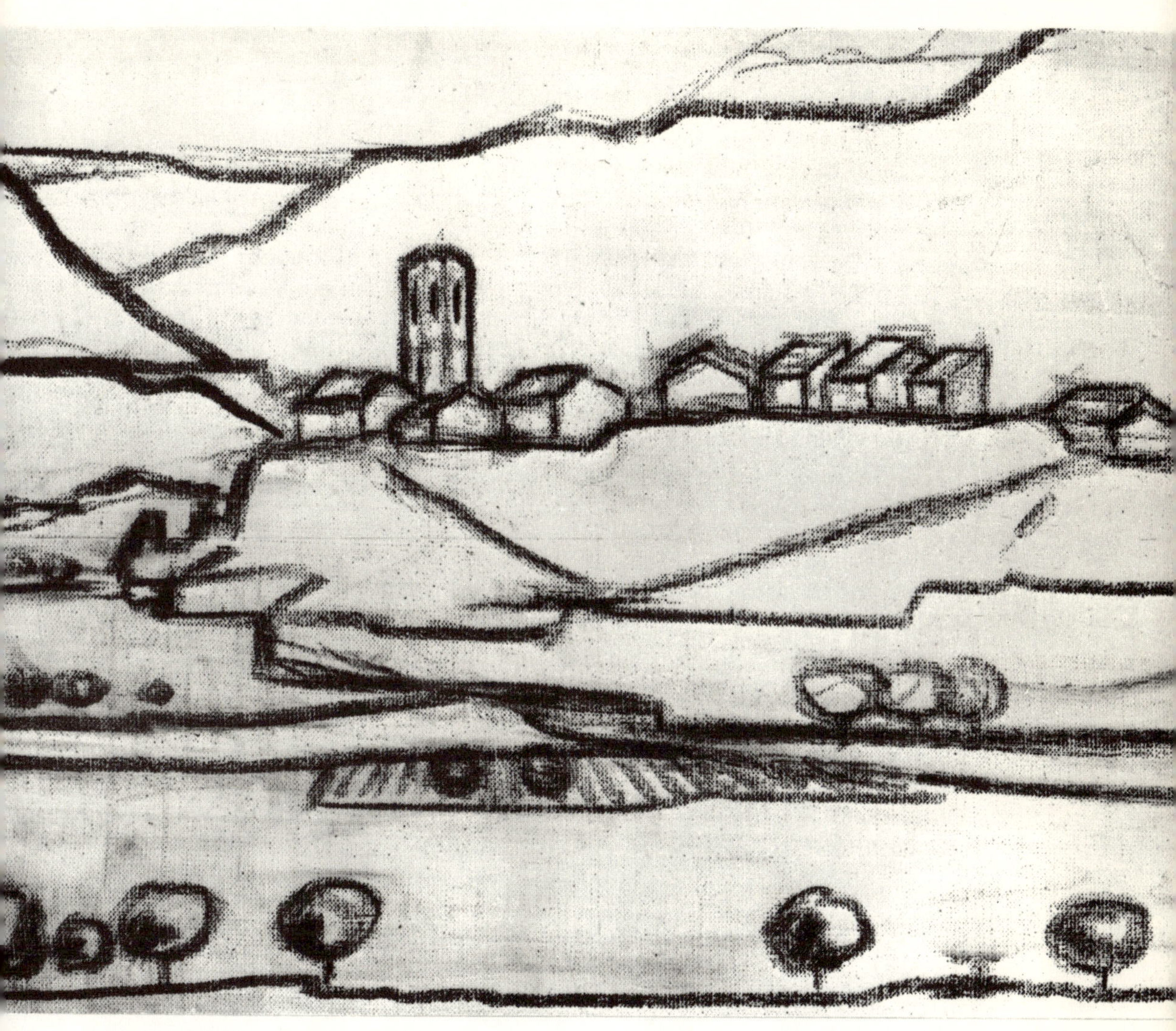

Fig. 170. Condition of the picture, the painting of which is explained below, on completion of the first stage of composition, interpretation and construction. This picture was painted on a No. 12 landscape canvas; during this first stage the material used was chiefly charcoal crayon.

---

erase, to emphasize a feature, and to reconstruct; charcoal crayon is easily erased, merely by wiping a cloth across the canvas. Once the construction of the painting has been definitely established and terminated, I have "fixed" the drawing by means of a special aerosol spray for fixing charcoal crayon. When the fixing material has dried — it does so in a few minutes — I will go over all the lines with extremely thin oil-paint, diluted in essence of turpentine, using a mixture of Prussian blue and burnt umber. In this way, we will definitely establish this linear contruction, with pronounced and thick strokes, which, as we shall see, will persist in some cases throughout the process of painting, and even appear in the finished picture.

SECOND STAGE

General harmonization of colours (Fig. 173)

I begin the painting of the picture with a thin coat of colour, on the basis of which I hope to build in the course of my last sitting. One must paint as an integrated process, colouring large and small spaces, but not yet including details and definite shapes.

I begin with the sky and the background of mountains, and then colour the small hill on which the village is situated: then I continue with the yellow and earthen colours of the meadows. I leave the houses and trees until last, in order to have the opportunity of putting in their final colours on the basis of fuller information. Indeed, once one has a broad background already painted, it is easier to determine the shade and contrast of some shapes in relation to others, and of the picture as a whole in relation to the background.

Some hints on this procedure

Two general principles related to the problem of beginning to paint a picture

The first principle is that one should begin by painting the bigger proportions, in order to "fill" the picture, and eliminate the strength and influence of the white of the canvas.

The second principle is that one should begin by painting the darker portions (those of a colour contrasting most sharply with the white of the canvas) and then go on to paint the smaller and lighter areas. In this way one comes closer to adjusting the colour, and the contrast between some colours and others.

At first, paint in broad strokes, without blending the colours

Apart from the fact that resolving the shape and colour of bodies by means of broad strokes, without any blending of colours and almost without transitions from one colour to another, can become part of a style (like that of Cézanne, in practice, in his last years) the process of colouring the canvas with flat brush-strokes, using the larger brushes (Nos. 8, 12 or 14), is the most advisable when one is beginning the painting of a picture to be completed in two or more sittings. The principle of "painting with flat brush-strokes" obliges one to visualize the picture as a whole, to paint with fewer strokes, as part of a somewhat schematic plan which, apart from encouraging in the artist a more intellectual and schematic vision of his work, paves the way for a more modern, more Impressionistic interpretation of the subject or motif.

Now decide on the range of colours to be used in the picture

A word of warning. The process of "daubing" the picture, of "filling" the canvas with colours, certainly does not mean that, at this first sitting, you can paint without any concern for the harmonization of colours, and think that "during the second sitting I will paint and repaint, adjusting the colours

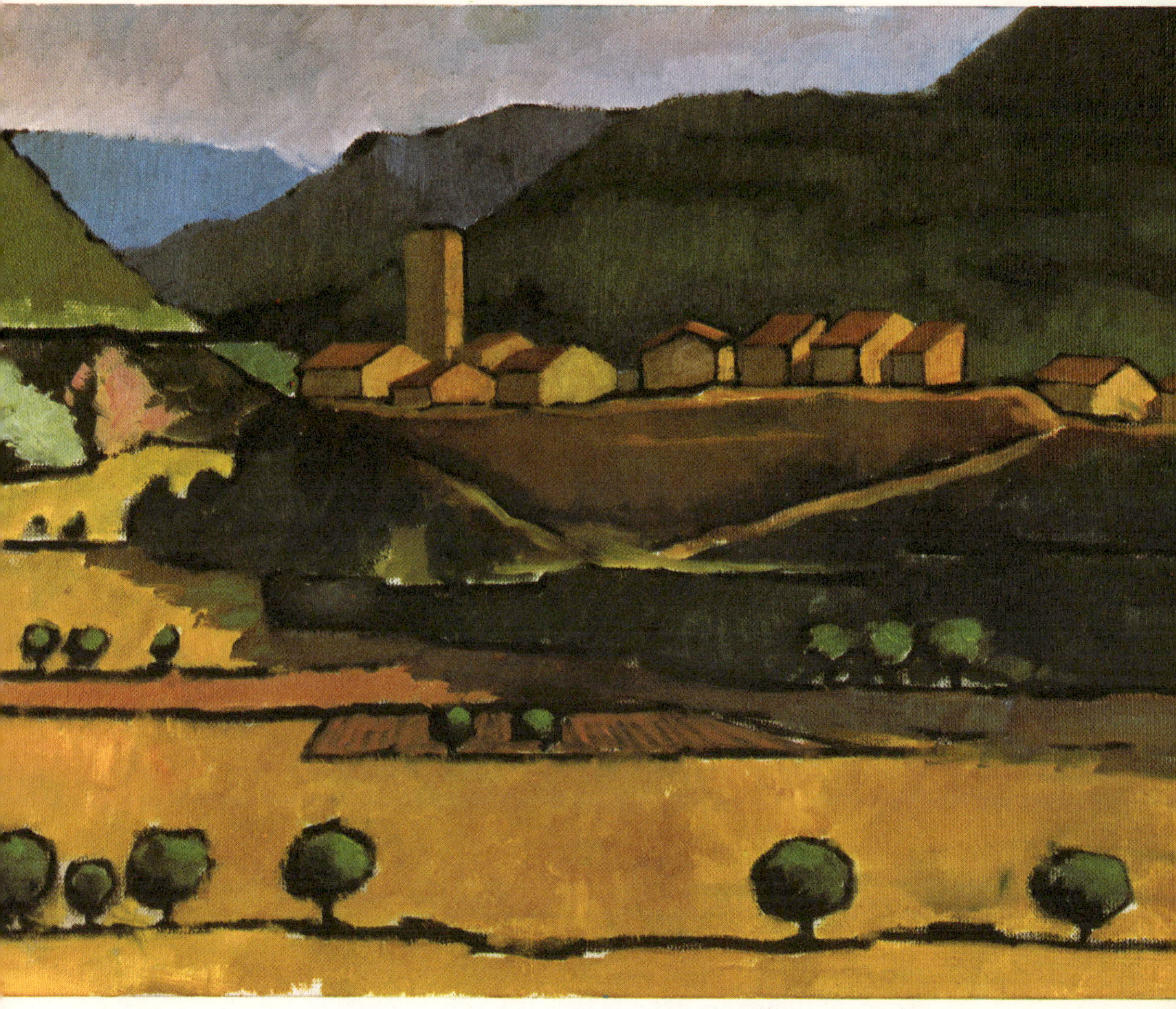

Fig. 173. Completion of the second stage. The work done so far makes it possible to anticipate the final result, the range of colours, and the contrast and composition. Thin paint has been used: this will dry quickly and make it possible to finish the picture at a second sitting.

---

more carefully". This is quite wrong: it is now that the harmonization of colours is decided and conditioned for the rest of the work. It is now that you can paint, visualizing the picture as a whole, without being obliged to include small details, resolving the problem of colour without being too absorbed in what the subject is "saying".

With this subject I did exactly that: imagining a range of warm colours, and putting on the palette more yellow, more ochre, and more sienna, red or carmine, thinking that these colours would predominate in the final picture.

As a secondary detail, I may mention that I spent just over two hours during this sitting, constructing, drawing and painting until I completed this first stage of the picture. Today is Friday; I am thinking of returning the day after tomorrow, Sunday, to finish the picture.

SECOND AND FINAL SITTING

Overall adjustment and finishing touches (Fig. 174)

It is Sunday, in September, at four o'clock in the afternoon.

The colours painted during the first stage of the painting are virtually dry, making it possible to paint over them easily. I will begin by emphasizing certain lines which delineate shapes, with the usual dark colour based on Prussian blue and burnt umber, to bring out the silhouette of the church tower, and of some of the roofs of the houses, and also using this dark colour to depict the silhouettes of the trees, shrubs and roads, which appear at the bottom of the hill.

I then adjust the colour and shapes of the hills in the background, "expressing" the differences in elevation and sudden slopes and dips in the mountains. I also adjust and determine the shapes and colours of the mountain on the left, under that somewhat luminous green in which there appears a series of bright and dark patches.

Then I clean the palette, and prepare a range of green colours to paint the trees on the small hill where the village is situated. I am working with thick paint, painting from dark to light: that is to say, superimposing the colours that reflect light on the green colours in shadow. I use the broader type of brush (No. 6 and, more especially, No. 8), so as not to fall into the temptation of drawing and painting with excessive detail. I am trying to avoid smooth blends and transitions which might lead to a finished picture which is soft and affected.

I clean the palette and the brushes, and put on new colours.

I mix and prepare the colours to repaint and adjust the tones of the houses and the church tower. I can see from the model that, in the light and shade of the houses, there are no two colours that are identical. And I try to accentuate these differences. I half-close my eyes in order to see better, and in its entirety, the contrast of these walls reflecting the light of the setting sun, against the background of the mountains in shadow, which are definitely blue in colour. And I try to emphasize this luminous effect, provoking contrasts, accentuating the darker parts of the mountains where they join the walls and roofs of the houses.

I make use of these ochre, yellow and pink colours to paint the earthen colour of the roads and the luminous outlines of the hill which I am painting.

Now I return to the trees on the small hill, modifying and darkening certain highly sunlit parts which, on account of their excess of clarity, "clashed" with the emphasis and contrast of the bright colours of the walls of the houses.

Then I paint the trees in the meadow and its earth-coloured edges.

I emphasize the lines dividing the fields...

I clean the palette and brushes, and apply new colours

I prepare the mixtures of yellows and ochres, with white and with small amounts of red and carmine, in order to paint the yellow colours of the fields with freshly-mown wheat. I then paint these fields.

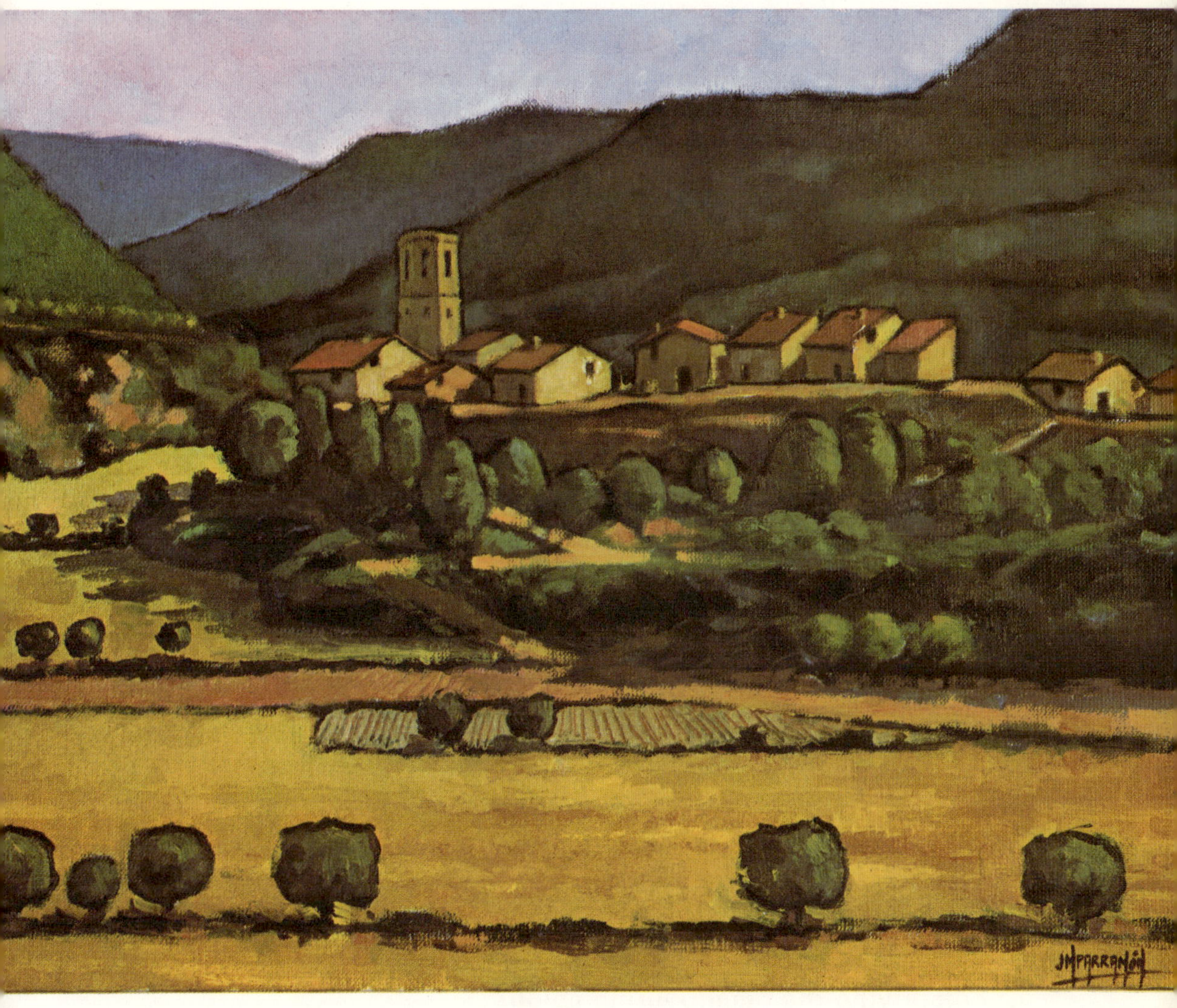

Fig. 174. The finished picture. This has been completed in two sittings: a first sitting of two hours, and a second sitting of three hours. In the course of this second sitting practically all the picture has been painted, following the principle of "beginning and finishing at one sitting". Hence, one employs the technique of direct painting.

Next, I paint the shadows cast by the hills over the yellow fields; then I turn my attention once more to the sky, repainting it with thicker paint, and harmonizing the colours.

I clean the palette and the brushes...

Now I go back to the houses, and draw and paint windows and doors. I still carry on painting certain parts of the mountains in the background... the chimney-pots of the houses... the row of trees on the little hill on the left... I draw the furrows on one of the plots of land, simply using the handle of the brush, as if it were a pencil... I make further modifications to the colour of the shadow of the church tower... and the sunlit walls of the houses near the tower...

It is now seven in the evening, and the colours are changing. I will leave it. I think I have finished, but it will be easier to see tomorrow, at home; then I can retouch the picture, if necessary.

A few hints on the procedure to be followed during this second sitting

"I clean the palette, I clean the brushes, I apply new colours"

This is an elementary, and purely mechanical, consideration; nevertheless, it is of great importance for the ultimate success of the picture, because cleaning the palette and brushes means that one is composing afresh the range of colours; it presupposes that one is "cleaning the colours"; it even means creating a fresh attitude, and starting afresh, without anything left over from the past, without mixtures of shades which will gradually turn grey. Moreover, to "change colours" means that one now has a clean white, a brilliant yellow, a vivid blue, etc. Do not neglect to do this; I have often seen the predicament of an amateur painter who could not mix, for example, a burnt green colour because there was no ochre left on his palette, and he was trying to make it out of yellow.

When you paint, "walk about in the picture"

As the reader will have observed in the above remarks about the gradual development of a picture, during this second stage there comes a moment when one wanders to and fro, painting the trees, then the houses, then the trees again, then the sky... going to and fro, as if one were "walking about in the picture" — to quote the words of Ingres to his disciples — that is to say, to paint in the cheerful and carefree manner of one walking about, without stopping in any particular place; so one avoids the risk of painting and repainting the picture until one forgets what one really wanted to paint.

The adjustment of a colour sometimes involves modifying the neighbouring colour

If you think, for example, that the blue background constituted by a mountain could be bluer and decide to rectify this, bear in mind also that, as a result of this adjustment, you will probably have "modified" the adjacent colour of another mountain, the sky, a tree, a house, etc. (on account of the law of simultaneous contrasts), so you must be prepared to alter the colours immediately adjacent to the first one.

Take care with interpretation; bear in mind the need for harmonization

Maintain until the very end that "firmly established concept of the picture", of "your" picture, as Cézanne did, and do not let yourself become absorbed by the model. From time to time pause, stop painting, look over the work already done... and if you find that the picture — "your" picture — is disappearing, and that the real model is dominating you, then leave the picture, take it home, and try to finish it at home, as was done by Bonnard and, at times, Monet.

Painting with the palette knife

Painting with the palette knife, in the sphere of landscape painting in oils, was first done by Courbet in the middle of the 19th century. Most of the Impressionist painters experimented with this process, finding in it a method of modernizing the handling or style of their pictures. The richness and brilliance of oil paints, when applied with the palette knife, also inspired the Fauvists to paint many of their works using this instrument. As you no doubt already know, the palette knife, used in this way, is a substitute and replacement for the brush and gives rise to a characteristic style.

In Fig. 103 we have observed that the palette knife is a type of knife with a wooden handle and a flexible steel blade, without a sharp blade, ending in a blunt edge or a rounded pointed edge. As can be seen in Fig. 175, the total lenght of a palette knife for use by artists is around 20-23 cm, and it is usually in the traditional shape of a stonemason's trowel. Note the length of the handle (about 10 cm). This makes it easier to grasp it firmly, with the handle in the palm of the hand.

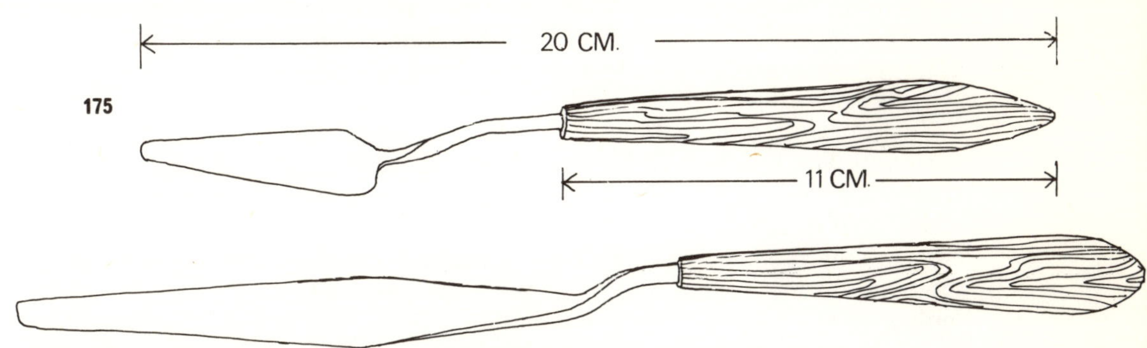

Using the palette knife for painting

The first consideration is that, when painting with the palette knife one does not use thinners; the colours are mixed and are applied undiluted, just as they come out of the tube. Secondly, the palette is also used for making mixtures, and collecting together and preparing colours; and one works with, at most, three or four palette knives of different shapes and with blades of di.ferent sizes: larger, smaller, long, pointed, etc. Generally, however, the palette knife has the shape of a stonemason's trowel.

Now observe, in Fig. 176 (A-G), how to use the palette knife to pick up the oil-paint, spread it as a paste, mix it, and paint with it.

Fig. A shows the position in which to hold the palette knife when picking up paint, with the blade inclined in relation to the surface of the palette... cutting, separating and taking up the required quantity of paint, as can be seen in B and C.

In the following illustration, C (ii), we put the paint on the palette, pressing it, mixing it to a paste and spreading it out.

If we wish to mix this colour with another, we take the necessary amount of the second colour and spread it on the first (D), beating the colours together, in a motion similar to that of a fork when one is beating eggs, continually supporting and rubbing the palette knife, collecting the colour into a pile when it has become too spread out, then beating and pressing it once again (E).

Now that we are going to paint, we put paint from the palette onto the palette knife, as shown in A; the paint is applied to the canvas in the same way as that shown in C (ii) with the possibility, as shown in F, of cutting and trimming, and of outlining and drawing shapes, especially rectilinear shapes. Or one colour can be applied on top of another, mixing them on the canvas itself, producing mottled colours, blends, etc.

This last process — that of painting and mixing the colours on the canvas itself — is characteristic of the technique of painting with the palette knife: it can produce lacquers, mottled colours and, in short, colours of extraordinary richness and vividness.

Two equally effective systems

One can, in fact, paint with the palette knife either directly or on a quick sketch made with very thin paint.

The procedure in each case can be summarized as follows:

Painting with the palette knife over thin paint: the first stage consists of painting with brushes, with oil paint diluted with essence of turpentine, i.e. with very thin colours, which lend a hue to the canvas but do not result in a thick coat of paint.

On this preliminary thin coat — using a carefully studied mixture of colours — one applies the paint with the palette knife, mixing the paint either on the canvas or on the palette.

It is most advisable to paint backgrounds and large areas with one operation of the palette knife, leaving until later stages the finishing touches for more complex and smaller areas and portions.

Similarly, it is best to apply the finishing touches with sable brushes.

The essential difference between painting on a surface of thin paint and doing so directly on the blank canvas is that in the former case one has a background, and hence a general harmonization of colours. So there is the possibility of the colours of this background being able to "breathe" — to fill in areas and resolve problems — in those parts, especially small areas and intersections, which the palette knife has not reached and, at the same time, construct without spoiling the general shape, which can be tricky.

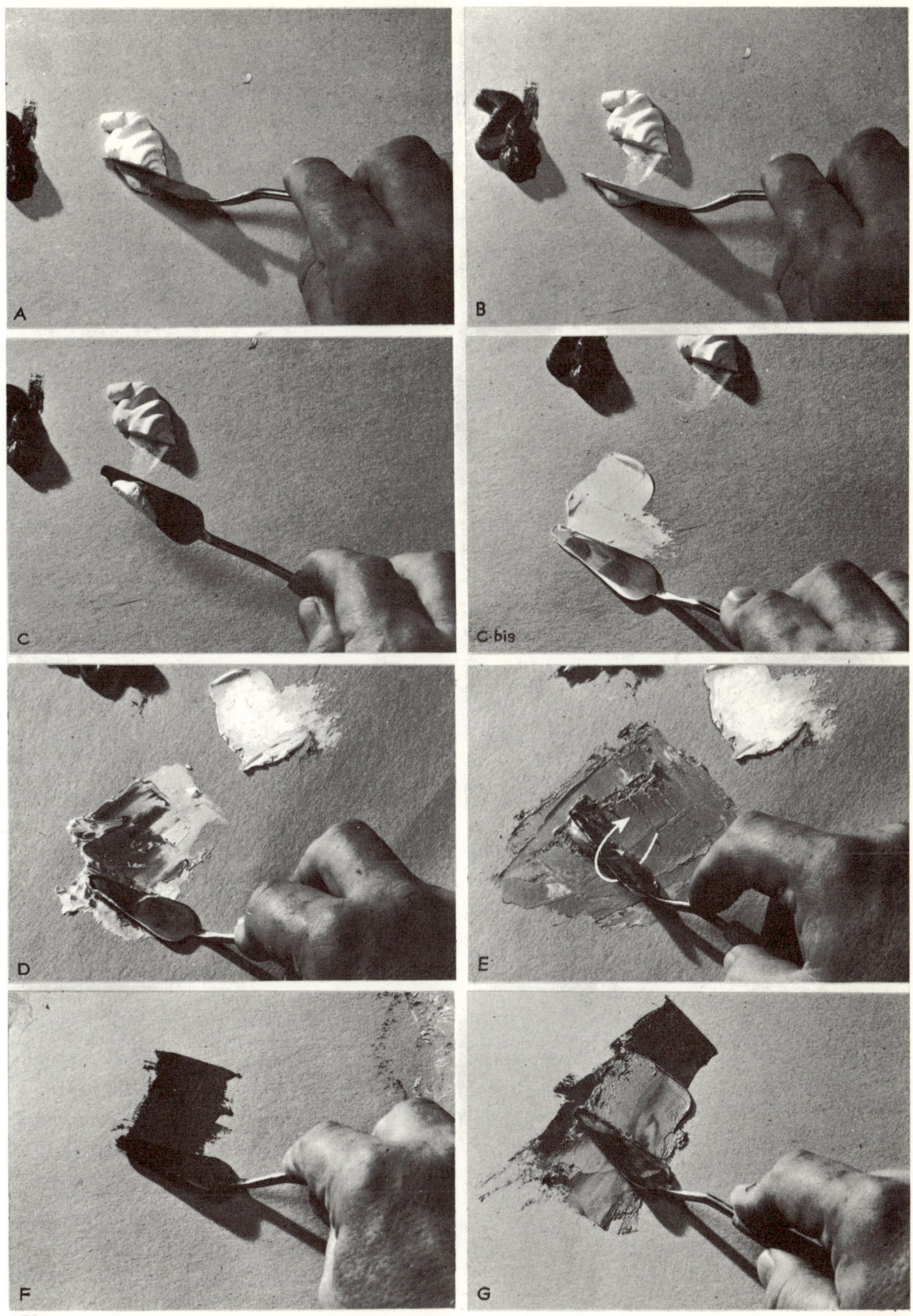

176

Painting with the palette knife directly on the canvas: in order to achieve a thoroughly modern style, it is advisable to effect mixtures and obtain shades of colours on the canvas itself, rather than on the palette.

Very extensive portions should be painted in one operation, during the first phase or stage, and one should try not to touch them up or retouch them during the subsequent stages.

The more fragmented areas or portions, with more diverse, small and complex shapes, should be painted with thin paint during the first stage. This makes it possible to emphasize the colours, painting on top of them, during the subsequent stages. In the case of the smaller areas, it would be preferable to apply colours already mixed and prepared on the palette. However, whenever it is possible, in order to get a more modern result, you should try mixing the colours directly on the canvas itself, as if it were a palette.

It is unnecessary to emphasize that this system is really difficult; it is inadvisable for the inexperienced artist, and should certainly not be attempted by the amateur who does not have a thorough command of the technique of oil painting with the brush.

During the last stage, in order to give the finishing touches, it is quite permissible to retouch and repaint with a sable brush. But one must try not to destroy the smooth, enamelled appearance characteristic of painting done with the palette knife.

In any case, use the "direct method"

As the reader will have understood from our earlier observations, painting with the palette knife must be done, in all cases, using the direct method, that is to say, at a single sitting, with the idea of starting and finishing in one operation... It means that this procedure is not suitable for the big picture or the major theme, for the laborious, broad and carefully terminated motif.

Cézanne used to paint portraits with the palette knife, but they were not portraits like those of Ingres — carefully studied, full of detail and highly elaborate — but really sketches, almost outlines, in which the artist presented and built up, using the edge and the flat surface of the palette knife and in a few minutes, the *impression* evoked by a particular face, or character, or man.

To conclude this brief summary, Fig. 177 shows a colour sketch which I myself painted with the palette knife, using the technique of painting directly with the palette knife on the canvas (a No. 5 board, in this case). Firstly, observe the thick parts and clots characteristic of painting done with the palette knife, and also the mixture of colours on the surface, which give rise to mottled hues and irregular blends... These factors, combined with this technique of painting in blurred outline, apparently without proper construction (partly as a result of the difficulty of drawing precisely defined lines with the palette knife) produce a "language" or appearance that is innocent, simple, primitive — this closely accords with present-day techniques of landscape painting. Lastly, analyse the com-

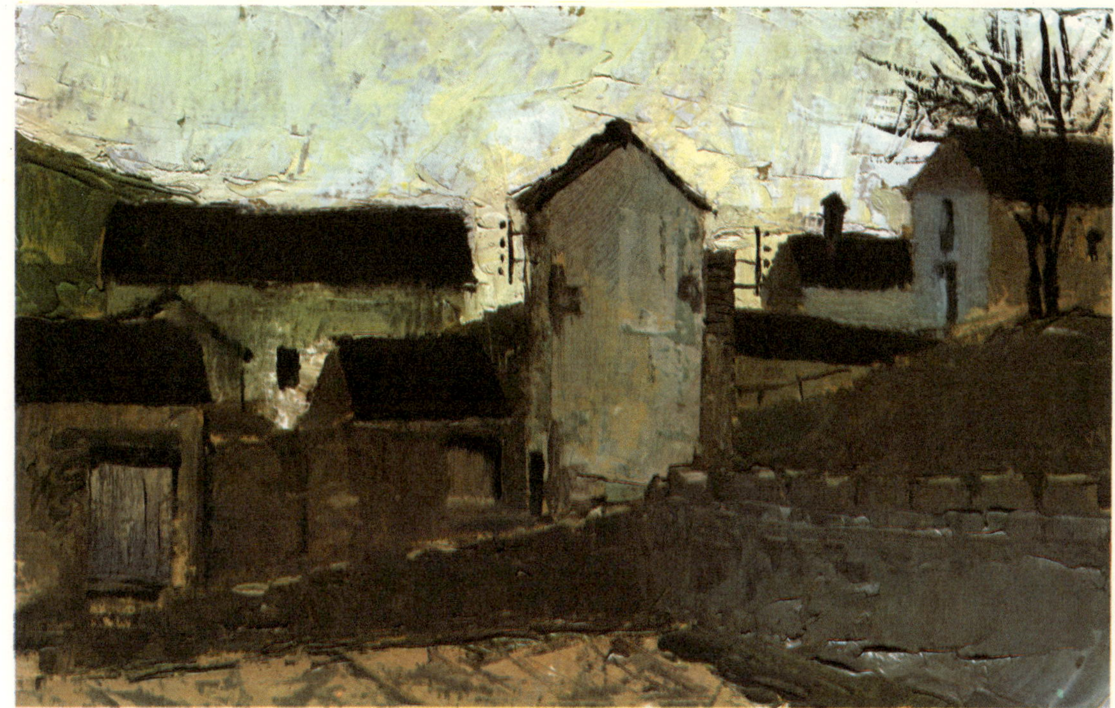

177

position, which has been resolved by building up the picture in planes, and the colour scheme, which is typical of colours broken up as a result of the mixture in unequal proportions of complementary colours.

There is not very much more to say. One could say more, but then one would need a book specially devoted to this technique, and this lies outside the scope of the present work.

Try it. Paint with the palette knife and it is certain that, without looking for anything, you will find a great deal ("And I do not seek; I find", Picasso used to say), since it is, without any doubt, the technique of surprises, full of those "happy accidents" of which Corot spoke.

...And that is all

I really do hope that this book will help you to paint landscapes. I hope, too, that reading it has inspired in you a great desire to paint, to go tomorrow, or the day after, or next Sunday, and every Sunday and holiday, to paint landscapes. Indeed, I hope that as soon as possible you will paint a landscape in one sitting, as the Impressionists used to do.

If that happens, then this book will have accomplished its object: it really will have helped you to paint landscapes. Because, quite honestly, what you manage to paint like a good professional, depends not so much on what this book can teach you as on the occasions and the amount of time that you can devote to painting. The writer Francis Jourdain once asked Cézanne "If a young painter asked your advice, what would you say to him?". Cézanne answered, "I would tell him to develop his skill, to draw a great deal, to copy and copy and re-copy the pipe of his stove until he gets it exactly right. Only then will he be in a position to talk about painting."

Yes, it is true that in drawing well and painting well there is a large element of skill, of continual practice, of abilities which range from how to load the brush with paint to how to achieve a particular colour. It is true that guidance regarding the art of composition, and interpretation can be obtained from the reading and study of such books as this: but, ultimately, it depends on experiencing the doing and redoing of many pictures. Courbet used to say:

Every artist must be his own teacher

Very well, then: the best teaching and the best apprenticeship is that which you yourself can acquire by everyday practice, and by your successes, which in the long run are the story of your failures.

. . . .

Is your easel set up? Is your carrying case ready, with the oil paints, the white in a big tube, the turpentine, the brushes, the palette, the canvas...? Well, get on with it! Go out tomorrow in the country, to that village you liked the look of, to the place where you saw that group of houses and that stream... and paint! Try to finish the painting in one sitting. Try to live the thrilling adventure of painting a landscape in oils.